CALDERÓN'S CHARACTERS:
AN EXISTENTIAL POINT OF VIEW

BIBLIOTECA UNIVERSITARIA PUVILL

DIRIGEN

Josep Puvill Valero. Puvill-Editor
Josep M. Sola-Sole. The Catholic University of America

II. ENSAYOS. 6

BARBARA LOUISE MUJICA
Georgetown University

CALDERÓN'S CHARACTERS: AN EXISTENTIAL POINT OF VIEW

PUVILL - EDITOR

Barcelona

© Barbara Louise Mujica
Publicado por Puvill-Editor. 1980.

DISTRIBUIDOR
LIBRERIAS PUVILL
Boters, 10; Paja, 29.
y Jaime I, 5
Barcelona-2

Publicado con la ayuda de Intercambios Culturales
Hispano-Americanos

Dep. Legal: Z-006-81
I.S.B.N.: 84-85202-25-2
IMPRESO EN ESPAÑA

Talleres gráficos: INO-Reproducciones
                    Sta. Cruz de Tenerife, 3
                    Zaragoza

To Mauro, Lillian and Mariana

ACKNOWLEDGMENTS

I wish to express my thanks to Dr. Antonio Regalado, who beyond a doubt has been the single greatest influence in my academic career. Many of the topics developed in this book germinated from ideas he suggested in lectures, conversations, and letters. Some of these are developed along very different lines in his own forthcoming book on Calderón. Dr. Regalado has often discussed his source materials with me, suggesting relevant readings and sharing the findings of his own research. It was his enthusiasm for and his profound understanding of Golden Age drama that initially sparked my interest in Calderón.

I also wish to thank Dr. James Stamm, Dr. John Hughes, and Mr. Robert Clark for reading this material and suggesting improvements.

Lastly, I wish to thank my husband, Mauro E. Mujica, and my dear friend, Marilyn Pérez-Abreu, for their patience and encouragement during the preparation of this study.

INTRODUCTION

The term "existentialism" refers to a specific, though many-faceted philosophical movement that developed out of a historical climate peculiar to the late nineteenth and twentieth centuries. The many thinkers who have been labeled "existentialists" —including Søren Kierkegaard, Karl Jaspers, Martin Heidegger, Gabriel Marcel, Jean-Paul Sartre, Albert Camus, Martin Buber, Paul Tillich— by no means represent a uniform view. On the contrary, they offer a variety of contrasting and often conflicting opinions. They share, however, the fundamental conviction that existence precedes essence, that the individual does not consist of inner or latent dispositions but rather is free to determine his own essence through conscious choices. In addition, they all stress the active role of the will rather than reason in their concern for the individual as he confronts a confusing and often hostile universe.[1]

The existentialist movement has its immediate origins in German romanticism, particularly in the ideas of such thinkers as Schopenhauer and Nietzsche. However, the first existentialist is generally considered to be Søren Kierkegaard. Kierkegaard's major concern was the relationship of the individual to God. Kierkegaard saw the individual as constantly confronting concrete ethical and religious demands that required a commitment on his part. The complexity and importance of these decisions were, for him, a constant source of anguish and dread. Kierkegaard illustrates the agony of the human predicament with the story of Abraham, ordered by God to put to death his own son. Abraham's continued faith in spite of the absurdity and hatefulness of the command was for Kierkegaard an example of the conscious commitment required by religion. The view of faith as the result of a conscious choice is also characteristic of other religious existentialists, such as Miguel de Unamuno and Gabriel Marcel. Paradoxically, in spite of —or, rather, precisely because of—

---

[1] Many existentialists, reacting against a prevailing tendency to deify reason and progress, undertake a reexamination of the role and efficacy of human reason. Nietzsche deplores modern man's "will to rationalize all things which have being." *Thus Spoke Zarathustra,* tr. by Marianne Cowan, (Chicago: Henry Regnery Co., 1965) p. 114, Miguel de Unamuno argues that, "La fe en la razón está expuesta a la misma insostenibilidad racional que toda otra fe," *Del sentimiento trágico de la vida* (Madrid: Austral, 1967) p. 90 Gabriel Marcel maintains, "Aujourd'hui nous abons je pense, a réagir de toutes nos forces contre la dissociation du vital et du spirituel dont se rendit coupable un rationalisme exsangue." *Le déclin de la sagesse* (Paris: Plon, 1954) p. 40.

their concern with religion, these are not the existentialists whose work is most relevant to this study. Seventeenth-century man did not question the existence of God; belief in God therefore did not require a conscious act of faith. The anguishing preoccupation with the validity of religion that characterizes the work of the religious existentialists is conspicuously absent from the work of Calderón.

In our own century, the best known exponents of existentialism are Heidegger and Sartre. Although Heidegger specifically rejects the label "existentialist," his work *Existence and Being* is generally considered to be one of the classics of the movement. Sartre, a self-avowed existentialist, is the more important of the two as regards this study. Sartre is an atheist and therefore does not cast the question of existence in terms of man's relationship to God, but rather, in terms of political and moral commitments. Sartre sees the individual as in constant confrontation with situations that require a choice in the light of personal commitments. The anguish and dread experienced by the individual results from his having to choose one mode of action or another without the absolute certainty that his choice or even his commitment is justifiable. It is, ultimately, the act itself that defines the individual. Each individual must proceed with the complete awareness that he alone is responsible for those irrevocable acts that will give meaning to his life.

Sartre's special importance with regard to this investigation lies in the fact that he, unlike most of the other major existentialists, has expressed his ideas not only in philosophical essays but also in a large body of fiction. Sartre's characters are typically faced with critical situations in which they must choose and act. They acquire life and meaning as characters only in terms of what they do or have done. The tension and sense of anguish that permeate Sartre's stories, novels and plays stem from the ultimate awareness of each character that he is responsible for the shape his life has taken, that he is condemned to bear the burden of his own freedom until he dies. It is this sense of the individual confronting a destiny which he alone must determine that so likens Sartre's characters to Calderón's.

Calderón was not, of course, an existentialist. No case is being made in this study to prove otherwise. However, the fact remains that the type of character —free and *en situation*— which is the hallmark of existentialist fiction is also the hallmark of seventeenth-century Spanish theater, in particular, Calderón's.

Certain historical factors contribute to this similarity. The sixteenth and seventeenth centuries witnessed a rupture in ages of unquestioned Church authority, giving rise to the Reformation, which in turn ignited the violent reaction of the Counter Reformation. The Reformation raised certain questions regarding the nature of man in relation to his destiny. The most debated of these was the matter of free-will vs. predestination. The latter was defended by such outspoken Protestant reformers as Martin Luther and John Calvin,[2] while the former was defended in varying degrees by a number of Counter Reformers, among them the founder of the Jesuit Order, Saint Ignatius of Loyola. It was precisely under the influence of the Jesuits that Calderón spent five formative years.

Calderón declares unequivocally his belief that the will is free in a number of his plays, including *La devoción de la Cruz, El mágico prodigioso,* and the *auto El gran teatro del mundo.* Yet, he repeatedly places his characters in situations in which they seem to act in predetermined ways. These

_____

[2] William Barret, historian of existentialism, sees the rise of Protestantism, capitalism and science as one consolidated trend toward the rational ordering of society that ultimately collapsed and left man face to face with nothingness. See *Irrational Man* (Garden City: Doubleday, 1962) pp. 27-30.

characters are not in fact predetermined, but in the face of devastating pressures —social conventions, astrological forecasts, their own passions— they often feel that they are. How the individual acts when confronted with such situations —the choices he makes and the way he performs— provides the substance of Calderón's theater.

Like Sartre's, Calderón's characters are, in the face of choice, besieged by doubts. The uncertainty experienced by Sartre's characters results from their awareness of the lack of finality of human existence and from the absence of moral absolutes. The feelings of uncertainty that plague Calderón's characters result from their inability to distinguish reality from appearance. The sixteenth and seventeenth centuries underwent a veritable crisis of skepticism that cast into doubt not only man's ability to comprehend reality through reason but also the reliability of sense perception and the very possibility of knowledge.[3] Although Calderón was not a skeptic, his work was influenced by the skeptical attitude toward the senses. Calderón's characters flounder in a world of confusion; in the face of ambiguous appearances, it sometimes seems to them that action is impossible. And yet, circumstances are such that they must make a decision. The moral dilemma of the individual *en situation* is timeless. Calderón's characters, as successfully as those of any modern existentialist writer, illustrate the perennial problem of man confronting his choices. Sartre has written: "...nous ne croyons pas au progrès; le progrès est une amélioration; l'homme est toujours le même en face d'une même situation."[4] The modernity of Calderón's characters, in spite of the fact that they were created in an entirely different historical context from, say, Sartre's or Camus', proves this point of view to be valid.

The focus of this study is, then, Calderón's characters: how

---

[3] See Richard H. Popkin, *The History of Scepticism from Erasmus to Descartes* (N. V. Assen, Netherlands: Koninklijke Van Gorcum & Co., 1960).

[4] *L'Existentialisme est un humanisme* (Paris: Nagel, 1966) p. 79.

they approach the situations with which they are faced, how they react, how they justify their acts. Like the existentialist theater, Calderón's theater is one of situation and one of action. The reasons for this are not only artistic, but also philosophical, for they relate to the playwright's concept of man as free to achieve or to fail to achieve salvation through his own choices and acts. As in the case of existentialist fiction, it is by observing the characters' acts that we can extract the meaning implicit in the work.

I have tried not only to analyze each character within the limits of his own particular context as developed in the play, but also to compare and contrast characters in different plays, pointing out similarities in approach and attitude of characters who superficially appear to be quite different from one another. As the study develops, it is hoped that a sense of the various types of characters created by Calderón will emerge, thus contributing to a greater understanding of the dramatist's philosophical position and of his dramatic art.

The six plays I have chosen to analyze are *La gran Cenobia* (1625), a historical drama; *La dama duende* (1629), a cloak and dagger comedy; *A secreto agravio, secreta venganza* (1635), an honor play; *La vida es sueño* (1635), a philosophical play; *El mágico prodigioso* (1637), a religious drama; and *La estatua de Prometeo* (1669), a mythological drama. These plays are all of different genres and cover a considerable time span. The first three present characters who are fixed or defined in their attitudes from the beginning of the play to the end. In the next two, *La vida es sueño* and *El mágico prodigioso,* there is an evolution in the characters, a kind of maturation process that takes place during the course of the drama, and a solution resulting from the characters' newfound consciousness both of their own powers and of the nature of the world around them. The last play, *La estatua de Prometeo,* is from Calderón's mature period and in it he incorporates many of the techniques he uses in the *autos sa-*

cramentales. Of the plays analyzed, *La estatua de Prome-teo* is perhaps Calderón's most perfect statement of the human condition and of his view of the proper use of will and reason.

In addition to the six plays by Calderón, I rely on a variety of texts by existentialist writers, ranging from the early or pre-existentialists such as Nietzsche to the most current of the well known existentialist psychoanalysts, Rollo May. The author on whose work I have relied most heavily is, of course, Sartre. In some cases I refer to writers who might be considered somewhat peripheral to the movement, but whose ideas are relevant to one or another of the aspects of Calderón's work being discussed. I have chosen passages from the works of Franz Kafka, for example, to illustrate the themes of alienation and absurdity and their use in modern fiction.

In addition, I have used a number of works by sixteenth and seventeenth-century writers in order to point out currents of thought prevalent during the period in which Calderón wrote. The most important of these writers is Francisco Suárez, whose *Disputaciones metafísicas* were used as a textbook in theological schools throughout Europe.

The similarities between Calderón's thought and that of the existentialists have not gone completely unnoticed by modern critics, although no major study exists on the subject. Albert Camus himself points out the element of gratuituousness that is present in both existentialist works and Calderón's *La de-voción de la Cruz* in his introduction to his translation of this play.[5] A number of scholars have explored similarities be-tween Camus' works and Calderón's, especially in refernce to *La devoción de la Cruz.* Manuel Durán discusses the themes of alienation and of gratuituousness rather superficially in an article published in *Yale French Studies.*[6] John Philip Couch

_____

[5] *La Dévotion à la croix* (Paris: Gallimard, 1953).
[6] "Camus and the Spanish Theater," *Yale French Studies,* No. 25, 1960, pp. 123-131.

13

compares Eusebio's alienation in *La devoción de la Cruz* with Mersault's in *L'Etranger,* and also sees similarities between the violent, sadistic love portrayed in Calderón's play and that in Camus' *Caligula.*[7] In an article appearing in *Symposium,* D. W. McPheeters discusses Camus' interest in Spanish theater and the reasons for the success of his translations. McPheeters emphasizes the dramatic and linguistic elements in Camus' translations rather than the philosophical ones.[8] Arturo Serrano Plaja explores the theme of absurdity in *Calígula* and *La devoción de la Cruz* in an article published in *Mélanges à la Mémoire de Jean Sarrailh.*[9]

Not all the criticism that deals with the existential. aspects of Calderón's work relates to Camus. Alexander Parker, who encouraged me to pursue this study, compares in a recently published article existential *angoisse* to the fear of acting blindly without a rehearsal expressed by Calderón's characters in the *auto El gran teatro del mundo.*[10] A. E. Sloman points out the eternal dilemma of man before his choices in his discussion of *La vida es sueño* in *The Dramatic Craftsmanship of Calderón.*[11] C. A. Jones develops the themes of didacticism and alienation in Brecht and a number of Golden Age playwrights, including Calderón, in an article entitled "Brecht y el drama del Siglo de Oro."[12] In a highly emotional and politically charged article, Ignacio Escobar López suggests similarities in the ideology of Calderón as ex-

---

[7] "Camus' Dramatic Adaptations and Translations," *The French Review,* XXXIII, i, Oct., 1959, pp. 27-36.

[8] "Camus' Translations of Plays by Lope and Calderón," *Symposium,* XII, 1958, pp. 52-64.

[9] "El absurdo en Camus y en Calderón de la Barca," *Mélanges à la Mémoire de Jean Sarrailh, II,* (Paris: Centre de recherches de l'Institut d'études hispaniques, 1967) pp. 389-405.

[10] "Commentary" to *El gran teatro del mundo,* in *Readings in Spanish Literature,* ed. by Anthony Zahareas and Barbara Mujica (New York: Oxford University Press, 1974).

[11] (Oxford: Dolphin, 1958).

[12] *Segismundo,* III, 1967, pp. 39-55.

pressed in *El gran teatro del Mundo* and that of the major existentialists. He discusses at some length the self-awareness of the individual in the face of his own freedom and his own temporality, and stresses that Calderón shares a common philosophical base with not only the religious existentialists but also the atheists.[13]

Other articles that deal with related topics include: *"La vida es sueño* de Calderón y los problemas del existencialismo actual,"* by Gregorio Martínez Almendrez;[14] "La angustia existencial por el no ser del ser y el teatro de Calderón," by J. Roig Gionella;[15] and "Schopenhauer, admirador de Gracián y de Calderón," by Joaquín Iriarte.[16]

---

[13] "Teatro sacramental y existencial de Calderón de la Barca," *Cuadernos hispanoamericanos,* CXXXIV, 1961, pp. 219-234.
[14] *Studium Generale,* Porto, Germany, I, 1953, pp. 97-125.
[15] *Gran mundo,* Madrid, VII, 1953, pp. 555-580.
[16] *Razón y fe,* CXLII, 1960, pp. 405-418.

CHAPTER I

WILL AND FANTASY: *LA GRAN CENOBIA*

Aureliano's Choice

La gran Cenobia is one of Calderón's earliest plays.[1] The plot revolves around the conquest of Palmyra by the Roman emperor Aureliano.[2] As the play opens, Aureliano appears in a cave in a forest near Rome. He is dressed in animal skins, symbolic of his animal-like existence far from society. Like Segismundo in *La vida es sueño,* he lives in a symbolic womb reminiscent of that period before birth when one is not yet master of one's will. In the first scene of the drama, the spectator is witness to the "birth" of Aureliano, to his awakening to the consciousness of his own freedom.

---

[1] *La gran Cenobia* was presented by the theatrical company of Andrés Vega on June 23, 1625, when the poet was only 25 years old. It appears in the *Primera Parte de Comedias de Calderón,* Madrid, 1636. See Angel Valbuena Briones, "Nota preliminar", in Don Pedro Calderón de la Barca. *Obras completas,* (Madrid: Aguilar, 1966) I, 70. Harry W. Hilborn gives 1634 as the year in which the play was written, but admits that this is only an approximation. See, *A Chronology of the Plays of Don Pedro Calderón de la Barca,* Toronto: University of Toronto Press) 1938, p. 73.

[2] For background material on the history of Palmyra see James Germain Février, *Essai sur l'histoire politique et économique de Palmyre,* (París: Vrin, 1931).

Aureliano, like all men, is confronted with a myriad of images. He sees things; he hears things:

> Espera, sombra fría
> pálida imagen de mi fantasía
> ilusión animada,
> en aparentes bultos dilatada
> no te consuma el viento
> si eres fantasma de mi pensamiento. (p. 71)[3]

But Aureliano cannot be sure the information conveyed by the senses corresponds to objective reality. He is surrounded by uncertainty. His vocabulary is riddled with terms which suggest subjectivity: *sombra, imagen, fantasía, ilusión, aparentes bultos, fantasma de mi pensamiento*. Faced with the possibility that the images he perceives may be illusions, he doubts:

> En tantas confusiones, ¿duermo o velo?
> aunque en mí ya es lo mismo
> cuando en tan ciego, en tan oscuro abismo
> de mi discurso incierto,
> lo que dormido vi, sueño despierto. (p. 71)

Aureliano's monologue contains some of the principal arguments of the Pyrrhonian skeptics against the possibility of human knowledge: sense perception is unreliable; one can never be sure whether or not one is dreaming.[4] Aureliano is thrown into a blind, obscure abyss of uncertainty. Awake or asleep, he is haunted by the same images.

[3] Page numbers refer to Don Pedro Calderón de la Barca, *Obras Completas*, Tomo, I, ed. by A. Valbuena Briones (Madrid: Aguilar, 1966).

[4] Although the sixteenth-century Pyrrhonian revival was felt principally in France, there is evidence that its impact also reached Spain. Pyrrhonian skeptics held that there is insufficient and inadequate evidence to determine if knowledge is really possible. All judgment, therefore, must logically be suspended. Two of the Pyrrhonists' principal arguments were that the information conveyed by the senses is unreliable and that an individual can never be certain whether or not he is dreaming. Regarding the senses, the Portuguese skeptic Francisco Sánchez wrote: "El sentido sólo ve lo exte-

The image which Aureliano sees is that of Quintilio placing the laurel of the emperorship of Rome upon his head. He recognizes this vision as nothing more than a projection or representation of the mind:

> sombra fue de mi dicha imaginada (p. 70)

And yet, as such —that is, as a projection of the mind— it has reality. Aureliano's dream corresponds not to an objective truth but to a subjective one. It is an *"ente de razón,"*[5] capable of moving the individual who assigns meaning to it.

Aureliano has already precast a goal for himself: he desires political power. His dream reflects his deep-seated wish to see himself crowned emperor:

---

rior, pero no lo conoce. La mente considera las cosas recibidas de los sentidos. Si éstos se engañan, también aquélla, y si no, ¿Qué se consigue? Sólo considera las imágenes de las cosas que admitió el ojo;..." *Que nada se sabe,* (Buenos Aires: Emecé Editores, 1944) p. 132. Michel de Montaigne expressed the same idea when he said: "...rein ne vient à nous que falsifié et alteré par nos sens." "Apologie de Raimond Sebond," in *Les Essais de Michel de Montaigne,* ed. Pierre Villey, Tome II (Paris: F. Alcan, 1922), p. 160.

Calderón assimilates many of the skeptics' major arguments. In a number of plays he shows himself to be skeptical toward the senses and in others he treats the difficulty in ascertaining whether or not one is dreaming (See analysis of *La vida es sueño*). When, in Calderón's *En la vida todo es verdad y todo mentira,* Heraclio affirms:

> que no sabe poco quien
> sabe que no sabe nada. (p. 1118)

he is echoing the skeptic contention. Calderón carries the skeptical premise to an extreme in this play by inventing a situation in which all characters are maintained in a suspended state of doubt.

On the skeptical crisis in the sixteenth and seventeenth centuries see Richard H. Popkin, *The History of Scepticism from Erasmus to Descartes* (Netherlands: Vangorcum Assen, 1960).

I wish to express my thanks to Professor Antonio Regalado for suggesting to me skeptical sources for Calderón's works.

[5] *"Ente de razón"* was a term used by the Jesuit philosopher Francisco Suárez to denote an entity invented by the mind but corresponding to no

19

Mas despierto o dormido,
¿no soy quien tantas veces atrevido,
no sin grande misterio,
señor me nombre del romano imperio,
cuya fuerte aprehensión, cuya porfía
me rinde a una mortal melancolía? (p. 71)

His melancholy is due to his inability to realize the potential
he believes is his. He yearns for the opportunity to realize
himself in the role of emperor. He seeks a role of power even
if it be only over the beasts.

Tanto, que, por no ver en las ciudades
la pompa de soberbias majestades,
vengo a habitar desierto horizontes,
y a ser rey de las fieras en los montes. (p. 71)

objective reality. An *"ente de razón"* is one which "tiene ser objetivamen-
te sólo en el entendimiento", *Disputaciones metafísicas* Tomo II, tr. from
the Latin by Sergio Rabade Romeo, Salvador Caballero Sánchez and Antonio Puigcerver Zanón, (Madrid: Gredos, 1960) p. 191 *"Entes de razón"*
could be the product of an imperfection in our understanding, as when we
take one thing for another ("...por no poder algunas veces conocer las cosas tal como son en sí, las concibe por comparación de una con otra, formando de esta suerte relaciones de razón donde no hay verdaderas relaciones." *Disputaciones*, VII, p. 395) or simply an invention of our understanding ("...el cual puede, partiendo de entes verdaderos, elaborar
otros ficticios uniendo partes que no pueden formar composición en la
realidad, a la manera como finge la quimera o algo semejante, formando así
aquellos entes de razón que se llaman imposibles y a los que algunos dan el
nombre de entes prohibidos." *Disputaciones*, VII, pp. 395-396). These
"entes de razón" are not dangerous as long as they are recognized for
what they are: fictions. They become problematic, however, when they are
taken for objective realities. See Suarez's chapter on "Falsedad" in *Disputaciones*, II. Calderón incorporates many of these ideas through the creation
of characters such as Aureliano who reject doubt and consequently insist
that their subjective projections constitute objective reality. Calderón uses the
term *"ente de razón"* in *El purgatorio de San Patricio*. The pagan king of Ire-
land has just witnessed the resurrection of Polonia and still he refuses
to believe in the power of God. Saint Patrick describes to him the principles of the Christian religion, but he dismisses this as mere inventions of
the mind:

But still he is not satisfied, for his is an obsessive passion to rule which, having failed to materialize into authentic temporal power, nevertheless haunts him in the form of a vision of himself as king:

> Pues si este soy, ¿qué mucho las pasiones
> que me oprimen despierto,
> entre las sombras del silencio muerto
> den cuerpo y voz a vanas ilusiones? (p. 71)

Aureliano recognizes his vision as a "vain illusion" only as long as the crown remains out of reach. But soon a new spectre rises before his eyes: the laurel wreath and the sceptre appear on a branch. Once more Aureliano hesitates. Are his senses still deceiving him?

> Pero ¿qué es lo que veo?
> O los ojos me mienten, o el deseo; (p. 71)

Are the symbols of power products, like his former dreams, of senses and desire? Are they, too, *"entes de razón?"* They seem to be enigmatic signs:

> Enigmas son de mi discurso errante
> tan declaradas señas, (p. 71)

> Y pues que puedes
> tanto con tu Dios, impetra
> su gracia, pídele tú
> que, para que yo lo crea,
> te dé un ente real que todos
> le toquen; no todos sean
> *entes de razón.* (p. 196).

I wish to express my thanks to Professor Antonio Regalado for pointing out to me Suárez's and Calderón's use of *"ente de razón."*

But signs are merely appearances which the individual interprets in accordance with his wishes.[6]

Aureliano chooses to accept the sign of the crown and sceptre as symbols of his own power. While recognizing that these symbols may be deceits of the senses, he chooses to cast aside doubt and to accept what he sees at face value.

[6] In a number of plays Calderón defends the notion that the future is inaccessible to any individual through signs. In *La vida es sueño* Basilio attempts to interpret astrological signs and is proven wrong in his predictions by Segismundo's eventual conversion. Segismundo tells his father that such attempts to ascertain what was "meant" to be is a presumption on man's part:

> Lo que está determinado
> del cielo, y en azul tabla
> Dios con el dedo escribió,
> de quien son cifras y estampas
> tantos papeles azules
> que adornan letras doradas,
> nunca engaña, nunca miente;
> porque quien miente y engaña
> es quien para usar mal dellas
> las penetra y las alcanza. (III, 971-980)

Calderón's attitude regarding astrological signs is related to his general skepticism regarding human knowledge and the unreliability of the senses. While the existentialists do not share the skeptic's view of the senses and of the impossibility of knowledge, they, too, deny the reliability of signs, portends or omens to reveal the future or "destiny." Sartre writes "...il n'y a pas de signe dans le monde... c'ést moi-même en tout cas qui choisis le sens qu'ils (les signes) ont." *(L'Existentialisme, p. 47)* Signs are simply a matter of personal interpretation: "l'homme déchiffre lui-même le signe comme il lui plait." *(L'Existentialisme, p. 38)* The existence of signs indicating destiny or inevitability would of course be in contradiction with the existentialist premise that man is absolutely free and subject to no kind of predetermination.

For Calderón, all men are free. Aureliano is free to reject the sign or to doubt its validity.[7] He chooses, rather, to grasp the crown and to place it on his own head:

> Soberana tïara,
> seña feliz de mi fortuna rara,
> perdona si mi atrevo
> a tu deidad; (p. 71)

Aureliano has chosen his own way. He has chosen to see in the "sign" an indication of a benevolent fortune, bestowing deity on her ambitious protégé.

Even when Astrea, the priestess, and the Roman soldiers appear to confirm that Aureliano is to be the new emperor, Aureliano maintains awareness that all may be illusory. He doubts:

> ¡Cielos!, ¿qué prodigios toco?
> Aqueste monte parece
> que da, preñado de asombros,
> espíritus a las peñas,
> que almas infunde en los troncos,
> o que de su centro duro
> va arrojando portentoso
> vasallos que me obedezcan. (p. 73)

---

[7] The controversy over the freedom of the will raged throughout the better portion of the sixteenth and seventeenth centuries. The Reformation brought with it the belief that man was saved or damned by the will of God, regardless of his own deeds. Luther wrote in *De servo arbitrio:* "...neither in a man nor in an angel, nor in any other crated being, can such a thing as free will exist." Calvin, in his *Institutes of the Christian Religion,* maintains: "inasmuch as the human will is fettered by sin and a slave, it can achieve no manner, of good: it is entirely devoid of this power of doing anything of a kind."
In opposition to this doctrine of *servo arbitrio* the Counter Reformation took a stand in defense of the doctrine of free will. Ignatius of Loyola, founder of the Jesuit order under which Calderón spent his formative years, wrote in the appendix to his *Spiritual Exercises:* "We should not lay so

23

much stress on the doctrine of grace as thereby to encourage the holding of that noxious doctrine which denies the existence of free will."

Suárez takes the same unequivocal stand as Loyola regarding freedom of the will: "Todo agente racional, y sólo él, es capaz de libertad." *Disputaciones metafísicas,* Tomo III, p. 368.

Calderón also defends the doctrine of free will. In *La vida es sueño,* Segismundo manifests his freedom in defiance of the stars and proves his father's deterministic theories wrong. See Chapter 4. In *En la vida todo es verdad y todo mentira* Heraclio sees freedom as a natural quality of man which no other can deny him:

>   ¿Hasta cuando?
> padre, negarnos intentas
> la libertad? (p. 116)

Julia takes the same stand in *La devoción de la Cruz:*
>   mal te puede negar
> la vida que tú me diste:
> la libertad que me dió
> el cielo, es la que te niego.

This concept of man as a free agent is fundamental to existentialist thought. Søren Kierkegaard wrote: "So by turning inwardly he (the genius; i.e., the epitome of "man") discovers freedom. Fate he does not fear, for he lays hold of no external task, and for him freedom is his bliss, not freedom to do this or that, to become king and emperor, or the exponent of popular opinion, but freedom to know himself that he is freedom." *The Concept of Dread,* tr. by Walter Lowrie (Princeton: The Princeton University Press, 1944) pp. 96-97.

For Karl Jaspers, freedom existed only insomuch as man rejected all preconceived notions, "scientific" formulae, social and philosophical systems which purport to define and predict: "For the *freedom of Existenz* exists only as identity with the origin on which thought founders. The freedom is lost to me the moment I rescind the lead and slide back into in-manence —for example into the deceptive idea of a universal, necessary and knowable totality of events (of the world, of existence, of spirit) in the face of which I surrender my freedom." *Philosophy of Existence,* tr. by Richard F. Grabau (Philadelphia: University of Pennsylvania Press, 1971) pp. 25-26.

Freedom, for these two thinkers, is the intimate relationship of the individual with himself, the awareness of conciousness of the self which disregards socially, scientifically and philosophically imposed systems and thereby permits the realization of personal authenticity.

Jean-Paul Sartre conceives freedom rather as a prerequisite to action: "La condition première de l'action, c'est la liberté." *L'Être et le néant* (Paris: Gallimard, 1943) p. 508. In *L'Existentialisme est un humanisme* he

The key woed here is *"parece,"* for there can be no certainty that what seems to be really is. Aureliano knows that the images confronting him are highly irregular; they are *"prodigios."* Vassals seem to be thrust up from the bowels of the earth, from the trunks of the trees. Power seems to come suddenly from nowhere.

Faced with such uncertainty, the wise course of action is to proceed with caution and weigh the probabilities. Doubt can be, and characteristically is in Calderón's theater, the richest source of knowledge.[8] By doubting the images projected by the senses the individual comes to realize that all worldly goods are temporal and illusory, and reaches that state of *desengaño* which, on a religious plane, makes possible his spiritual awakening.

states categorically: "il n'y a pas de déterminisme, l'homme est libre..." p. 36; In another section of the same book he states: "l'homme est liberté..." p. 37.

[8] In *La vida es sueño* it is only when Segismundo learns to doubt his senses and maintain a skeptical attitude with respect to the reality of his life at court that he becomes aware of the transitory nature of the world and opens his way for salvation. See Chapter 4. In *El mágico prodigioso* it is only when Cipriano doubts and then rejects the creations of the devil that he becomes ripe for revelation. See Chapter 6. Calderón's characters are frequently haunted by doubts. Semiramis, in *La hija del aire,* laments:

> Ya me deja este pesar
> que temer y que dudar. (p. 727)

And then:

> En duda me ha puesto
> acaso. (p. 727)

And in the third act:

> Quién se vio
> en tal duda? (p. 744)

But Aureliano rejects wisdom, for he rejects doubt. Consciously and deliberately he chooses to accept the information provided by the senses, to discard the possibility of deceit. He imposes certainty where none is possible. He invents a self-made truth which is nothing more than an invention of his will. He chooses to reject doubt and to accept the image offered by the senses:

> En efectos tan dudosos,
> ¿pueden mentir los oídos?
> ¿pueden engañar los ojos?
> No, pues es cierto que veo;
> no, pues es verdad que oigo. (p. 73)

An then, to use what he now asserts as reality as justification for seizing power:

> ¿Qué aguardo, pues le merezco?
> ¿Qué dudo, pues le conozco? (p. 73)

For, maintains Aureliano, it is enough for something to *seem* a reality to him in order for it to *be* a reality, albeit a subjective one. 'If all kingdoms are dreams, why shouldn't he dream his? If a madman sees himself as king, he *is* king, at least within the context of his own reality.

> Sea César, aunque luego
> despierte; que al cabo todo
> los imperios son soñados.
> ¿Qué busco ejemplos más propios,
> si es en su concepto Rey,
> si piensa que es Rey, un loco? (p. 73)

The success or failure of Calderón's characters in terms of personal fulfillment or, in the religious plays, in terms of religious salvation, depends on how they deal with doubt. Characters such as Segismundo, Cipriano and Heraclio who come to accept the uncertainty of the temporal world are successful; those such as Aureliano, Semiramis, Leonido, Focas, who reject doubt, are not. Religious truths are not, of course, subject to doubt. It is precisely the acceptance of the uncertainty of the temporal world which, in the religious plays, enables the protagonist to accept on faith and by means of divine revelation religious truth.

Aureliano invents a system —in which he is king and all others are vassals— using the senses as a convenient criterion for judging the validity of information[9]. He chooses to act as if he were dealing with a permanent indisputable reality while in fact he disregards the evanescent, illusory quality of all temporal power.

[9] Montaigne maintains that all human science is only an invention, no more real than poetry. Human systems are mere "songe et fumée." (Montaigne, p. 285) This stand put extreme skeptics in direct opposition with the advocates of the "new science." Eventually several compromising views were developed. Marin Mersenne, in his *La Verité des Sciences contre les Sceptiques ou Pyrrhoniens* (1625), tried to bridge the gap between the "new science" of such figures as Copericus and Galileo and the theories of the skeptics. Mersenne maintained that, although the claims of the skeptics could not be refuted and although it was indeed true that the senses conveyed to the brain mere appearances, a scientific attitude could be adopted that could be satisfied to study these appearances without endeavoring to ascertain the essence or true nature of things. See Popkin, *A History of Scepticism.*

Two hundred years later, when science again came under attack, certain early existentialists argued that science could not solve the most fundamental human problems. Kierkegaard wrote: "Science cannot explain such things. Every science has its province either in immanent logic, or in an immanence within a transcendence which it cannot explain..."
The Concept of Dread, p. 46 Nietzsche criticizes the desire of the scientist to reduce life to formulae: "It is just the same with the belief with which at present so many materialistic natural-scientists are content, the belief in a world which is supposed to have its equivalent and measure in human thinking and human valuations, a "world of truth" at which we might be able ultimately to arrive with the help of our insignificant, four-cornered human reason!" *Joyful Wisdom*, tr. by Thomas Common, (New York: Frederick Ungar Publishing Co., 1964) p. 339. The Spanish philosopher Miguel de Unamuno argued that science was incapable of reaching what is vital, alive in man. It is oblivious to sentiment, trancendence, need for God: "Lo vivo, lo que es absolutamente inestable, lo absolutamente individual, es, en rigor, initeligible. La lógica tira a reducirlo todo a entidades y a géneros, a que no tenga cada representación más que un solo y mismo contenido en cualquier lugar, tiempo o relación en que se nos ocurra... La ciencia es un cementerio de ideas muertas, aunque de ellas salga vida." *Del sentimiento trágico*, p. 73. Like Montaigne, Ortega y Gasset, whom the existentialist historian, William Barrett, classifies as a "pre-existentialist,"

Will and Representation

One means by which the will manifests itself is through fantasy. Aureliano's projections and reprojections of the image of Quintilio placing the laurel on his head are his means of making the world conform to his will.[10] This is evident in the first scene of *La gran Cenobia,* already discussed:

> Espera, *sombra* fría,
> pálida imagen de mi *fantasía,*
> *ilusión* animada,
> en *aparentes* bultos dilatada,
> no te *consuma el viento*
> si eres *fantasma de mi pensamiento.* (p. 71)

sees science as invention and poetry: "todos esos mundos, incluso el de la ciencia, tiene una dimensión común con la poesía, a saber: que son obra de nuestra fantasía." *Ideas y creencias,* (Madrid: Austral, 1964) p. 58; "la ciencia está mucho más cerca de la poesía que de la realidad." (*Ideas,* p. 31). These thinkers saw science as an invention, a "system" superimposed on reality, which was no less a fantasy than any other human invention.

[10] In the traditional concept, will is movement toward a good. Juan Luis Vives, writing in the sixteenth century, summarizes the traditional view when he writes: "Creado el hombre para la eterna bienaventuranza, le fue otorgada la facultad de aspirar al bien con el fin de que desee unirse y como pegarse con él. Esta facultad recibe el nombre de voluntad." *Tratado del alma, Obras completas,* II, (Madrid: Aguilar, 1948) p. 1182. But will itself is a blind force. It cannot move toward good if it does not recognize it as such. Intelligence, understanding, judgment, and memory work together to light the way for the will (See pages 1182-1183) That is, the aspects of reason guide the will; will is "aquella facultad o energía del alma por la cual deseamos lo bueno y aborrecemos lo malo, guiados por la razón." (p. 1214). Will cannot be forced. It can move in any direction, provided it is in the direction of some good — but not necessarily the good recommended by reason. The senses, too, reveal good things, although they may be temporary or relative goods: "Como efectivamente sean tantos los objetos que se presentan a nuestra elección, por más que la razón demuestre con poderosos motivos que uno de aquellos es el bueno y aconseje su adopción, si se ofrece otro que tenga algunas apariencias aunque muy tenues y adelgazadas de bien, es señora la voluntad de inclinarse a él y

Each of the underscored words in the passage above suggests an entity which is sensually perceptible and yet does not correspond to objective reality. Quintilio appears to Aureliano as a "shadow," a dark, obscure, undefined mass; a "fantasy," the product of the imagination in conjunction with the senses and the will; an "illusion," defined by a no less pedestrian source than Webster as "an unreal or misleading image presented to the vision"; a "mass" or undefined form which is only *aparente,* or visibly, seemingly there. The nebulous suggestion of Quintilio's presence may suddenly "dissolve into the wind," a "phantom" or delusion, a representation of an ideal produced by "thought," characterized elsewhere in Calderón's work as a potentially frivolous manifestation of the functioning of the mind.[11] In this passage Calderón uses

abrazarse con él con esa tan leve sospecha, mientras rechaza al otro que presenta una excelente forma y sustancia de bien." (p. 1215). Will, then is not necessarily subject to reason. Reason may be made to bow to will. Aurealiano's behavior may be explained as follows: In the hierarchy of good things, power must indisputedly be included. But power, like beauty, wealth, and a host of other favors, is a temporal good, far inferior to salvation. Nevertheless, it is the good Aureliano's will craves. He moves, guided by the senses ever in the direction of more power. This movement toward power is what we call ambition. The senses reinforce this drive by conveying images which feed it.

In 1818 Arthur Schopenhauer defines "representation" as a function of the will. Schopenhauer divides the world into two faculties: representation is everything that can be known or perceived, all that is object or phenomenon; will is the "representer," the "being-in-itself" which cannot be represented. The representation exists for the service of the will; it is a mirror of the will, a reflexion of what the will wills. See *The World as Will and Representation,* tr. by E. F. J. Payne, Vol I, (New York: Dover Publications, Inc., 1958).

The existentialist psychotherapist Rollo May uses Schopenhauer's theory as a point of departure for his concept of fantasy: "I use fantasy here not as meaning something unreal to which we escape, but in its original meaning of *phantastikous,* "able to represent," "to make visible." Fantasy is the language of the total self, communicating, offering itself, trying on for size. it is the language of "I wish/I will." Rollo May, *Love and Will,* (New York: W. W. Norton & Company, 1969) p. 281.

[11] Calderón represents the frivolous aspect of thought by dressing *Pensamiento* as a *loco* in a number of *autos.* In *La cena del rey Baltasar,*

a technique characteristic of much of his work: the amassing of synonyms or near synonyms to create an impression of excess, unrestraint or immoderation, precisely the qualities which characterize Aureliano and other Calderonian characters who resemble him.

Aureliano's imagined coronation by the wounded Quintilio corresponds not to what is, but to what Aureliano wishes. Fantasy, as a function of the will, is a means by which we relate ourselves to the world, by which we make our wishes visible to ourselves.[12] That the scene Aureliano projects corresponds to a wish is evident from his grasping at it, from his desire to retain it, expressed by *"Espera,"* and *"no te consuma."*

Calderón shows that thought is not in itself mad, although it may function as madness in the minds of characters such as Baltasar:

> Andar de loco vestido
> no es porque a solas lo soy,
> sino que el público estoy
> a la prudencia rendido;
>   pues ningún loco se hallara
> que más incurable fuera
> si ejecutara y dijera
> un hombre cuanto pensara; (61-68)

Thought, when subjected to prudence, need not be mad. But there is always the possibility that thought may break loose from prudence. The seeds of madness are in all of us:

> y así lo parecen pocos,
> siéndolo cuantos encuentro,
> porque vistos hacia dentro,
> todos somos locos,
> los unos y los otros. (69-73)

The same device of disguising *Pensamiento* as a madman is used in *El día mayor de los días.*

[12] The following comments by Rollo May define "wish" and "will" as they are used here: "The wish is the beginning of orienting ourselves to the

30

The image of Quintilio is not a happy but an anguished one.
The emperor appears:

> el rostro ensangrentado,
> y por varias heridas
> vertiendo horrores, derramando vidas. (p. 71)

The blood-stained face, the wounded body, the tremulous, anguished voice of Rome's fallen ruler as imagined by Aureliano reflect the violence and passion not of Quintilio, but of Aureliano, who projects the image. The violence of the fantasy is an indication of the violence of the will which represents it.

The fact that Aureliano's fantasy does not correspond to objective reality does not mean it corresponds to no reality at all. It does reflect a deeply felt, vividly experienced psychological reality. In the first place, the image he projects now is one he has projected repeatedly, which indicates it has become almost an obsession for him. In the second, this projection causes him very real inner torment resulting from both the intensity of his desire to rule and from his awareness that this desire may never be realized. The image haunts him, for it reminds him of a failure, a kingdom coveted and not attained, a goal projected and not achieved.

future, and admission that we *want* the future to be such and such; it is a capacity to reach down deep into ourselves and preoccupy ourselves with a longing to change the future. Note that I say *beginning,* not the end; I am perfectly aware of "wish fulfillment," wishes as a substitute for will, and so on. I am saying that there is no will without a prior wish." (*Love and Will,* p. 211; italics May's).

May goes on to define will and wish as follows: *"Will is the capacity to organize one's self* so the movement in a certain direction or toward a certain goal may take place. *Wish is the imaginative playing with the possibility* of some act or state occurring. (*Love and Will,* p. 218; italics May's.)

Faced with the dichotomy between the world as he wills it and the world as it is, Aureliano withdraws into himself. He returns to the womb, so to speak. He rejects a kingdom which will not have him as ruler and retires to a rustic setting. The set of the first scene is in itself significant, for it is an example of how Calderón uses costumes and scenery to reflect psychological reality. Aureliano's surroundings are not the soft, green undulating hills of the pastoral novel, but rather a wooded mount, bordered by steep cliffs. The asperity of the scene reflects the agitation of Aureliano's inner self: He has retired to the woods to become king of the beasts, since men will not have him as their king. And it is fitting that Aureliano should become king of the beasts, for he is a beast himself. Dressed in animal skins and giving rein to his unbridled will, he is no different from the animals that surround him.[13]

Isolated in the harsh confines of the woods —or of the inner self— Aureliano leaves his will free to fantasize:

> Pues si este soy, ¿qué mucho las pasiones
> que me oprimen despierto,
> entre las sombras del silencio
> den cuerpo a vanas ilusiones? (p. 71)

His passions are ignited and stimulated by the fantastical projections of the will. From the will to power springs forth a passion for power: a burning, a longing, an ardent desire. Passion is suffering and Aureliano's passions oppress him ("que me oprimen despierto"). Lost in a nightmare of unsatiated wanting, Aureliano agonizes, victim of his own will. When at last the crown and sceptre appear, Aureliano is confused. Are they real or simply another representation of the impassioned will?

> O los ojos me mienten, o el deseo; (p. 71)

[13] Schopenhauer saw will as a faculty of every animal and vegetable being. Will alone is therefore insufficient to confer a being with "human" status. *The World*, p. 275.

He chooses, as we have seen, to accept the objects as signs that he was destined to rule. This grasping at fantasy is the distinguishing characteristic of the willful individual.[14]

Aureliano is elated and encouraged:

> un aliento nuevo,
> un espíritu altivo que me inflama
> el corazón, a tanto honor me llama. (pp. 71-72)

Just as Aureliano's previous despair was unalleviated by any sense of hope, his elation is untempered by any sense of precaution. He calls forth the very beasts of the earth to witness his coronation.

Man's acts acquire value when they are performed before a witness.[15] For the Christian, the omnipresent witness and ultimate judge is God. But Aureliano, functioning outside the Christian framework, seeks temporal witnesses, and for lack of men, beasts will do.

Aureliano is different from kings who are born into positions of sovereignty, for he does not simply accept power; he seizes

[14] Rollo May's discussion of Father Williams Lynch's observations on willfulness provides us with some useful definitons: "willful (is) the insistence of one's own wish against the reality of the situation... The defiant willful act, says Lynch, is correlated with fantasy rather than with imagination, and is the spirit which negates reality, whether it be a person or an aspect of impersonal nature, rather than sees it, forms it, respects it, or takes joy in it." *Love and Will,* pp. 216-217.

[15] Not all philosophical currents assign equal importance to the witness. The atheistic altruist, for example, finds fulfillment in the good deed perfomed precisely in the absence of all witnesses. The deed is seen as an end in itself rather than as a means by which one proves oneself worthy of praise or religious salvation. For the Christian, all deeds are witnessed by God. For the Sartrian existentialist, all acts must be performed in the presence of others, for it is others, not we ourselves, who pass judgment on us in terms of our acts. Aureliano seems to sense a need for witnesses to validate his new-found power.

it.[16] He seeks power as a means of self-gratification because he is egocentric and considers himself a world unto itself:

> Pequeño mundo soy, y en esto fundo
> que en ser señor de mí, lo soy del mundo. (p. 72)

Aureliano's attitude does not reveal true recognition and domination of the self. Aureliano never sees himself as he really is, but only as he represents himself to himself. Immediately upon placing the crown upon his own head, he proceeds to the fountain, where he admires his reflection.

> En este lisonjero
> espejo fugitivo mirar quiero
> cómo el resplandeciente
> laurel asienta en mi dichosa frente.
> *Mírase en una fuente.*
>
> ¡Oh sagrada figura!,
> haga el original a la pintura
> debida reverencia,
> cuando, llevado en mis discuros, hallo
> que yo doy y recibo la obediencia,
> siendo mi emperador y mi vasallo.
> Narciso, en una fuente,
> de su misma belleza enamorado.
> rindió la vida; y yo más dignamente,
> dando toda la rienda a mi cuidado,
> si no de mi belleza,
> Narciso pienso ser de mi fiereza.
> *Quédase mirándose.* (p. 72)

[16] The individual born into a position of power is not at fault in accepting it. On the contrary, he is obligated to accept it and to use it as a means of doing good. In the *auto El gran teatro del mundo,* God, whom Calderón depicts as the stage director or *Autor,* symbolically assigns a role to each player who must accept it and use it to his best advantage in terms of religious salvation. That is, it is God's prerogative to assign the roles, not man's.

For Sartre, an individual who assumes a role which is not his own acts out of bad faith. Each individual is free to define or realize himself, but only in

This extremely significant episode points up two important facets of Aureliano: first, his desire for an audience or judge, a function he himself takes over for lack of vassals, and second, his fascination with his own reflection. Aureliano is obsessed with his own image, or representation of himself. He sees himself only as he wills himself to be: as king.[17]

the role which is authentically his. In Sartre's *Les mains sales,* for example, the bourgeois antihero pretends to be a revolutionary but is betrayed by his own conservative upbringing and middle-class values.

[17] A valid comparison could be made between Aureliano and Cervantes' Don Quijote. Both have their own particular view of themselves, product of their wills, to which their representations of the world conform. Don Quijote sees himself as a knight errant and a windmill as a giant appropriate for a knight errant to fight. Aureliano sees himself as a tyrant and every living thing, from the beasts of the earth to the monarchs of other lands, as potential vassals.

In *Don Quijote,* as in *La gran Cenobia,* fantasy is unmistakably the manifestation of the will, which makes possible self-realization. When Don Quijote goes forth for the third time in search of wrongs to right he asserts: "Yo tengo más armas que letras, y nací según me inclino a las armas, debajo de la influencia del planeta Martes; así, que casi me es forzoso seguir por su camino, y por él tengo de ir a pesar de todo el mundo, y será en balde cansaros en persuadirme a que no quiera yo lo que los cielos quieren, la fortuna ordena y la razón pide, y *sobre todo, mi voluntad desea.* (Libro II, Cap. VI, italics mine). The determining factor for Don Quijote is not the inclination imposed on him by the planet Mars, but his own will. Don Quijote's invention and definition of the self is an act of the will manifested and made real through acts of the body —the actual physical going forth to combat evil forces. In order to realize his objective he relies on fantasy. He represents the world as he wills it to be for the realization of the acts necessary for his self-definition as a knight-errant. In the episode of the *"encamisados,"* Sancho is afraid, but "Lo contrario le avino a su amo, al cual en aquel punto se le *representó* en su *imaginación* al vivo que aquella era una de las aventuras de sus libros. *Figurósele* que la litera eran andas donde debía de ir algún mal ferido ·o muerto caballero..." (I, XIX, italics mine). And when he arrives at the inn: "...el agujero que a él le *pareció* la ventana, y aun con rejas doradas, como conviene que las tengan tan ricos castillos como él se *imaginaba* que era aquella venta; y luego en el instante se le *representó* en su loca *imaginación* que... la doncella fermosa, hija de la señora de aquel castillo, vencida de amor, tornaba a solicitarle. (I, XLIII, italics mine). The abundance of words denoting or con-

Aureliano sees his sovereignty as absolute —in no way illusory and in no way temporal. When the priestess Astrea appears with Roman soldiers and presents him with evidence to the contrary, he chooses to ignore it.[18] Astrea tells how Quintilio's treacherous conduct provoked the hatred of the masses and of his own soldiers. She concludes by telling how Quintilio was murdered by his own men. The lessons to be gleaned from this account of Quintilio's career are that good fortune may be short-lived and that cruel, ambitious emperors do not inspire love and respect in their subjects. But Aureliano does not grasp, or even consider, the meaning of the example. He chooses, rather, to disregard it.

noting fantasy and representation should make it obvious that fantasy is a means by which the will, through acts, realizes self-definition in *Don Quijote.*

Yet, in spite of the important similarities between Don Quijote and Aureliano, there are very significant differences. Don Quijote —ridiculous and pathetic as he may be at times— is a pleasing character. He encompasses the loftiness, the idealism which can result from the will's manipulation of fantasy. And, although he is frequently lucid and reasonable, it is precisely at those moments of irrational idealism when he most endears himself to the reader.

Don Quijote recreates the wolrd in accordance with his will's image of himself, but unlike Aureliano, he recognizes a reality outside himself: beauty. Don Quijote's awareness of moral and physical beauty give him something to strive toward, for beauty is something which the will can function in terms *of,* but cannot function *on.* Beauty remains untouchable. Beauty as a concept lies outside the realm of Don Quijote's will to transform, for although he recreates the world in terms of his ideal, beauty, he does not create beauty itself. In this sense Don Quijote is truly erotic, Eros being, as Rollo May puts it, "a desiring, longing, a forever reaching out, seeking to expand." *Love and Will,* p. 73 Eros is an uplifting force. It was, for Saint Augustine, the force capable of uniting man with God. It is something outside us which attracts us. (*Love and Will,* p. 74) Dulcinea is the personification of Eros for Don Quijote.

Aureliano, in contrast with Don Quijote, is a negative character, for unlike him, he maintains no ideal which remains above and beyond his ability to manipulate. For him, there are no Dulcineas.

[18] Like Aureliano, Don Quijote disregards evidence which contradicts his own particular vision of the world. When Don Quijote experiments with his helmet and coat of armour, he proves beyond doubt that it is inauthentic

Aureliano's weakness does not result from his projection of fantasies, but in his unwillingness to go beyond the image.[19] This is evident in the episode in which he chooses to discard doubt and accept the crown and vassals. Instead of refusing temporal power because, as he is aware, it is illusory, Aureliano insists that it is real, since it is real in his concept. Aureliano's error lies in refusing to accept the representation of power for what it is: a representation. Consequently, Aureliano never fully achieves his freedom but rather becomes hindered by the image of himself projected by his will: that of a ferocious, violent, uncontrollable warrior:

> y yo más dignamente,
> dando toda la rienda a mi cuidado,
> si no de mi belleza,
> Narciso pienso ser de mi fiereza. (p. 72)

Once he has cast the mold, he is destined to become a tyrant —unless, of course, by a subsequent act of the will he were to reject the image. But as long as Aureliano chooses to adhere to his image of himself as a tyrant and to accept the image as a reality, he will be bound by it.

and incapable of resisting stress. Yet, instead of giving up his ideal, he gives up his experiments.

[19] Schopenhauer maintained that recognition of the world as one's personal representation was the first step toward wisdom. (See note 10.) For Heidegger, who denied all ties with the existentialists but who nevertheless has much in common with them, freedom consists in recognizing the image and rejecting it. In *Existence and Being,* he maintains, "Freedom reveals itself as the 'letting-be' of what-is." (tr. by W. B. Barton, Jr. and Vera Deutsch, Chicago: Henry Regnery Co., p. 305). That is, only by controlling one's representations and fantasies, only by desisting from imposing one's personal projection on what is outside the self, can one attain freedom and exercise strength. Heidegger differs considerably from Schopenhauer in that he recognizes a world beyond will and representation. He is similar to him, however, in recognizing the importance of achieving awareness of one's own images.

Aureliano, Le Salaud

The term "bad faith" as used by Sartre and other existentialist writers accurately describes Aureliano's attitude. Sartre defines "bad faith" as the invention of any kind of determinism which causes or enables the individual to deny his own liberty and consequently responsibility for his acts. Sartre divides men of "bad faith" into two catagories. Those who hide behind a determinism —who invent excuses for their actions— are *lâches,* or cowards. Those who hold their existence to be inevitable or necessary rather than totally gratuitous are *salauds,* or bastards. [20]

It is, of course, ticklish to apply such terms to creations of a playwright who had no notion of them and was not trying deliberately to illustrate them. [21] Nevertheless, if we bear in mind that we are not using these terms to refer to concepts consciously invented by Calderón but rather to specific types of thinking which might occur in any culture during any period of history, they may be useful. [22]

Aureliano is a *salaud* in the sense that he believes he was meant to occupy a position of power. The doubt he experiences stems from his uncertainty regarding the in-

---

[20] *L'Existentialisme,* p. 84.

[21] One important difference between Calderón's outlook and Sartre's must be noted in reference to this discussion: For Calderón, no existence is gratuitous. All men are on earth for the purpose of attaining salvation. Calderón does not share Sartre's belief in the gratuitous nature of human existence but rather his rejection of predetermination. Aureliano is a *salaud* because he believes he will inevitably fulfill a particular destiny.

[22] The reality of the individual in the face of choice is timeless. Even though man's frame of reference changes, his predicament remains the same: l'homme est toujours le même en face d'une même situation." *L'Existentialisme,* p. 79 Aureliano, in this sense, is no different from any twentieth-century man; he is free to accept or reject what he believes to be his "destiny."

formation conveyed to him by his senses, not regarding what he believes to be his destiny.

That he merits the emperorship, he is positive:

> Divina Astrea,
> no dudo yo de mi heroico
> ánimo merecimientos
> para el laurel que corono;
> antes, porque le merezco,
> dudo tenerle; (p. 73)

As far as Aureliano can see, the vassals which appear before him are an indication that heaven itself approves his ascension to the throne:

> Pero si el cielo permite
> esta elección, y vosotros
> la obedecéis, desde luego
> vuestro emperador me nombro. (p. 73)

He adds his own "Viva" to the shouts of his soldiers, for he is, in effect, his own greatest admirer. He then reiterates the image of himself as a violent warrior:

> Viva, para ser azote
> sangriento y mortal asombro
> de la tierra (p. 73)

There is, however, an important difference between this speech and the one that highlights the scene in which Aureliano admires himself in the fountain. In the latter, Aureliano merely projects an image of himself, representing himself as he would like to be. But Aureliano's new speech is more than a projection; it is a plan of action, for he now has soldiers at his disposal. Through action he will attempt to bring the image to life, to make it real.[23]

[23] "...il n'y a de réalité que dans l'action," Sartre, *L'Existentialisme*, p. 55.

Aureliano has his first opportunity to prove himself a tryant in the scene in which Decio, one of his generals, arrives and tells of his defeat. Aureliano shows himself to be unsympathetic and unpardoning. His attitude is typical of the *salaud*. Aureliano sees himself as a conquerer. Decio's defeat is in conflict with the way Aureliano thinks things were meant to be. It is a blow to his self-image that he cannot accept. Because he has a preconceived notion of his own destiny, he becomes inflexible. He becomes incapable of considering each circumstance as it arises. He sees the future, rather, as an unwaivering trajectory toward triumph. No deviation from the course can be tolerated. Therefore, he cannot accept Decio's defeat —especially humiliating because it was suffered at the hand of a woman—, nor is he willing to listen to his explanation. Compassion is impossible. When Decio suggests that Cenobia is a woman so magnificent she might conquer even the emperor, Aureliano mocks him brutally.

Because he sees his success as inevitable, Aureliano rejects the notion of changing fortune and dismisses the suggestion of his own possible conquest by Cenobia as absurd. Decio warns Aureliano that fortune is fickle. He warns him to cease his cruel mockery, for someday the two men may see their positions reversed. But the *salaud,* because he sees his destiny as fixed, can conceive of no modification in the present circumstances. So certain is Aureliano of his own future that he spares Decio's life only to put fortune to the test:

> Vive muriendo, y advierte
> que no te mato, por ver
> de la fortune el poder.
> Ni la temo, ni respeto; (p. 76)

But Aureliano does not experiment in good faith —that is, out of curiosity and with an open mind. On the contrary, he is certain the tables will never turn.

40

In an act of extreme arrogance he takes away Decio's sword. Aureliano chooses to humiliate Decio instead of pardoning him not only because Decio's defeat has challenged his self-image, but also because he is unable to imagine himself in Decio's unfortunate position. Therefore, he is unable to empathize and unwilling to grant pardon.

The *salaud*, convinced of his own merit, sees others as simply instruments for his own self-realization or personal gratification. He sees his abuse of others as justified because he believes himself preordained to occupy a position of privilege. When he mistreats others, he believes himself to be merely exercising his rights. Decio is, in this sense, Aureliano's instrument. By humiliating Decio, Aureliano demonstrates how uncompromising, how fierce, how arrogant he is. Decio is a tool for Aureliano's realization of his self-image, a means by which Aureliano proves he really is

> azote
> sangriento y mortal asombro
> de la tierra (p. 73)

from whom no one may expect compassion.

Cenobia: The Alternative

Cenobia, like Aureliano, occupies a position of power. But while he is characterized by lack of restraint, she is characterized by self-control. Decio speaks of her "cuerdo atrevimiento" and describes her as:

> cuerda al vencer, al governar valiente (.) (p. 75)

Her self-restraint is suggested in metaphor by Decio's description of her horsemanship, the horse being a traditional symbol of passion:[24]

[24] See the discussion of Rosaura's lack of horsemanship in Joaquín de Casalduero, "Sentido y forma de *La vida es sueño." Cuadernos del Congreso por la Libertad de la Cultura,* No. 51 (1961) pp. 3-13.

mostraba, aunque de furia lleno,
que se pudiera governar sin freno. (p. 75)

While Aureliano sees power as a right, Cenobia sees it as a responsibility. When a soldier approaches her with papers testifying as to his service to the crown, Cenobia has already been informed of what he has to tell her. She is aware of all developments in her kingdom. Unlike Aureliano, she does not see her subordinates as instruments for her self-gratification, but as subjects to whom she has a duty.

Unlike Aureliano, Cenobia does not crave power. She accepts her authority without overstepping her bounds. She is aware that it is Abdenato, her husband, who must make all decisions:

Tened, amigos, paciencia,
que es el Rey quien lo ha de ver. (p. 77)

Cenobia understands the natural order of things and her place in it.[25] Wife of an infirm king, she could easily seize power; yet, she is content to remain second in command. Such moderation elicits admiration and respect from her subjects.

Just as Aureliano reveals himself, or to use an existentialist term, defines himself in a specific situation in which he is

---

[25] Calderón inherited from the Middle Ages the view of a rationally ordered universe. For him, universal harmony is established by God. The *auto sacramental La vida es sueño* opens with the image of the warring elements:

Agua:	¡Mía ha de ser la corona!
Aire:	¡El laurel ha de ser mío!
Tierra:	¡No ará mientras yo no muero!
Fuego:	¡No será mientras yo vivo! (1-4)

But the war is put to an end with the intervention of Poder, Sabiduría and Amor, who, controlled by one divine will, rule the world.
Calderón also expresses this view of a rationally ordered world in which each being has a place in the drama *La vida es sueño:*

forced to act, so does Cenobia. Aureliano proves himself a tyrant in his confrontation with Decio; Cenobia proves herself a stateswoman in her confrontation with Libio.[26]

Libio and his consort Irene have been plotting to assassinate Abdenato in order to enable Libio to assume power. Libio requests an audience with the Queen. In their meeting,

> no hay
> animal, planta ni piedra
> que no tenga calidad
> determinada (II, 23-26)

Furthermore, each individual has his place in the hierarchy and God has provided him with what he needs to play his part. In *El gran teatro del mundo* the Autor distributes their roles to the players:

> Ya para que no les falten
> las galas y adornos juntos,
> para vestir los papeles
> tendré prevenido a punto
> al que hubiere de hacer rey,
> púrpura y laurel' augusto;
> al valiente capitán,
> armas, valores, y triunfos; etc. (243-250)

This concept of the universe as a well-ordered machine in which each thing has a reason and a place offers a dramatic contrast with the existentialist view of an "absurd" universe in which there is no finality.

[26] "Define oneself" is a term frequently used by French existentialists such as Sartre to mean "give meaning or form to one's life." Within a Christian framework individuals can be said to "define" themselves as either worthy or unworthy of salvation. For both Calderón and the twentieth-century existentialists this process of self-definition depends on choices and on the acts which result from them. Calderón makes the point that salvation depends on one's deeds at the end of the *auto El gran teatro del mundo*. In the final scenes of the play the characters are required to return to the world those things which had been loaned to them; only Discreción has something she can take with her to the final judgment: her good deeds. Mundo says to her:

> No te puedo quitar las buenas obras.
> Estas solas del mundo se han sacado. (1374-1375)

43

Cenobia, always alert and cautious, immediately notices something is awry. But rather than give vent to her rage, as Aureliano did, she manipulates the situation to gain time and information. The dialog between the Queen and Libio reveals extraordinary restraint on her part. Libio tells her he has been waiting to see her alone, to which she replies he may always count on an audience with her. Her directness and apparent confidence in him are aimed at shaming him out of any evil intentions he may have, for what kind of a man would turn against such a generous superior? Libio begins by implying that people are talking about Cenobia. But instead of indignation or anger, Cenobia shows trust.

By losing control Cenobia might provoke an angry confrontation which might be disastrous both for her and the nation; by maintaining it she gains insight into the situation.

Good deeds are not the result of any kind of predetermination, but of a choice on the part of the individual. In the same *auto*, God, the Autor, specifically refuses to intervene in human affairs, preferring to leave each one free to play his role as he chooses:

> Yo, bien pudiera enmendar
> los yerros que viendo estoy;
> pero por eso les di
> albedrío superior
> a las pasiones humanas,
> por no quitarles la acción
> de merecer con sus obras; (929-935)

Acts, as Calderón sees them, are neither predetermined by outside factors nor the inevitable result of the passions, but are the responsibility of the individual.

For existentialists such as Sartre, self-definition is dependent entirely on one's acts: "l'homme n'est rien d'autre que ce qu'il se fait" (*L'Existentialisme*, Paris, 1966, p. 22); "il n'est rien d'autre que l'ensemble de ses actes." (*L'Existentialisme*, p. 55) Each act is the result of some previous choice: "Je peux vouloir adhérer a un parti, écrire un livre, me marier, tout cela n'est qu'une manifestation d'un choix plus originel." (*L'Existentialisme*, p. 24).

44

In a comparable situation, Aureliano gives vent to his furor and incurs the wrath of Decio, his future assassin. Cenobia, who displays magnanimity, obligates Libio's apparent good will, at least temporarily. When Libio begins to imply that it is not Cenobia's praises the crowds are singing, she corners him by commenting she is certain no one would dare to criticize her in his presence, for she knows him to be her loyal servant. When he argues one cannot be always drawing one's sword, she argues that for the same reason some things are better left unsaid. He argues that the people object to being governed by a woman; she, that they seem not to mind vic- tories won by a woman. The debate reveals Cenobia's dex- terity in the application of logic, her quick thinking, and, above all, her self-control. Through logic, Cenobia reduces her adversary to shame:

> Bien es que vean,
> pues los hombres no pelean,
> que goviernan las mujeres. (p. 75)

The accusation is aimed directly at Libio, who, by his own account, has failed to draw his sword in defense of the Queen. In a situation in which men are slow to fight, it is fitting that a woman take charge of the government. Libio understands the insinuation perfectly well. He argues that he is only repeating what he has heard; Cenobia, that since he brings the charges, he will hear the answers. She ends by making it clear that any traitor will be punished:

> que he (de) dar leyes, y asombros
> les daré también y horror,
> cuando quite a algún traidor
> la cabeza de los hombros. (p. 78)

This tactic allows Cenobia to avoid a direct accusation and an immediate, violent confrontation. It also enables her to prepare her defenses, for Libio has betrayed his intentions:

45

¡Qué ciegamente ha mostrado
su intento! (p. 78)

Libio's exit is followed by a comic scene with the buffoon
Persio in which Cenobia once again uses the technique of
obligating the good will of another by expressing confidence
in him. Persio is in many ways a comic parallel of Libio. He,
like Libio, pretends to be what he is not and carries testimony
from others in order to prove a false identity. Libio comes
with gossip from the crowd, posing as a loyal subject of the
Queen. Persio bears false papers, posing as a valiant soldier.
Both buckle under the Queen's wary cross examination. But
Libio is dangerous while Persio is not. Libio is treacherous
while Persio is simply ingenious. Libio is thrown out of the
court while Persio is allowed to stay, for although Cenobia is
aware of the absurdity of Persio's far-fetched tales, she knows
that such characters are best controlled by obligating them
through generosity than by alienating them through antagonism.

The culmination of the first act is the meeting between Decio
and Cenobia. Decio arrives at Cenobia's court a man without
an identity, for he has been robbed of his honor and good
name by Aureliano. Decio's claim to honor is not the
obsessive preoccupation with reputation of Calderón's honor
characters, but rather the earnest longing of an individual for
his self-respect.

Cenobia: Pues, ¿quién eres?
Decio: No lo sé;
tan ajeno de mí estoy,
que lo dudo. Decio fui
el tiempo que tuve honor;
mas después que no lo tengo,
no sé, Cenobia, quién soy. (p. 80)

46

Decio is, in a certain sense, out of role. He has been forced into an unmerited position of inferiority by Aureliano's insult. This is the significance of his doubting his own identity.

Decio attributes his defeat to ill fortune, but unlike Aureliano, he is aware that fortune can change:

> Tal hizo, por ir vencido,
> como si tuviera yo
> en mis manos mi fortuna,
> sin considerar que son
> inconstantes sus efectos. (p. 80)

Decio tells Cenobia of Aureliano's impending attack. Cenobia once again shows herself to be reserved and generous. Rather than making immediate preparation for the imminent danger, she concerns herself with Decio's wounded pride. She does not boast arrogantly of her victory. Instead, she recognizes the roles of fortune and emotion in all human endeavor. While Aureliano had ridiculed both Decio's view of fortune and his great admiration for Cenobia, the Queen shows compassion and understanding:

> ¿Porque te vencí se afrenta,
> y con necia a la Fortuna
> y por cobarde al amor
> aun sin haberle tenido? (p. 81)

The Renaissance considered love an ennobling force. To conquer Aureliano through love would be in a sense to humanize him. Aureliano's disparagement of love is a reflection of his crudity, of his beast-like quality.[27]

[27] See, for example, Boccaccio's story in which Cimone, who is "almost stupid and beyond hope" and has a voice which is "loud and uncouth, more like an animal's than a man's" is ennobled by love. Giovanni Boccaccio, *The Decameron*, tr. by Richard Aldington, (New York: Dell Publishing Co., 1930) pp. 309-317. Love has a similar civilizing effect on Erastro in Cervantes' *La Galatea*, (Madrid: Espasa-Calpe, 1961) Rennaissance literature provides numerous examples. Since Aureliano rejects love he remains in his uncivilized or "animal" state.

Cenobia urges Decio to stay and help her, but he is unwilling to betray his own men. Decio despises Aureliano as an individual, but he recognizes political allegiance to him and knows he has a responsibility to his soldiers. Cenobia understands and respects his position. Unlike Aureliano, she is not so self-seeking that she disregards others' sense of duty and self-respect. Consequently, she permits him to return to his men and to accept his place in battle.

The Structure of the First Act

Symmetry is fundamental to Calderón's dramatic technique. The first act of *La gran Cenobia* provides an excellent example of Calderón's use of symmetry. However, here as elsewhere in Calderón's work, the symmetry has not only an artistic function but also a philosophical one. It is fundamental to the intellectual content of the play.

There are five main episodes in the first *jornada* of *La gran Cenobia*. They occur in the following sequence: Introduction of character/ Confrontation/ Introduction of character/ Confrontation/ Unification.

In the first episode Aureliano is introduced and assumes power. Aureliano is a negative character. This major episode is followed by a confrontation with Decio. Decio is a positive character whom Aureliano will alienate by his harshness and egotism. This confrontation will lead to a crisis of which Aureliano is completely unconscious. Blinded by the vision of what he believes to be his own destiny, Aureliano cannot foresee any negative development which might deprive him of his power.

The second and third episodes are the reverse of the first and second. In the third episode Cenobia is introduced. Cenobia is a positive character. In the fourth episode there is a confrontation between Cenobia and Libio. Libio is a negative character whom Cenobia will attempt to assimilate —that is, make into a loyal subject— by her confidence and generosity. The result of this confrontation is to ward off a potential crisis of which Cenobia is completely aware. Alert to the whims of fortune and the instability of every human situation, Cenobia can foresee a negative development which would be dangerous to her husband and to the state. The confrontation with Libio is shadowed by the meeting with Persio. This is not a major episode, but a comic parallel of the scene between Libio and Cenobia. It relieves the tension built up during the four previous scenes, which include two tense confrontations.

The symmetry is enhanced by the sets. The first two scenes take place in a harsh, craggy, mountainous, wooded area. There, the willful Aureliano is surrounded by the beasts whom he resembles. The second two scenes take place in the court. This set reflects the civilized or reasonable, as opposed to the uncivilized or primitive.

The fifth scene has a unifying function. Decio, who has confronted Aureliano, now meets Cenobia. Decio links the action of the first two scenes with the action of the second two. He establishes a relationship between Aureliano and Cenobia. It should be noted that the scene which ends the first act is paralleled by a similar scene which is not presented on stage but which is described: the first meeting between Decio and Cenobia in which the former is defeated in battle. The form of the first act may be summarized as follows:

Unifica-tion	Introduction	Confronta-tion	Introduction	Confronta-tion	Unifica-tion
Decio and Cenobia	Aureliano (antagonist)	Aureliano vs. Decio (2nd protagonist)	Cenobia (protagonist)	Cenobia vs. Libio (2nd anta-gonist)	Decio and Cenobia

This symmetrical structure is essential to the meaning of the play. It illustrates that in Calderón's theater it is always possible for a character to make a decision different from the one he does make. Calderón often shows this through the juxtaposition of two characters who in similar situations act in different ways. Both Aureliano and Cenobia are in positions of political power, but one displays selfishness and recklessness while the other displays generosity and caution. The choice is up to the individual. Decio and Líbio are also parallel characters who display the same polarity as Cenobia and Aureliano. Both are political subjects in conflict with their monarch. Decio is a loyal subject who proves his loyalty by returning to his troops in spite of the insult he has suffered at the hands of the emperor. Libio is a disloyal subject who proves his disloyalty by plotting against the state in spite of the confidence and generosity the queen has shown him. Decio puts the good of others before his own well being and desire for vengeance. Libio puts nothing before his own ambition. Thus in the situation in which Decio and Libio find themselves —that of vassal— various modes of conduct are possible. Which one each follows is entirely up to him: it is a matter of choice.

Will and Vengeance

Aureliano's career as emperor is characterized by a series of acts of vengeance. The first of these is the affront against Decio made during the first *jornada*. Decio, aware he has failed the emperor by suffering defeat in battle, asks Aureliano's forgiveness. Aureliano answers with an insult:

> ¿Qué disculpa habrá que aguarde
> hombre que vencido viene?
> Di, por ver si alguno tiene
> disculpa de ser cobarde. (p. 74)

The emperor not only fails to comprehend the reasons for Decio's defeat, but attacks him brutally. He is not satisfied simply not to forgive; he must insult. Three times he accuses Aureliano of cowardice. The third is followed by an even graver insult: he throws Decio on the ground and steps on him. Then he relieves him of his sword.

These acts, performed intentionally and in the presence of witnesses, constitute an affront requiring vengeance.[28] But seen in another perspective, they are acts of vengeance in themselves.

Vengeance is a means of setting things right, of making another pay up for something he has done. After vengeance is taken, things are once again "even." By taking vengeance, Aureliano attempts to restore things to the way they were, to preserve his fantasy of himself and of the world.

Aureliano finds Decio's defeat offensive to his self-image of conquering hero. A king is, of course, official commander of his army. Decio is responsible to Aureliano, who is ultimately responsible for all defeats suffered by his soldiers, whether or not he leads a particular campaign. Thus, Decio's defeat is Aureliano's defeat. To have one of his generals conquered, and, graver still, by a woman, is an insult to his own reputation. Aureliano's humiliation of Decio is, then, a true act of vengeance; it is a punishment inflicted in return for an offense, a means of "getting even."

The second act of vengeance occurs during the second *jornada*. Aureliano is to go forth into battle against Cenobia. Astrea, having consulted the oracle, predicts victory:

> "Irás y vencerás: no
> serás vencido en la guerra." (p. 84)

---

[28] According to the seventeenth-century concept of honor, an affront is aggravated by the presence of witnesses. See Julian Pitt-Rivers, "Honour and Social Status" in J. G. Peristiany, *Honour and Shame*, (Chicago: The University of Chicago Press, 1966) pp. 19-79.

The battle, however, turns out to be disastrous for Aureliano. Astrea had misread the oracle, whose real message was:

> "Irás y vencerás no;
> serás vencido en la guerra." (p. 84)

Aureliano, in his zeal to accomodate reality to his own particular view of it, had sought reassurance from the priestess. But no individual can fully penetrate the mysteries of the future. No mortal has access to the secrets of the gods.[29]

Aureliano refuses to accept evidence which conflicts with his views. He had chosen, in the first act, to renounce doubt in favor of intellectual certainty. ·For him, the image of himself as conquerer is an unquestionable certainty. As in the episode with Decio, the evidence to the contrary is met with rage. He takes vengeance on Astrea by throwing her over a cliff. It is, of course, he and not she who has lost the battle; yet, it is she who must pay the consequences:

> Muere, infame, y vengue en ti
> de aquese Apolo crüel
> rabia, que no puedo en él;
> en esta gruta.
> *Arrójala por una cueva, despeñada.* (p. 84)

Aureliano himself defines the punishment as an act of vengeance *(vengue en ti).* But why does he take vengeance on Astrea? Vengeance is a form of shifting the responsibility, of making another pay for one's own humiliation. Aureliano preserves his self-image by shirking the responsibility for his defeat. He does not admit, as the evidence suggests, that he cannot know the future and that there is always the possibility of either victory or defeat in any conflict. Rather, he hangs on to his belief that his future is fixed and to his confidence in his image of himself. In order to do so, he must

---

[29] See discussion of this point in reference to *La vida es sueño* in Chapter 4.

shift the responsibility for his defeat to another person on whom he takes vengeance, thereby restoring things to what he sees as their normal order.

Aureliano's third act of vengeance is his attempted murder of Libio. Toward the middle of the second act Libio approaches Aureliano with the promise of helping him penetrate Cenobia's camp and taking her prisoner. After this treacherous act is effected, Libio comes to ask Aureliano for his reward. Aureliano makes a mockery of Libio's request by first granting him favors, thereby building up his confidence, then by having him thrown from a cliff:

> Mas con lo que hago y digo,
> premio el favor y la traición castigo.
> ¡Con ella desde el monte
> > *(A los Soldados.)*
>
> que opuesto a las estrellas
> es en sus luces bellas
> término al horizonte,
> le despeñad! Con esto
> te vienes, Libio, a ver en alto puesto. (p. 92)

Aureliano's mockery is intensified by his choice of words: the reference to "high places" is meant to deride Libio's ambition.[30]

This act of vengeance, like the previous ones, is a reaction to a failure on the part of Aureliano. The emperor had shamed Decio because the latter had not the military know-how to conquer Cenobia. And yet, Aureliano himself triumphs not by force, but by an act of treachery. Such a victory is not a victory at all, but a stunning defeat. The presence of Libio in Aureliano's court would be a constant reminder of that defeat.

---

[30] In a similar scene toward the end of *La vida es sueño*, Segismundo punishes the soldier who had liberated him. Calderón seems to possess a Machiavellian awareness of the danger of trusting traitors.

Once again, Aureliano must take vengeance as a means of preserving his image of himself as conquering hero.

But there is a second reason for eliminating Libio: Aureliano recognizes in him a scoundrel like himself. Libio is, like Aureliano, ambitious, willful, treacherous. Like him, he believes that fortune is fixed. Like him, he is guilt-ridden. Libio is tortured constantly by his feelings of guilt. In the scene in which Astrea, having been hurled from a precipice by Aureliano, calls out for help, Libio mistakes her description of Aureliano for a description of himself:

> Astrea: Ven, traidor; y si te queda
> más rigor, muéstrale aquí;
> que huyendo, tirano, de esto,
> te verás en alto puesto.
>
> Libio: Parece que hablan de mí. (p. 85)

Astrea calls out again:

> Sé soberbio, sé tirano,
> sé riguroso, sé fiero
> de una vez. (p. 85)

And once again, Libio believes the strange words refer to him:

> ¡Cielos! ¿Qué espero?
> Hoy, nuevo espíritu gano,
> pues me anima el cielo a ser
> cruel, pues me ha persuadido
> con voces, quizá ofendido
> de una soberbia mujer. (p. 85)

Libio, like Aureliano, has a rigid view of the universe and his place in it. He, like Aureliano, interprets signs in accordance with his image of himself and the world. It is not surprising, then, that he takes Astrea's words as a mandate to act treacherously. As in the case of Aureliano, all appearances seem to second the fantasies of his will. Consequently, Libio

54

determines to realize his ambition to see himself in a "high place" through means of treason. The very fact that Libio mistakes Astrea's description of Aureliano for a reference to himself is an indication of the similarity between the principal and secondary antagonists.

Aureliano recognizes this similarity and fears it. He also knows that a man who has betrayed one monarch will betray another.

> Pierda yo los recelos;
> que quien en tanta pena
> su sangre vende, venderá la ajena. (p. 92)

He knows this especially well because he himself uses treachery to achieve his aims.

In summary, Aureliano's vengeance on Libio reflects a double sense of guilt and corresponds to a double defeat. In the first place, it reveals his sense of guilt at having failed to triumph over Cenobia on the battlefield. This is a *past* defeat. In the second place, it corresponds to a fear of treachery on the part of Libio. This would be a *future* defeat. Thus, in the case of Libio, exactly as in the cases of Decio and Astrea, Aureliano resorts to vengeance in order to eradicate a failure and to preserve the fantasy of himself his will has created.[31]

---

[31] Nietzsche discusses the relationship between will and vengeance in *Thus Spoke Zarathustra:* "So the will, the liberator, came to hurt others; because it cannot move backwards, it takes revenge on anything capable of suffering. In fact, this —this alone— *is* revenge; the will's unwillingness to yield to time and time's "It was."' Vengeance, as Nietzsche sees it, constitutes an admission of the will's impotence to change the past: "Impotent toward what has already been done, the will is the unhappy spectator of the past. The will cannot will backward; that it cannot break through the enslavement of time and time's greediness is the will's loneliest tribulation." p. 143.

For Aureliano, vengeance is not only will's rage against the "enslavement of time," but also assurance against the possibility of future failure. If the past constitutes one unsurmountable obstacle to the will, so does the reality

The fourth and most significant act of vengeance performed by Aureliano is his humiliation of Cenobia in the last *jornada* of the play. From the very beginning of the second *jornada,* Aureliano's motive for seeking Cenobia's defeat is vengeance:

> ¡Altiva Cenobia, hoy llega
> tu castigo y mi venganza! (p. 84)

Once Cenobia has been taken prisoner, Aureliano must repress the feelings of love and compassion she awakens in him:

> O muera mi deseo,
> o viva mi esperanza;
> que amor pide piedad y honor venganza. (p. 91)

To show pity is a normal human reaction. Love, manifested in its purest form as charity, is an elevating force which differentiates man from beast.[32]

Aureliano, attracted by Cenobia's great beauty, is, for a moment, "purified" or "civilized," and reason triumphs momentarily over will:

> El que constante estuvo
> y sordo tiempo tanto
> de una mujer al llanto,
> perfecta alma no tuvo;
> ni es racional, ni es hombre
> a quien de la mujer no rinde el nombre. (p. 91)

---

of another will. Libio, through an act of his own will, may check the possibilities of Aureliano's success. Thus, Aureliano's vengeance is not only a reaction against past defeats but also a precaution against future defeats. The concept of vengeance as an enragement of the will against an obstacle is the same in either case.

[32] The highest form of love is traditionally considered to be charity or concern for the welfare of another. This form of love was called *agape* by the Greeks and *caritas* by the Latins. The most perfect expression of *agape* is considered to be God's love for man.

Only the rational soul may be moved to pity. A being who cannot be moved to pity does not have a perfect soul, and the human soul, by its very definition, is perfect. Therefore, he who does not feel pity has a less than perfect soul —that is, is less than human.[33]

But Aureliano rejects the natural leanings of his heart and reverts to his original brutish state. By a conscious choice, he rejects the rational faculty and gives rein to his will to power. Instead of allowing himself to succumb to beauty, Aureliano represses his good inclinations and subjects reason to will:[34]

> Si Cenobia es tan bella,
> si tú tan valeroso
> que la excedes, procura
> que iguale tu valor a su hermosura. (p. 92)

> No, ni su fuego entero
> me hará querer, si yo querer no quiero. (p. 92)

Aureliano remains a brute by choice. If he would yield to Eros,[35] with its power to elevate, he could avoid the catastrophe he brings upon himself. But instead, he allows his will to crush the very beauty that might save him.

[33] See Vives, *Tratado*, p. 1218-1219.

[34] Vives defines love as "la inclinación o progreso de la voluntad hacia el bien." (*Tratado*, p. 1249) Goods, as we have pointed out in note 10, could fall into distinct categories, ranging from the mere gratification of the senses to *agape*. Beauty was thought to be one of the highest goods, for physical beauty was considered to be a reflection of moral beauty: "La hermosura de los cuerpos refleja la hermosura de nuestras almas y casi la pone delante de nuestros ojos con su aliños, con su elegancia, con su proporción y su armonía. La perfección interior engendra la perfección exterior." (*Tratado*, p. 1251) Calderón does not uniformly portray physical beauty as a reflection of moral perfection. (See, for example, the *autos El gran teatro del mundo* and *No hay más fortuna que Dios*.) In *La gran Cenobia*, however, he does adhere to this concept of physical beauty.

[35] See Note 17.

Vengeance, like fantasy, is a means of attempting to make the world conform to the will's representation of it. By projecting fantasies, the will "makes visible" what it wills. By acts of vengeance, it eradicates evidence that the world is not as it wills it. It reacts against its own impotence to change incidents which have occurred or may occur.

An individual who systemizes the world to make it conform to his will's representation of it negates his own freedom, for he acts only in accordance with the system he himself has invented. He binds his hands. He becomes victim of the determinism he himself has invented.

This is evident in the scene in which Aureliano refuses to allow himself to be moved by Cenobia's beauty. Beauty is an essence beyond the will, a purity the will is incapable of blemishing. To admire beauty is to control the will, to hold it back in awe. To be moved by beauty, to love it, to respect it, is to step aside and recognize it as something outside one's realm of willing. The individual who leaves beauty untouched by the will, who allows beauty to act upon his will rather than allowing his will to act upon beauty, has reached the ultimate control of the will. His restraint of the will is so great that he can effect a state of non-willing. To control the will in this way is to achieve total freedom. For the person who controls his will is no longer the dupe of his will's fantasies; rather, he recognizes the existence of something —some purity or unnamed essence— beyond his own representation. He is no longer bound by his own system. He is no longer the victim of any self-inflicted determinism.[36] The opposite of freedom,

[36] For Nietzsche real liberation could take place only when the will mastered itself, when it could will itself to stop willing. Otherwise, it would be a slave to its own blind movement. Beauty was precisely the essence by which the will could be tamed. Recognition and respect for beauty could halt the passionate movement of the blind will: "His awareness (the exalted man's) has not learned how to smile and get rid of jealousy; his streaming passion has not yet come to rest in beauty. Truly, I want his demands to

58

total liberty to act, is impotence, inability to act. The individual who, like Aureliano, is slave to his will's representations, is doomed to total impotence. Before his own image, Aureliano remains unbending. A word frequently used by Calderón to refer to this quality of inflexibility is *rigor*.[37] In *La gran Cenobia, rigor* is used in reference to Aureliano. Astrea calls out to Aureliano:

> Hoy ha de triunfar de ti
> el *rigor*... (p. 85)

And then:

> Ven traidor; y si te queda
> más *rigor,* muéstrale aquí; (p. 85)

And then:

> Basta, invicto Emperador,
> la furia perdona ya,
> que más fama te dará
> la clemencia que el *rigor.* (p. 85)

submerge silently, not in satiation but in beauty!... it is precisely the hero who finds beauty his most difficult task. Beauty is unattainable to the violent will." This new-found control was what could convert the hero into a superhero: "The descent of power is what I call Beauty, power become gracious and descending into visibility... For this is the soul's secret: Only after the hero has left, there approaches in a dream... the Super-Hero." *Zarathustra,* pp. 119-120.

Martin Heidegger develops a related idea in his essays: Beauty is something beyond the individual which he can attain only by ceasing to project his own images and fantasies. By controlling the will and willing only a state of non-willing, he can become sensitive to a reality beyond the will which is Truth or poetic beauty. (See Martin Heidegger, "Hölderlin and the Essence of Poetry," tr. by Douglas Scott and "On the Essence of Truth" tr. by R. F. C. Hull and Alan Crick in *Existence and Being* (Chicago: Henry Regnery Company, 1949) pp. 290-324.

For these thinkers, as for Calderón, power over the self and consequently freedom lies in controlling the will rather than being controlled by it.

[37] *Rigor* and its derivatives are applied not only to individuals but also to circumstances which a character sees as inflexible. Often it is used with reference to the honor code, which is seen as "rigorous" in the sense that it

Aureliano's *rigor* is the inevitable product of his willfulness. It is the necessary outcome of his refusal to part with the representations of his will.

That Aureliano's willfulness constitutes not a strength but a weakness becomes increasingly evident toward the end of the play. At the beginning of the third *jornada*, Aureliano achieves the vengeance he seeks over Cenobia. He humiliates her by forcing her to pull his triumphal chariot like a beast of burden. Shamelessly he brags about his victory, as though he had conquered her in honest battle instead of through treachery:

> más su vitoria estimo
> que si en campaña venciera
> en defensa de los dioses,
> brazo a brazo y fuerza a fuerza,
> los gigantes de Sicilia
> o los cíclopes de Fiegra. (p. 93)

But Aureliano's arrogance masks the knowledge that his victory is really a defeat. To pretend to value a prisoner taken by deceit more than a giant slain in battle is to admit one's inability to take that prisoner any other way. Aureliano has taken vengeance on Cenobia for three defeats she has in-

---

is —for certain characters— a reality with which no compromise is possible. In *A secreto agravio, secreta venganza*, Leonor laments:

> Esto, Sirena, es forzoso
> declárese mi rigor
> porque mi vida y mi honor
> ya no es mío, es de mi esposo.

Don Juan Roca expresses the same idea in *El pintor de su deshonra:*

> ¡Mal haya el primero, amén,
> que hizo ley tan rigurosa!

Rigor is often used in conjunction with terms which refer to astrology, such as *estrella, fatalidad, hados*. These, too, connote the concept of rigidity or inflexibility.

flicted on him: the first, in the battle against Decio; the second, in the battle whose outcome was wrongly predicted by Astrea; the third, in the moral battle Aureliano has just lost by having had to resort to treachery.

Aureliano has had to cheat in order to force reality into the mold he has cast for it. Yet he sees his triumph over Cenobia as the fulfillment of his domination over fortune:

> Esta que veis a mis pies
> mujer humillada, esta
> que, a ser mortal la fortuna,
> la misma fortuna fuera,.... (p. 93)

In the first act he had also compared fortune to Cenobia, conquerer of Decio:

> témela tú, que en efecto
> es la fortuna mujer. (p. 76)

Now he reiterates his disdain for fortune by recalling Decio's prediction that the wheels of fortune would change and that he, Aureliano, would someday be at Decio's feet:

> ¿Cómo ese tiempo no llega?
> O no osa ya fortuna,
> o me teme o me respeta.
> Ni la estimo ni la aprecio;
> ¡bueno fuera que temiera
> a una mujer y a un cobarde! (p. 93)

Since Aureliano sees fortune as his slave, existing only for his own fulfillment, he refuses to grasp the concept that fortune can quite unexpectly and gratuitously change.

Once on the throne, Aureliano's willfulness makes it impossible for him to achieve an equitable government. He cares only for power and not at all for the responsibilities involved in ruling:

> ¿Qué más premio han de tener
> los soldados? ¿El servirme
> no basta para interés? (p. 98)

61

His rigorousness makes compassion impossible:

> Si son pobres, no nacieran:.
> demás de ¿qué importa a un Rey
> que haya pobres en su imperio?
> Sufran y padezcan, pues;
> que pues el cielo los hizo
> pobres, él sabe por qué. (p. 98)

Unlike Cenobia, who is acutely aware of her responsibilities as queen, Aureliano is interested only in the pampering of his will. Just as Cenobia cultivates admirers, Aureliano collects enemies desirous of his downfall.

At the end of the play we see him once more haunted by fantasies. First Libio attempts to murder him, provoking in the sleeping emperor visions and apprehensions:

> (¡Qué terrible aprehensión es
> esta, que el ánimo mío
> rinde pesada y crüel!) (p. 99)

Waking and sleeping, images pursue him:

> (¿Imaginación,
> qué pretendes?) (p. 99)

Libio, acting out of cowardice and vengeance, is unable to carry out the plot.

Astrea also approaches, and Aureliano continues to be tortured by specters:

> Espíritus que en eterna
> cárcel habitáis, después
> de dar el común tributo
> a la tierra, que debéis
> en pálidos desengaños,
> ¿qué buscáis? ¿Qué pretendéis?
> Sombras, ¿qué me perseguís?
> Fantasmas, ¿qué me queréis? (p. 100)

The vocabulary of these last scenes is strikingly similar to that of the first: *aprehensión, espíritu, sombras, fantasmas* all connote something visible but which does not necessarily correspond to objective reality. Aureliano's will has led him nowhere. The play starts and ends in the same place, with a tortured Aureliano struggling against uncertainty.

> ¡Ay cielos! Pero ¿qué temo,
> si ilusión del sueño fue? (p. 100)

Just as in the first scene, Aureliano finds himself in the semiconscious state between dreaming and waking, unable to distinguish the fantasies of his own will. He has gone from the eternal nothingness that precedes life to the eternal nothingness which follows it.[38] The structure of the play encompasses its very meaning. The untamed will leads man from one void to another. There is no salvation, no progress, no sense of "having arrived," no striving toward an ideal for Aureliano.

The untamed will leads to total impotence. Victim of his fantasy, Aureliano can no longer act. In vain he lashes out against the specters.

Fantasy, we have said, is a manifestation of the will, and now there is nothing left for Aureliano to will but his own death. Once on the throne, there is nowhere else for him to go. Aureliano's last fantasies manifest a will to death as surely as his first fantasies manifest a will to power.

As we have already shown, Libio, the secondary antagonist, mirrors Aureliano. Toward the middle of the third *jornada*, in

---

[38] Nothingness is a scholastic term of primary philosophical importance. To Calderón, death was not followed by nothingness, but by afterlife. Yet, the pagan character Aureliano, functioning totally without reference to the Christian framework, is confronted with a kind of empty death in which there is neither hope of future salvation nor fear of future damnation and no sense of satisfaction at having completed a life well-lived. In this sense he is indeed confronted with "nothingness."

the scene in which Libio plots Aureliano's murder, Irene warns him that such an act of treason against the state most surely amounts to suicide. But Libio has lost the will to live:

> Necia estás;
> véame una vez vengado,
> que no quiero vivir más. (p. 96)

This death wish is the ultimate manifestation of the impotence of the will.

Aureliano, too, yearns for death. When at last Decio arrives to commit regicide, Aureliano participates in the act of destruction. His words reveal his will to die:

> Con mi mano arrancaré
> pedazos del corazón,
> y en desdicha tan crüel,
> para escupírsela al cielo,
> de mi sangre beberé;
> que hidrópico soy, y en ella
> tengo de aplacar mi sed. (p. 100)

His "system" has failed. His representation has been shattered. And for Aureliano there is nothing beyong the image. No fantasy, no vengeance, can save him from the final *desengaño* of death. His will is still unsatisfied; he still thirsts *(hidrópico soy)*; yet, there is nothing left for him to thirst for but his own end. [39]

---

[39] Calderón often describes his willful characters as "hydropic." These characters suffer from an unsatiable thirst, an uncontrollable desire which cannot be defined, an undirected, unchecked will which even in the face of death goes on thirstily willing. In *La hija del aire* Semíramis is referred to as hydropic:

> ...que está
> el corazón anhelando,
> *hidrópico* de victorias.

Decio: Another Alternative

Decio provides an example of an alternate mode of action in the face of disappointment and humiliation. In the first act of the play, Decio is twice put down. First, he is defeated in battle by Cenobia; then, he is shamed by Aureliano. But in neither case does he resort to brash violence.

Decio does not consider his military defeat at the hands of Cenobia a cause for revenge, but rather for admiration of the magnificent woman who accomplished it. He recognizes that a military battle necessarily results in a winner and a loser; to lose a fairly and wellfought battle is no cause for shame.

Furthermore, Decio recognizes that his defeat was partially due to ill fortune and that fortune can change. Unlike Aureliano, Decio does not have a "system." He does not see fortune as fixed and at the service of his will. This is obvious in the dialogue in which Aureliano mocks fortune. Decio, taking examples from Aureliano's own experience, shows how fortune is constantly shifting:

> Tú eras ayer un soldado;
> y hoy tienes cetro real;
> yo era ayer un General,
> y hoy soy un hombre afrentado;
> tú has subido, y yo he bajado. (p. 75)

In *La cena de Baltasar,* the king is described as hydropic. Idolatría says:

> En los aparadores
> la plata y oro brillan resplandores,
> y con ricos despojos
> hartan la *hidropesía* de los ojos.

In *En la vida todo es verdad y todo mentira,* Focas, like Aureliano, dies in a state of hydropsy:

> Un *hidrópico* de sangre,
> que, por no poder beber
> la de todos, en la suya
> está apagando su sed.

He warns Aureliano that they may someday find their positions reversed. If fortune renders presumptuous confidence absurd, so does it obviate any reason for despair.

Aureliano, however, does see military defeat as cause for vengeance and therefore inflicts humiliation on Decio as punishment for having lost the battle against Cenobia. Both Aureliano and Cenobia triumph in a sense over Decio. However, Cenobia gives Decio no reason to seek revenge, while Aureliano does. For while Decio is defeated by Cenobia in a battle between equals, he is humiliated by Aureliano as an inferior unable to defend himself. He is bullied and insulted unjustly. His conflict with Aureliano is not the impersonal confrontation of two soldiers on the battlefield but a very personal one between individuals. Furthermore, Aureliano's insult occurs before witnesses.

Yet, Decio does not see vengeance as an immediate necessity. When vengeance is finally taken, it must be deliberate and man to man. Vengeance, we have said, is a means of preserving one's self-image. Decio's failure to take immediate vengeance does not indicate that he attributes no importance to his self-image. On the contrary, self-respect *is* largely a matter of self-image. But Decio is not a slave to the will's images. He recognizes and appreciates beauty. He recognizes and respects duty. He is therefore able to control his will. When Cenobia suggests he stay in her ranks and help realize Aureliano's defeat, Decio declines:

> ¿Pues he de ser
> contra mi patria traidor? (p. 81)

Decio's concern for the well-being of his men is evidence that he is not disposed to pamper the will. The matter of his self-image will have to wait. What is more, Decio recognizes honor —understood as self-respect— as a complex matter. Strength resides not in the giving in to the will but in the control of the will. To give in to the will would be to prove correct Aureliano's accusation of weakness. To control the will, to consider first his duty to his state, is to show strength:

> Contra Aureliano, bien puedo,
> como ofendido; mas no
> contra los míos, que fuera
> confirmar su presunción. (p. 81)

Decio will wait for the opportunity to face Aureliano alone without endangering the lives of others.

Decio's most extraordinary show of control of the will occurs during the scene on the bridge in the second act of the play. Fleeing after a defeat, Aureliano meets Decio but does not recognize him. Unaware of his identity, he leaves him to guard a bridge from Cenobia's advancing army. Decio has the perfect opportunity to take vengeance on his superior. He has only to let Cenobia pass. Yet Decio feels a sense of duty to his emperor; he respects his position as head of state even though he despises him as an individual. When Cenobia arrives with her men, she reasons with Decio that if he allows her to advance, they will both be satisfied, for Aureliano's defeat will assure her victory and his vengeance. But Decio's ultimate triumph must be over his own will:

> ya Aureliano está vencido;
> ese triunfo ya le tienes;
> déjame ganar, Cenobia,
> ahora el de defenderle
> siendo mi contrario: así
> quedaremos igualmente
> tú, contenta; honrado yo,
> y él vencido; con quien vienen
> tres medios a conseguirse
> más noble y más cuerdamente. (p. 87)

Cenobia's arguments do not persuade Decio, for he knows that in order to be worthy of her he must regain his self-respect. And this cannot be achieved by a treacherous act of vengeance but by adherence to his word. While Aureliano succumbs to ultimate impotence through the pampering of the will, Decio attains strength through the domination of the will. Aureliano, left with a hydropic will thirsting for power where there is no power to be had, faces annihilation and nothingness. Decio, left with a powerful will, attains beauty and fulfillment in the form of Cenobia's admiration.

In the third act of the play Decio witnesses Cenobia's hideous humiliation by Aureliano. Decio does not despair,[40] but he is indignant at this affront to beauty. Once more Decio confronts Aureliano, this time not as a general who has been conquered in battle but as a subordinate who has performed with courage and loyalty. Aureliano owes Decio his life, for Decio faithfully defended the bridge to Aureliano's camp from attacking soldiers.

Decio approaches Aureliano as a worthy subject to be rewared for his achievement. He asks to be judged on the basis of his acts,[41] not on the basis of past animosity:

> di que Decio es un cobarde,
> que no importa; mas no ofendas
> al soldado que te dio
> la vida... (p. 94)

---

[40] Decio recognizes the transitory nature of the world; he knows all play a role they must eventually give up:

> a Roma llegas a tiempo
> de ver la mayor tragedia
> que en el teatro del mundo
> la fortuna representa. (p. 92)

Calderón develops the metaphor of the world as a stage in a number of other plays, including the *auto El gran teatro del mundo* and the *comedia La vida es sueño*.

[41] See note 26.

Aureliano reasserts that Decio is a coward, unworthy of
praise, because he was defeated by a mere woman. Decio attacks Aureliano's logic by arguing that if his defeat by a
woman showed weakness, then Aureliano's triumph over a
woman is hardly cause for boasting.

Aureliano answers this allegation with arrogance:

> Para vencer basta, Decio,
> que cualquier contrario sea;
> para ser vencido, no. (p. 94)

Aureliano's will to power feeds on the need to destroy and
subjugate, to control everything and to remain itself uncontrolled. Any adversary is fair game; any victory is valid;
any defeat is unacceptable.

Aureliano refuses to reward Decio's act of valor as he had
promised, alleging that his general is an "hombre sin honor"
on whom he does not intend to lavish "honra alguna"
(p. 95). Aureliano resorts to this excuse once again in order
to preserve his own self-image. Decio's strength makes
manifest Aureliano's weakness. To reward Decio would be to
admit he had requested his aid in a moment of urgency. It
would be to admit he was wrong about Decio's cowardice. It
would be to compromise with his representation of himself
and the world. He resents Decio's presence because it confronts him with a truth he dare not admit:

> Decio, tú solo a mis glorias
> te opones, tú solo intentas
> oscurecer la alabanza
> que me da Roma... (p. 95)

Decio confronts him with his impotence to recreate the world
as he wills it and to project his will into the past; that is, to
change the fact of his own failures.

Decio has faced Aureliano man to man. He has presented him with proof of an act of loyalty. He has given him the opportunity to pardon. He has asked for clemency not from a position of weakness but from a position of strength. He has proven his worth through his acts. But Aureliano has refused to yield. Now Decio feels justified in taking vengeance, not as a means of camouflaging his own failures and weaknesses, but as punishment for Aureliano's willfulness and for his profanation of beauty:

> ¡Que así un bárbaro procura
> profanar con tal fiereza
> las aras de la belleza,
> los cultos de la hermosura!
> ¡Qué locura!
> ¡Ay Cenobia! Pienso, rabio,
> mataré al Emperador;
> y mejor
> en venganza de tu agravio
> que en venganza de mi honor. (p. 95)

It is significant that it is Decio, and not Libio or Astrea, who finally murders Aureliano. For it is only Decio who acts out of idealism rather than out of purely personal motives. What is more, it is only he who possesses the moral strength to govern once the tyrant is dead.

One further proof of Decio's self-control is his failure to take immediate vengeance in the scene in which he witnesses Cenobia's attempted seduction of Aureliano. Cenobia has decided to use the only means left to her in order to gain power over Aureliano: she will feign love. Decio witnesses the scene with his eyes but has no knowledge of the motives:

> ¿Pero, qué veo
> ¡cielo!, entre desdichas tantas? (p.96)

His senses, of course, are fooling him. Cenobia is not in love with Aureliano.

70

But the senses ignite the imagination[42] and Decio's immediate impulse is to take vengeance.

Shortly afterward, Cenobia witnesses a scene between Astrea and Decio she believes to be a declaration of love. Immediately her imagination, embellishing the information provided by her senses, begins to work:

> Mas no, mayor daño fue,
> pues ya imagino que sé
> qué es amor y qué son celos. (p. 98)

This is the moment of anger and potential tragedy which in Calderón's honor plays starts the mechanism of vengeance. In an atmosphere of secrecy and dissimulation, honor heroes contrive to take revenge on their women and their women's suspected lovers.[43]

The situation in La gran Cenobia is different. Instead of secrecy, there is openness. Cenobia accuses Decio. Decio ex-

---

[42] The relationship between sense and imagination was well understood in the sixteenth and seventeenth centuries. Vives, describing the normal functions of the human writes: "existe una facultad que consiste en recibir las imágenes en los sentidos, y que por esto se llama imaginativa; hay otra facultad que sirve para retenerlas, y es la memoria; hay una tercera que sirve para perfeccionarlas, la fantasía, y, por fin, la que les distribuye según su asenso o disenso y es la estimativa." (Tratado, p. 1170) Imagination and fantasy are simply the faculties by which the human represents and elaborates the information conveyed by the senses. But Vives knew that imagination and fantasy could excite the passions and cause psychological as well as physical harm: "...para excitar una pasión no siempre se necesita un juicio determinado en virtud de un cúmulo de razones. Bastan y es lo más frecuente para moverla las representaciones de la imaginación. Así, con sólo que la fantasía arrastre consigo tumultuosamente una cierta especie de opinión o juicio de que es bueno o malo el objeto que se le presenta, andamos entre toda suerte de perturbaciones anímicas;" (Tratado, p. 1245) Cervantes, like Calderón, illustrates these ideas through fiction. See Don Quijote, the entremeses El celoso extremeño and La cueva de Salamanca, the short story El viejo celoso and the jealousy episodes of La Galatea.

[43] See Chapter 3.

plains the circumstances of his intimacy with Astrea and in turn accuses Cenobia. She explains the deceit she has planned in order to mislead Aureliano. By facing the situation openly, the senses are belied and the tragedy is avoided. The two lovers are undecieved and communication is made possible. The scene ends in a declaration of love.

Decio's righteousness is illustrated one final time at the end of the play when, having killed Aureliano, he is named the new Caesar. Libio and Irene are certain of pardon for they see in Decio a coniver of their own ilk. But Decio, acting now as chief of state, grants no clemency to traitors. As a king he had respected Aureliano and proven himself a worthy subject. As a man he had despised him and proven himself a worthy adversary. Decio has no use for henchmen such as Libio and Irene who are moved by personal ambition. He therefore condemns them to the end they deserve.

Decio's domination of the will proves that there is an alternative to Aureliano's willfulness, even in the face of defeat. Through control of the will Decio achieves the strength which enables him to make himself worthy of Cenobia's love. Instead of emptiness, frustration and violence, Decio's career culminates in spiritual and political fulfillment.

The Ultimate Strength: The Principle of Clemency

Cenobia illustrates yet another alternative to willfulness; she acts on the principle of clemency. Vengeance is traditionally considered a masculine prerogative[44] while clemency is con-

---

[44] On the relationship between masculinity and vengeance in the seventeenth century honor code see Julian Pitt-Rivers, "Honour and Social Status" and Julio Caro Baroja, "Honour and Shame: A Historical Account of Several Conflicts" in *Honour and Shame*.
Woman as the incarnation of forgiveness and generosity is topical in seventeenth-century drama. Tirso de Molina's play *La prudencia en la*

sidered a feminine attribute. But clemency must not be mistaken for weakness. Clemency is, on the contrary, the ultimate strength. It requires total domination of the will and the capacity to part with the will's images. It requires relinquishment of the image by disdaining to take vengeance.

Cenobia's career is characterized by clemency, that is, by acts of leniency or mercy. In the first act, Cenobia answers Libio's treacherous insinuations not with chastisement but with displays of confidence. Immediately afterwards, she responds with understanding to Decio's entreaty to return to his soldiers. Cenobia recognizes Decio as an important ally and at first proposes he remain in her court to help her combat their common enemy, but when he explains his motives for wanting to rejoin his troops, she grants him leave:

> Pues, alto, vete, y advierte
> que vuelvas por tu opinión
> y para que ocasión tengas,
> tu mayor contrario soy.
> Vete, pues. (p. 81)

mujer is conceived entirely around this concept of woman. Cenobia is perhaps one of the best examples of the same concept in Calderonian theater. Other examples of magnanimous women in Calderón's plays, capable of forgiving even the inhuman *rigor* of their husbands' application of the honor code, are Mencía in *El médico de su honra* and Rosmira, Curcio's wife in *La devoción de la cruz*. In *La hija del aire*, Semíramis, who is power hungry and vengeful, describes her son Ninias, who is generous and reasonable, as

> cobarde y afeminado; (p. 756)

The traditional sex roles are reversed in this play, Semíramis representing the vengeful and masculine and Ninias, the magnanimous and feminine;

> yo mujer y él varón,
> yo con valor y él con miedo,
> yo animosa y él cobarde
> yo con brío, él sin esfuerzo,
> vienen a estar en los dos
> violentados ambos sexos. (p. 756)

73

Cenobia recognizes that Decio's self-image or *opinión* —and consequently his self-respect— depends on his compliance with his duty.

At the beginning of the second act Cenobia is once again confronted by Libio. She answers him first with a warning, then makes it clear that she is aware of his intended treason.

> Yo soy tu Reina; y advierte
> que te dejo de matar
> con mis manos, por no dar
> a un traidor tan noble muerte,
> y podrá ser que algún día
> a las de un verdugo muera. (p. 83)

But when Libio stammers, revealing he has understood her warning, she changes her tactic and lavishes praise and expressions of confidence upon him. By displaying leniency rather than rigorousness Cenobia obligates her adversary and wards off danger. By showering him with compliments rather than insults she corners and controls him. By banishing Libio, she would give him the oportunity to unite with her enemies. By praising him, she keeps him at court under her watchful eye, thus exercising some control over his movement.

Cenobia's strength lies in her recognition of her role for what it is: a role. And while she plays the role of queen splendidly, she does not for a moment take it to be permanent and inalterable. Thus, she does not display the arrogance and cockiness that characterize Aureliano. She is willing to compromise with her self-image when her moral or political sense requires her to do so. As queen she could command Decio to stay and Libio to be punished. Yet she does not give in to her will. She is content to part with her role of all-powerful head of state in order to allow another to comply with his duty and to assure the beholdenness of a potential enemy. While the willful individual rushes mindlessly toward his goal, the

74

rational individual thinks ahead. And if willfulness is impotence, then domination of the will is freedom.[45]

Cenobia's most dramatic sacrifice occurs in the scence on the bridge. Total victory is at hand. Cenobia is in a position to take Aureliano captive. Decio guards the bridge alone, while Cenobia is accompanied by an escort of soldiers. But Cenobia sends her men away and reasons with Decio. And when he agrees to do what she would do were she in the same situation as he, Cenobia advises him to comply with his duty:

> Dec.   Considérate en mi puesto
> que lo mismo que tú hicieres
> haré yo.
>
> Cen.   Si yo me viera
> con la obligación que tienes,
> en este puesto empeñada,
> muriera hasta defenderle.
>
> Dec.   ¿Y si el rendirle importara
> a un grande amigo?
>
> Cen.   No puede
> nadie acudir a su amigo
> más que a su honor. (p. 88)

The scene is artistically exquisite. In it Calderón pits against one another two positive characters each with valid reasons for obstinance and each in love with the other. Decio and Cenobia vie with one another through subtle intimations, through inferred challenges. For each, the true battle is with his own conscience. It is a scene of great tension, for the dilemma must be solved either by direct combat between the two lovers or by the withdrawal of one. In the end, it is Cenobia who makes the sacrifice. She surrenders her moment of glory not out of a position of weakness but out of an understanding of Decio's need to comply with his duty. Cenobia

---

[45] See notes 19 and 36 on Heidegger and Nietzsche.

is not bound by an inflexible image of herself as conquerer. She is willing to compromise, even to sacrifice victory in order that another may preserve his self-respect.

Cenobia makes yet another sacrifice once she is taken prisoner by Aureliano. She is willing to endure personal indignity, provided that vengeance be taken on her alone and not on her people. Cenobia is not guided by a great thirst for temporal power for she is not beguiled by the image of herself as queen. Her capacity to make sacrifices is precisely her strength and the most convincing manifestation of her freedom.

Cenobia makes still another sacrifice in the final scene of the play. Aureliano assassinated and Irene and Libio taken prisoner, Cenobia asks one favor of the new emperor:

> Si yo merezco, Señor
> que a Libio y a Irene den
> tus manos la vida, ésta
> pongo rendida a tus pies. (p. 101)

Cenobia is willing to sacrifice her glory and her life in order to save the lives of those very persons who betrayed her. This is Cenobia's culminating act of clemency.

Cenobia's acts of clemency grow progressively greater. Her flattering of Libio in the first and second scenes is primarily a matter of political expedience. Her acceptance of Persio in her court involves little risk to herself. Granting Decio leave to return to his troops, however, represents both a risk and a displeasure. And allowing Decio to protect Aureliano in the scene on the bridge represents a true sacrifice —a relinquishment of total victory, of merited vengeance— and a risk that Aureliano may once more attack her troops. Her acceptance of humiliation at the hands of Aureliano in return for the protection of her people represents still another magnificent sacrifice. And finally, her request that Decio spare Libio and

Irene represents the sacrifice of her total victory for the well-being of her enemies.

Willfulness results from a refusal to dominate the will by reason, to accept responsibility for one's acts, to control one's fantasies. While Aureliano may be characterized as willful, Cenobia may be characterized as reasonable. This is obvious from the self-control she displays in the episodes just discussed. There are also a number of other indications of Cenobia's rationality. At the beginning of the second act Irene mentions that Cenobia is writing a journal called *Historia oriental*. The significance of this fact is twofold. First of all, it establishes Cenobia as an intellectual queen, a woman who uses her mind. In the second, it introduces the metaphor of life as a book.[46] Cenobia's diary is the history of her people and herself, their queen. She recognizes that she is responsible for the text. No one else can write her story for her:

> Libio: ¿Pues soy yo
> quien ha de escribir su historia?
> Cen: Quien la tome de memoria;
> quien ha de escribirla, no. (p. 83)

Cenobia does not attempt to write what has not yet occurred. Unlike Aureliano, she does not attempt to prognosticate her destiny. She knows that she, through her acts, will mold her story within the unforeseeable circumstances presented by fortune. The metaphor of the unfinished book emphasizes both Cenobia's awareness of her freedom as well as her understanding of her own responsibility and the functioning of fortune.[47]

---

[46] Ernst Robert Curtius attributes the abundance of metaphors associated with the book in Spanish *siglo de oro* literature to both the influence of medieval Latin poetry and to the Islamic culture which flourished for centuries in Spain. For a discussion of the book metaphor in Spain and in particular in Calderón see *European Literature and the Latin Middle Ages*, tr. by Willard R. Trask (New York: Harper Torchobooks, 1953) pp. 340-347.

[47] In modern existential literature Unamuno develops the metaphor of life as a book in *Cómo se hace una novela*.

Another indication of Cenobia's rationality is her reluctance
to be moved by fantasies. In a scene almost identical to the
one in which Libio, overhearing Astrea's condemnation of
Aureliano, concludes she is speaking of him, the queen reacts
quite differently. Passing near the same cave as Libio,
Cenobia hears words which seem to refer to her. Yet, she
rejects them as fantasies:

> Ilusión fue;
> venza yo con el valor,
> que nada temo ni creo
> hasta que sea trofeo
> de un tiráno y de un traidor. (p. 85)

Cenobia is not the dupe of the senses. The echoes and reflections she perceives do not deceive her.

In the scene in which the ghost of Abdenato appears to
Cenobia, she again attempts to reject the vision:

> Ahora, vanos temores,
> dejad de perseguirme. (p. 90)

And indeed, the apparition disappears:

> Resulta en humo finge
> una nube la sombra,
> dejando el aire libre. (p. 90)

Cenobia does not give in to the senses, and although she suffers a temporary defeat at the hands of Aureliano and Libio,
her strength to reject images results in her eventual triumph.
While Aureliano becomes extatic over signs of his good fortune and despondent over the specter of his own death,
Cenobia maintains her mental equilibrium in the face of appearances and is therefore able to cope with the situacion at
hand.

Another indication of Cenobia's domination of the will
through reason is her attitude toward fortune. Like Decio,

78

Cenobia knows that fortune is the henchman of no one and therefore, she makes no predictions about the future. She neither boasts nor despairs, but faces each predicament as it arises. She is able to maintain her dignity in the face of both triumph and defeat:

> mostrar quiero advertida
> que quien en pena grave
> supo vencer, hoy ser vencida sabe. (p. 91)

She exercises self-discipline in all situations. In this sense, she is prudent. Aureliano, in the scene in which he sentences Libio to death, warns Cenobia:

> Ten, Cenobia, prudencia,
> que esto es mundo. (p. 92)

Prudence for Aureliano is self-protection and political expedience. It is shrewd caution, devoid of moral overtones. But for Cenobia, prudence is to be understood as a cardinal virtue:

> Si tengo;
> y a más rigor prevengo,
> más valor, más paciencia;
> que quien tuvo soberbia en tantas dichas
> sabrá tener paciencia en las desdichas. (p. 92)

Cenobia's definition of *"prudencia"* reveals her understanding of the changing nature of circumstance.[48]

---

[48] In the sixteenth and seventeenth centuries the word "prudencia" begins to take on a new meaning. Formerly it had been considered that virtue characterized by discretion and sacacity. But by the 1500's it has already come to mean political expedience. Juan Luis Vives writes in *Tratado del alma:* "La prudencia sin justicia es sospechosa, pues se le considera como astucia y engaño." (p. 1255) For Machiavelli, prudence is a means of preserving one's own prestige and power by outguessing one's rivals; it is one of the principal lessons to be learned from *Il Principe*. In 1647 Baltasar Gracián gives to press *Oráculo manual y arte de prudencia*. Gracián's book is a kind of political primer concerned with getting on in

This awareness that the wheel of fortune turns at the most unexpected moment makes clemency paramount. For one may always find oneself on the bottom of the wheel. One must be flexible, not rigid, for the future is always uncertain. *Rigor* robs the individual of freedom to act in unforeseeable circumstances.

Flexibility, lenience, magnanimity, clemency —these are the principles that must guide the lives of men and women who, like Cenobia, hope to survive the tricks of fortune. And these virtues can be attained only through the domination of the will.

Conclusion

The preceding analysis of *La gran Cenobia* points up some fundamental aspects of Calderón's view of the human condition. Calderón places his characters in situations in which they must make choices. Aureliano turns out to be a tyrant and Cenobia a benevolent ruler because of the choices they make. Aureliano chooses to reject doubt and give credence to only that evidence which substantiates his will's precast image of him. Cenobia, in contrast, chooses to confront each situation as it arises, maintaining a certain skepticism regarding her own biases and fantasies.

the world. As the name implies, Gracián views prudence as an art to be cultivated. The *Oráculo manual* advises the would-be man-of-the-world to make people dependent on him, to avoid victories over superiors, to cultivate those from whom he can learn something, to appreciate the need for artifice, to make use of the wise, to avoid raising exaggerated expectations, to be able to recognize the fortunate in order to associate with them and the misfortunate in order to avoid them.
Aureliano sees prudence as this kind of political one-upmanship, while Cenobia understands it in its more primitive sense.
Professor Antonio Regalado discussed the changing meaning of the word *prudencia* in a lecture on Cervantes' *Don Quijote* given at Columbia University in 1970.

What Aureliano chooses in effect is not to choose. He denies his freedom through an act which is in itself a choice. By precasting an image of himself from which he refuses to deviate, Aureliano limits his possibilities of action. He becomes a pawn of what he believes to be his destiny.

Generalizing from *La gran Cenobia*, we might conclude that Calderón sees each individual as responsible for his own acts and his own life. Predetermination is largely a mental attitude, but a mental attitude with very real repercusions, for it robs the individual of his vitality and freedom. Aureliano, in reality, never does attain the unlimited power he seeks so hungrily, but rather degenerates, as we have shown, into a state of total impotence. At the end of the play we see him reduced to terror, a victim of his own fantasies, totally alone, unfulfilled and seeking death.

Twentieth-century existentialist literature has produced characters who, although different in context, are surprisingly similar to Aureliano in terms of their outlook and their own personal dilemmas. One example is Lucien in Sartre's novella *L'Enfance d'un chef.*

As a literary creation Lucien is in some ways very different from Aureliano. He is the product of twentieth-century bourgeois society; his context— family, social position, provincial background, education—are of primary importance. Aureliano, in contrast, seems to come from nowhere and it is precisely this lack of "context" which helps to give him universality. What these two seemingly very different characters have in common is a will to power which is nourished by fantasy.

Very early in life Lucien becomes aware that everyone plays a role and that he, too, has a role to play. "Role" is, for Sartre, very different from what it is for Calderón. For Calderón one's role is one's station in life, the situation into which one

81

is born, one's place in the natural hierarchy of things. One's role is to be accepted and made the most of. "Role", then, has no negative connotation for Calderón, although his concept of "role" contains an inherent danger: the individual may take his temporal "role" for an eternal reality and consequently use it to justify selfish behavior. This is what happens to the king in Calderón's auto *El gran teatro del mundo*. Properly understood, however, "role" is simply the social context into which one is born and is in itself neither good nor evil.[49] Calderón is very much a medieval poet in the sense that he sees the world as a rationally ordered hierarchy in which every being has its rightful place.[50]

For Sartre, in contrast, "role" is associated with hypocrisy. One's "role" is what one is expected to do and feel, whether those actions and feelings reflect one's authentic self or not. One's "role" is one's social image. It is one's place in society with all the artifical formalities that go with it.

[49] The role itself is inconsequential. Every role provides possibilities for salvation. No role is better than another. In the *auto El gran teatro del mundo*, the Autor tells the characters:

> En la representación
> igualmente satisface
> el que bien al pobre hace
> con afecto, alma y acción
> como el que hace al rey, y son
> iguales éste y aquél
> en acabando el papel. (409-415)

Discreción conveys the same message in *No hay más fortuna que Dios* when she says:

> ...naciendo
> en su estado cada uno
> capaz del Bien; pues es cierto
> que ningún estado es malo
> como el hombre en él sea bueno. (1659-1663)

[50] See note 25. For a further discussion of Calderón's "medieval" characteristics and his efforts to reconcile his medieval Latin and Catholic heritages, see Curtius, pp. 547-570.

Young in life Lucien learns to play his role. He learns to pretend he loves his mother, although he does not, because that is what is expected of him. He learns to go through the motions of religiosity even though religion is meaningless to him. He learns when to show obedience, when to show anger, when to show arrogance. He learns to comply with the image his family and society have of him.

Aureliano forms an image of himself and refuses to part with it. Lucien forms an image of himself in accordance with society's image of him and he, too, dares not part with it. Aureliano's image of himself is the product of his will to power. Lucien, too, wills power. He knows he is someday to command. He is to become a factory boss, like his father. Lucien wills an image of himself in accordance with his role as future factory boss and acts in consonance with that image.

Lucien, like Aureliano, suffers anguish and doubt. Aureliano's uncertainty comes from a skeptical attitude toward the senses. He suspects that the information relayed by the senses may be false and correspond to no objective reality. Perhaps there are no crown and scepter, no vassals. Perhaps his power is only an illusion, his "destiny" only a fantasy. Most twentieth-century existentialists do not share the skeptic's distrust of the senses. Their doubt stems rather from a lack of sense of finality, a feeling that nothing was "meant to be."[51] Lucien senses that to be factory boss is not his destiny, that there is no such thing as "destiny." He suspects the gratuitousness of human existence. He becomes acutely aware that he is not

[51] This sense of lack of finality was due at least partially to the religious crisis of the nineteenth and twentieth centuries which robbed man of his certitude of a divine plan and an afterlife. Nietzsche signaled the bankruptcy of religion as a vital force in Western thought with his declaration "God is dead." Søren Kierkegaard signaled the vacuity of contemporary religion in *Attack upon Christiandom*. Miguel de Unamuno described perhaps better than any other writer the anguish of modern man before this sense lack of finality.

his role. He —what he thinks, feels, wants— does not correspond to what society dictates he ought to be. He knows he is playing a role by complying with the image. He knows it is all a game. This gives him the sensation of not existing.[52] To exist is to be free, to reject the role, to determine one's future in accordance with one's "real self." Not to exist is to be a pawn of fate, to be unable to effect any change, to be incapable of affecting anyone or anything. Lucien becomes aware, furthermore, that everyone plays a role, that everyone "doesn't exist." No one seems to lead an authentic life: "le monde est une comédie sans acteurs."[53]

Like Aureliano, Lucien, faced with doubt, is free either to accept it or to reject it. Aureliano, as we have seen, rejects doubt and adheres to his own precast representation of himself, thereby limiting his possibilities of action and self-fulfillment. Lucien does the same. He decides to accept the role. The next time he sees the son of Bouligaud, a factory worker, he flaunts the authority and arrogance of a future factory boss. This experience is totally unsatisfactory; the young Bouligaud does not even recognize Lucien. Lucien slips into further anguish and doubt. Once more he flirts with "non-existence." He decides that in order to prove the inexistence of everything, an act is needed. This act must be his own suicide. A gratuitous ceasing to exist of a young boy would be a perfect manifestation of the utter senselessness of the world.[54]

[52] "Qu'est-ce que je suis, *moi?*' Il y avait cette brume, enroulée sur elle-même, indéfinie. 'Moi!' Il regarda au loin, le mot sonnait dans sa tête et puis peut-être qu'on pouvait deviner quelque chose comme la pointe sombre d'une pyramide dont les côtes fuyaient, au loin, dans la brume. Lucien frissonna et ses mains tremblaient: 'Ça y est, pensa-t-il, ça y est! J'en étais sûr: *je n'existe pas.*' "L'Enfance d'un chef," *Le Mur,* (Paris: Gallimard 1939) p. 172; italics Sartre's.

[53] *"L'Enfance"* p. 172

[54] "On ne pouvait pas compter sur un traité de philosophie pour persuader aux gens qui'ils n'existaient pas. Ce qui'il fallait c'était un acte, un acte

To make such a choice would be to accept doubt, to accept the lack of finality of the world and to reject one's "image" or "role." Lucien chooses not to commit suicide. Even toying with the idea of suicide is converted into a game. He invents a new image of himself, that of "martyr." He begins to play a new game, in which he sees himself as a romantic hero. But Lucien's flirtation with this new role is short-lived.

Life offers Lucien a variety of experiences which might permit him to reject his role as future factory boss in favor of another or in favor of real authenticity—that is, the acceptance of freedom through the rejection of all roles. Lucien becomes involved with a literary type, then a homosexual against whom he dares not rebel out of fear of being taken for a prude. He learns to enjoy the homosexual experience, but upon returning home to his own ambiance after a trip with his homosexual friend, rejects it violently because it is in conflict with his image of himself as future factory boss. He is filled with shame and fears for his reputation. Like Aureliano, Lucien attempts to negate an experience he considers a failure in terms of his self-image. Just as Aureliano turns against Decio because he represents a threat to his "image," so Lucien turns violently against Bergère, the homosexual, and prays for his death and the death of Berliac, the literary friend who might find out about his unsavory experience through Bergère. Aureliano performs an actual act of vengeance and Lucien a mental one. But they are essentially the same: a means of "covering up" a failure and

vraiment désespéré qui dissipât les apparences et montrât en pleine lumière le néant du monde. Une détonation, un jeune corps saignant sur un tapis, quelques mots griffonnés sur une feuille: Je me tue parce que je n'existe pas. Et vous aussi mes frères, vous êtes néant!" ("L'Enfance" p. 174) Note Sartre's use of the word "apparences." For Sartre the world of appearances is hypocritical society in which individuals are convinced that they are their role. For Calderón, as for the skeptics, all information conveyed by the senses was merely appearance. Both insist on the necessity of going beyond "appearances."

making things right again; a means of denying one's own responsibility, a means of preserving the image.

Aureliano is haunted by visions. Lucien is haunted by words. He becomes obsessed with words such as *"complex,"* *"sadico-anal,"* *"pédéraste,"* words which for him carry a new image of himself in conflict with the old one. Lucien does his best to cast these words away. He tries to assure himself that he is not really a pederast, and his triumph over the conflicting image is achieved when a former philosophy teacher assures him that Freud's theories are just a passing fad. Like Aureliano, Lucien accepts that evidence which reenforces his self-image and rejects that evidence which does not.

Once he has succeeded in pushing aside those experiences, words and images which threaten his image of himself as a future factory boss, Lucien makes every effort to reenforce the latter. He nourishes a myth about his concern for high moral standards and the importance of family. This not only re-enforces his self-image but also prevents him from having to make decisions. His "moral standards" serve as a ready-made excuse whenever temptation threatens. He begins to conceive of his position as future factory boss as moral duty. His father assures him that profit is not only a right but a duty. By making money, he keeps the factory going and provides jobs for his workers. Exploitation is a God-given responsibility.

Aureliano, we have seen, reduces people to instruments for his image cult. Cenobia must be subjugated in order for him to maintain his image of conquerer. Decio must be humiliated in order to permit him to preserve his self-image. Lucien, too, sees others as instruments for the realization of what he now conceives —in spite of periodic doubts— as his destiny. The factory workers are there for him to take command of. Working-class women are there for him to prove his sexual prowess. His homosexual experiences were in violent conflict which his image of himself as factory boss. Workers would not respect a homosexual. Social peers would not fraternize with one. Working-class women are the obvious instruments by which he can regain confidence in his normal sexuality.

His first potential victim is Berthe, a maid. But once Berthe shows herself willing Lucien drops the matter, since there is risk to his reputation involved in getting the daughter of a factory worker pregnant, or even giving one the opportunity to brag about an adventure with him. To have sex with such a girl is not in his role: "Je n'ai pas le droit de la toucher."[55] It would be too risky to his image. Anyhow, her willingness alone constitutes a victory for his ego.

Lucien's first real adventure is with Maud, a working-class girl to whom he gives a false name in order to avoid complications. Lucien finds the affair easy to handle; he manages, as usual, to avoid taking responsibility for little failures by inventing absurd excuses, as, for example, in the comical episode in which he and his friend Guigard compete to see who can hold a kiss longer: ("J'ai laché Maud par discrétion, pensa-t-il, mais ce n'est pas malin, une fois qu'on sait respirer, on peut continuer indéfiniment.")[56] The second time, Lucien wins. His self-image cannot reconcile itself to his being a loser. Through false displays of tenderness and pretty words, Lucien accomplishes his goal. Maud awakens in Lucien not only sexual self-assurance but also feelings of social superiority. He feels sorry for her; she inspires him with romantic sentimentality. He feels toward Maud a kind of healthy piety. He is not moved in the same way Aureliano is when he is confronted with Cenobia's beauty. He does not recognize in her a superior force. Maud inspires Lucien with a kind of self-righteous good will that enables him to reenforce his image of himself as strong and superior, yet understanding.[57] And, of course, when it is convenient for him

[55] "L'Enfance" p. 212
[56] "L'Enfance" p. 217
[57] The strong, superior, yet understanding boss is the image Mr. and Mrs. Fleurier teach Lucien to project from the time he is a little boy.

to do so, Lucien abandons Maud without a second thought.

Lucien, like Aureliano, is moved by a will to power. Although Aureliano's will to power is purely personal while Lucien's is nourished by family and society, both men have in common the creation of a self-image based on a drive to command to which they deliberately give in. Both men wish to rule. Both men desire subjects and unquestioned obedience. Lucien, within the context of twentieth-century provincial society, is a tyrant.

Lucien becomes acutely aware of his "destiny" through means of his political activity. Like Aureliano, Lucien is a basically weak person. He easily falls under the influence of others. His new hero is Lemordant, a rightist activist who fits Lucien's vision of what a leader should be. The rightist line reenforces still further Lucien's image of himself as a future factory boss. He becomes increasingly aware of the purity of his race, of his "Frenchness," of his moral standards, of his physical force inherited from his magnificent ancestors. The rightist doctrines of the *Action Française* reenforce his view of the world as made up of those who command and those who obey. He learns not to discuss, to close his mind to argument and to rely securely on the party line.

Lucien's self-realization is further aided by the wave of anti-Semitism in which his group participates. In the Jews Lucien finds an easy scapegoat. He gains approval of his comrades by putting out the eye of a young Jew and the undying respect of his friend Guigard when he refuses to shake the hand of a Jew at a party. After this second incident Lucien is

---

This is necessary "(pour) te faire obéir et te faire aimer." See the episode in which one of the workmen gets two fingers cut off in the factory: "Lucien lui parla sérieusement et doucement, en le regardant tout droit dans les yeux et en l'appelant Morel. Maman dit qu'elle était fière d'avoir un petit garçon si bon et si sensible." Lucien's goodness and sensitivity are part of his role. (*"L'Enfance"*, p. 161)

overcome with doubt for fear he has made a fool out of himself. His hate for the Jews increases. Once again, vengeance recompenses for a failure by taking the responsibility off the individual. Lucien sinks into a sea of hate. His vengeance is not actual, but mental. He forces himself to meditate on his hatred for the Jews. His bad behavior wasn't *his* fault, but *their* fault. But Lucien cannot convince himself.

All of a sudden the situation changes when Guigard praises Lucien for his action. His doubts are dispelled. According to Guigard, he has acted out of conviction. A man of "conviction" fits Lucien's image. He has become somebody; he is Lucien, who hates Jews. Now, full of pride and self-respect, he is ready to take over the factory. He will realize his destiny. He is convinced, now more than ever, that he was born to rule: "Mais si je ne devais être que ce que je suis, je ne vaudrais pas plus que ce petit youtre."[58] The rest of the world, by its obedience, will legitimatize that destiny:

> Le vrai Lucien —il le savait à présent— il fallait le chercher dans les yeux des autres, dans l'obéissance craintive de Pierrette et de Guigard, dans l'attente pleine d'espoir de tous ces êtres qui grandissaient et murissaient pour lui, de ces jeunes apprentis qui deviendraient *ses* ouvriers, des Férolliens, grands et petits, dont il serait un jour le maire.[59]

Just as Aureliano needs witnesses, so does Lucien. A witness makes an act real, consummate. Lucien needs Guigard and Pierrette just as Aureliano needs the beasts of the forest to accomplish self-realization, to fix the image. To rule, one must have vassals who are at the same time witnesses of one's power.

Lucien sees his power as something inevitable, as something predetermined:

[58] "L'Enfance," p. 238
[59] "L'Enfance," p. 23

"Des génerations d'ouvriers . pourraient, de même, obéir scupuleusement aux ordres de Lucien, ils n'épuiseraient jamais son droit à commander, les droits c'était par delà l'existence, comme les objets mathématiques et les dogmes religieux... Bien avant sa naissance, sa place était marquée au soleil, à Férolles. Déjà —bien avant, même le mariage de son père— on l'*attendait;* s'il était venu au monde, c'était pour occuper cette place: J'existe, pensat-il, parce que j'ai le droit d'exister."[60]

Lucien finishes his meditations by imagining a sweet, pure, country girl of good family and pure linage, whom he will marry.[61] Lucien is now prepared to assume his place in the sun.

Lucien and Aureliano are obviously different types of literary creations. They are products of different epochs, different genres, different types of writers. And yet they illustrate similar problems of human existence.

Both Lucien and Aureliano demonstrate a will to power. Their self-images are manifestations of that will. Each doubts his self-image but chooses to accept it rather than to reject it. Both use vengeance —mental or actual— to eradicate events in conflict with their image and to absolve themselves of responsibility. Both are weak. Both relinquish their freedom to the image they have invented for themselves— for although Lucien is a product of society, it is in his power to reject society's values. By accepting them, he revalidates them for himself.

---

[60] *"L'Enfance,"* p. 239

[61] Along with his sexual education attained through his experiences with Berthe and Maud, Lucien has developed a high regard for virginity in girls of good family. These are girls not to be touched before marriage. Lucien's new-found respect for women gives him a sense of purity: "Les jeunes filles qui sortaient de la messe levaient parfois vers lui leurs beux yeux francs; alors Lucien se détendait un peu, il se sentait pur et fort; il leur souriait. Il expliqua à la bande qu'il respectait les femmes..." (*"L'Enfance"*, p. 232)

Both Aureliano and Lucien are *salauds*. They are convinced of their own destiny. Both see themselves as "chosen" and use this idea to justify to themselves their abuse of others. Other people become in their eyes simply instruments of their own self-realization.

For the existentialist, authenticity is the acceptance of one's liberty and responsibility. To achieve authenticity is to go beyond the role or image and to use to the optimum one's possibilities of action. In this sense, both Aureliano and Lucien are inauthentic, for they both reduce drastically their possibilities of action by rejecting those in conflict with the image. They hide behind the representation, thus making the realization of the authentic self impossible. Perhaps Aureliano could have been moved to pity before Cenobia's beauty had not his "image" of himself rendered mercy impossible. Perhaps Lucien could have become a professor of philosophy —a subject of real concern to him— or a tolerant pederast, had he not been limited by his "image."

Authenticity and inauthenticity are timeless problems of human existence. Calderón and Sartre both explore, through the creation of literary figures, the question of choice and authenticity, and they come to strikingly similar conclusions. Calderón casts the problem largely in terms of appearance and substance; precisely those characters who are repeatedly swayed by appearances are those whom we might validly term "inauthentic." To the extent that Aureliano faces and resolves —or, more accurately, fails to resolve— the same problems as Lucien, he is a percursor of this type of literary character. Calderón illustrates through literary creation one aspect of the problem of will and choice. In this sense, he is a truly "modern" playwright, concerned with many of the same problems which concern us today.

CHAPTER II

FREEDOM AND REASON: *LA DAMA DUENDE*

Doña Angela's Quest for Freedom

La dama duende is a comedy about a wily young widow, doña Angela, who is determined to enjoy herself in spite of the zealous vigilence of her honor-obsessed brothers, don Luis and don Juan. In spite of the apparent superficiality of the plot, *La dama duende* touches on many of the same philosophical issues Calderón elucidates in more serious plays.[1] The central theme of the comedy is the quest for freedom and self-realization, developed dramatically through doña Angela's constant maneuvering in order to escape the watchfulness of her brothers.

---

[1] At the beginning of his career Marcelino Menéndez Pelayo wrote, in reference to *La dama duende*, "Estas comedias (de capa y espada) no son las más trascendentales de Calderón. Ciertamente que sería vano buscar en ellas el pensamiento sublime de *La vida es sueño*, que es cifra y compendio de toda la vida humana, con sus caídas, tormentos y desengaños; ni el de *El mágico prodigioso*, con sus dos tesis de la victoria del libre albedrío sobre todas las sugestiones diabólicas, y de la razón natural como preparación para los caminos de la gracia y de la fe." *Calderón y su teatro* (Buenos Aires: Emecé, n.d.), p. 285 Menéndez Pelayo's opinion that Calderón's comedies are vacuous and without philosophical interest has gone almost unchallenged over the years.

Doña Angela lives with her two brothers in the home of the elder, don Juan. She is watched over and protected to such an extreme that she feels as though she had been buried alive. The symbolism is somewthat reminiscent of Segismundo's tower, signifying both the womb and coffin. Don Luis's and don Juan's protectiveness is socially justifiable, since young widows were considered to be particulary vulnerable. But doña Angela sees the social conventions which prevent her from living her life to the fullest as tricks of an unjust fate.

> Vuelve a amortajarme viva,
> ya.que mi suerte crüel
> lo quiere así.

(Primera jornada, 371-373)

> ¡Suerte injusta, dura estrella!

(Primera jornada, 401)

However, doña Angela does not accept her fate resignedly. She learns to lie and scheme, donning a veil and slipping out to the Court whenever she can. As the play opens, doña Angela is hurrying home from the celebrations in honor of the baptism of Prince Baltasar,[2] followed by her brother don Luis who, ignorant of her identity, feels attracted toward her. On her way she encounters don Manuel, an unknown gentleman, who, it turns out later, is to be a guest in don Juan's home. Doña Angela beseeches his aid, thereby obligating his honor.

There have been two significant exceptions: Angel Valbuena Briones compares the confined, repressive quarters in which the action takes place to Segismundo's tower. He also discusses Calderón's attack on superstition. Introduction to Calderón de la Barca, Pedro, *La dama duende*, ed. Angel Valbuena Briones (Madrid: Espasa-Calpe, 1962), pp. xiii-xxxii and xlii-lxxi. Edwin Honig identifies one of the themes of the play as freedom and relates *La dama duende* to Calderón's other honor plays. Introduction to Calderón de la Barca, Pedro, *Four Plays*, tr. and intro. by Edwin Honig, (New York: Hill and Wang, p. 1961), p. xxii. He also explores the implications of incest in doña Angela's brothers' zealous vigilence of her honor. Introduction to *Four Plays* and "Flickers of Incest on the Face of Honor: Calderón's Phantom Lady," *Tulane Drama Review*, VI, iii (1962), pp. 69-105.

[2] Prince Baltasar Carlos was baptized on November 4, 1629.

Don Manuel challenges don Luis to a duel, leaving doña Angela ample time to reach home and take off her finery. When don Luis arrives home, he goes right to his sister's room in order to check up on her activities. When he tells her how he met don Manuel while pursuing a veiled lady he had seen at Court, she reprimands him for chasing evil women, perfectly aware of the fact that she herself is the one her brother was following. Posing as a virtuous widow, she assures him she has spent the afternoon in her room crying, as becomes a woman in her position.

The disparity between the reality of the situation and the appearance of virtue doña Angela seeks to project is the source of much of the humor of the scene. Her hypocrisy is conscious, calculated, and defiant, totally unhindered by moral remorse. Don Luis is also a hypocrite, but his is a kind of hypocrisy accepted in a society in which sexual liberty is considered a male prerogative. He reproves his sister at the very moment he laments not having been able to make contact with an unknown woman of dubious reputation. Throughout the play doña Angela manipulates appearances in order to escape the watchful eye of her brothers, while don Luis makes illicit passes at ladies, particulary at doña Isabel, his own brother's fiancée. Both are hypocrites, but while doña Angela is totally lucid, don Luis is unaware of the contradiction between his behavior toward his sister and his own conduct.

Doña Angela has a goal: her freedom. Her escapades and flirtations —that is, her quest for erotic love— are primarily a manifestation of her quest for freedom. The system she devises in order to realize her goal depends on her ability to keep up with the goings-on in her brother's house while maintaining the other characters in ignorance. In the beginning, the system is relatively simple. She ventures out to Court concealed by a veil without her brothers' knowledge. She knows, of course, everything that goes on with respect to her own activities, while her brothers know nothing. During the first *jornada* of the play, don Luis comes in to tell her

95

what she already knows: that he was following a woman with whom he wished to converse when don Manuel and his servant Cosme intervened. He next informs her that the duel was prevented by don Juan, who arrived just in time to tell him that don Manuel is his friend and is to be their guest. Don Luis, then, reveals to his sister all that has happened up until that moment, permitting her to see clearly the relationship between don Manuel and the members of the household. She, on the other hand, reveals nothing. Maintaining social decorum by deceitfully playing the role of the virtuous widow, she is able to probe her brothers for information while always remaining one step ahead of them.

Like Eusebio in Calderón's *La devoción de la Cruz,* doña Angela is forced into a role by unfortunate circumstances resulting from social conventions imposed by the law of honor. But, Calderón shows in his *auto sacramental El gran teatro del mundo,* the role of each individual is to be assigned by God alone, not by other individuals. If doña Angela rebels against a role she cannot play honestly, she is justified, since society has placed her in a situation which is hardly a normal one for a pretty young girl of her wit and charm.[3]

Doña Angela is reduced to a life of deceit in order to appear moral before society. If, like Mersault in Albert Camus' *L'Etranger,* she refused to play the role which society assigned to her, she would be, like him, condemned to death, for transgressions of honor by women are almost always punishable by death in seventeenth-century honor plays.

But Angela does not rebel openly. Without ever abandoning the role which she is condemned to play, she continues to struggle for her freedom. When Isabel, her servant, indicates

[3] Parts of this and the following section have been adapted from my article "Tragic Elements in Calderón's *La dama duende,*" *Kentucky Romance Quarterly,* XVI, iv, (1969), pp. 303-328.

to her that there is a way to enter don Manuel's room secretly, Angela pries out of her all the information she can, at the same time making a conscious effort not to appear overanxious. First she tells Isabel that she cannot possibly believe that don Manuel is in her house, guest of her brother, without seeing him with her own eyes. Then she pumps Isabel for futher information, insisting all the while it is merely out of curiosity that she asks so many questions. Here and in other scenes, Angela justifies her curiosity with the familiar proverb "seeing is believing." In this way she gathers information without risking her honor and without having to offer her informant any additional explanation.

When Angela and Isabel at last enter don Manuel's room, it is under the pretext of curiosity. Doña Angela is not in love with don Manuel. In fact, she does not even know who he is. It is her desire for freedom that leads her to become involved in escapades of this nature, not her passion for don Manuel. The search for love which follows this first adventure is, in reality, a search for freedom. Throughout the entire play, don Manuel is for Angela a sort of "prince charming" who might rescue her from her misery. In short, don Manuel represents for Angela a path toward freedom.

It is not until Angela enters don Manuel's room that her desire is awakened. With extreme care and great interest, she and Isabel examine don Manuel's personal effects. It is at this moment that doña Angela's womanly desires are ignited, for by manipulating these intimate masculine objects —shaving equipment, undergarments, letters— doña Angela becomes aware of the man himself. And she reacts with jealousy when Isabel discovers a packet of letters with a portrait of a woman among don Manuel's belongings. But, as usual, doña Angela dissimulates and pretends not to be interested in the discovery.

When doña Angela and her maid enter the room, Isabel asks the purpose of their visit and doña Angela answers,

97

> A volvernos solamente;
>> (Primera jornada, 796)

It may be that the excursion to don Manuel's apartments began as a simple adventure, but it is not the case that doña Angela has come only to return to her own quarters. Doña Angela, as always, plays the role of the virtuous widow, but in reality she is already formulating the plan that will liberate her from her cloister.

Doña Angela does not leave don Manuel's room without writing him a note, thereby initiating the game that will make her the Dama Duende and free her from her brothers. The constant entering and leaving don Manuel's apartments are a continual provocation. Doña Angela will use every trick of coquetry in order to free herself from the situation to which she is condemned. And, as she excites don Manuel's interest, she excites her own, for each entry into the forbidden room is a stimulus for her passions. By entering don Manuel's room, doña Angela realizes the forbidden act which symbolically signifies her liberation.

Don Manuel replies to Angela's provocation with a note in chivalric language. That is, he responds to her invitation to play. Don Manuel, unlike don Luis and don Juan, participates in doña Angela's game and little by little discovers her secrets. In spite of Cosme, who is certain that the mysterious entering and leaving his master's room are the acts of some supernatural being, don Manuel insists that there is a key to the mystery; that everything will become clear when the key is discovered. Doña Angela sums up this idea when she tells the story of Juanelo's egg:

> Las grandes dificultades,
> hasta saberse lo son:
> que sabido, todo es fácil.
>> (Segunda jornada, 162-164)

Throughout the play, doña Angela is the character who

98

knows most and the one who manipulates the action, while don Manuel approaches her vantage point step by step. She is a kind of stage director who controls the movements of the other characters.

The penultimate time that doña Angela enters don Manuel's room, he surprises her. Don Manuel, confused, draws his sword and doña Angela fears that he might kill her. In order to make him desist, she resorts to saying that she has come to his quarters because she is in love with him, and loving is not a crime (Segunda jornada, 1014-1054). This is the first time that doña Angela defines her passion as love. The game of entering and leaving don Manuel's room is born of curiosity and develops into an adventure. On discovering don Manuel's personal effects, her sexual desire becomes inseparable from her desire for freedom; that is, after discovering don Manuel, doña Angela no longer ventures out simply for the sake of venturing out, but directs her passion toward don Manuel. She no longer escapes to the Court, but to don Manuel's room. Her goal has been modified. Now, standing before don Manuel and with no way out, she defines her desire, which until now has been manifested in the form of a simple flirtation, as love.[4] Love, for doña Angela, is merely an escape hatch which, first of all, replaces her obsession with freedom —since she now projects her desires toward don Manuel instead of toward the Court— and secondly, justifies her actions. Indeed, a lovely young girl can hardly be judged harshly for being in love with a charming young bachelor. Here, doña Angela not only justifies her actions within the context of the play but also assures herself of the sympathy of the audience.

That the objective that was freedom has been replaced by a

---

[4] Until this moment doña Angela's adventure has been no more than a lark, a flirtation, a means of expressing her desire for liberty. But now Angela is faced with the reality of don Manuel's existence as a man. Surely the sword is an obvious Freudian symbol here.

new objective which is love is evident in the following lines. Doña Angela is now ready to reveal her identity to don Manuel:

> Fuerza al decirlo ha de ser;
> porque no puedo llevar
> tan al fin como pensé
> este amor, este deseo,
> esta verdad, esta fe.
>
> (Segunda jornada, 1058-1062)

The "truth" that she was seeking was freedom; now it is love.

But although doña Angela has redirected her passions, she still finds herself in the same tragic situation: she is a prisoner in her own home, a human being without freedom.

Neither the hopes of the audience nor those of the Dama Duende are to be too aroused at this point: Isabel interrupts the scene with the news that don Juan is looking for his sister, and Angela disappears without don Manuel's or Cosme's knowing how or why.

Having spoken with don Manuel, doña Angela feels more desperate than ever. Still concealing her identity and the fact that she lives in the same house as he, she formulates a plan to bring him to her apartments. The ingenious way in which Isabel brings don Manuel to her mistress is comical. Nevertheless, the third confrontation between don Manuel and doña Angela reveals the tragedy of doña Angela's predicament. Don Manuel greets her with gallantries and courtly clichés, to which she answers,

> No soy alba, pues la risa
> me falta en contento tanto;
> ni aurora, pues que mi llanto
> de mi dolor no os avisa;
> no soy el sol, pues no divisa
> mi luz la verdad que adoro;

100

> y así, lo que soy ignoro;
> que sólo sé que no soy
> alba, aurora o sol; pues hoy
> ni alumbro, río ni lloro.
>
> (Tercera jornada, 101-110)

Doña Angela is, in essence, a character as lost as Segismundo in *La vida es sueño* or Eusebio in *La devoción de la Cruz.* She can no longer "shine" or "laugh" or "cry," for society and her brothers have deprived her of her identity. Her self-realization is impeded by an exterior force which does not allow her to discover herself as a woman and as an individual. *"Y teniendo yo más vida/ ¿tengo menos libertad?..."* complains Segismundo. Angela's lament is essentially the same. *"Lo que soy ignoro,"* she says. What doña Angela wants most is to be herself. Like Segismundo, doña Angela is a person of character, a self-willed determined woman who rebels against Fate in search of her own destiny. She does not react to her situation in such an overtly violent way as Segismundo. Her problem is not to learn to control her will (although it is true that at the beginning of the play she behaves in an impulsive manner and exercises more and more control as the play develops), but rather to direct her will in a way that will permit her to achieve her objective: freedom.

> ni soy lo que parezco
> ni parezco lo que soy.
>
> (Tercera jornada, 133-134)

Doña Angela, like Segismundo, lives in a tover. Later on she says, Doña Angela, like Segismundo, and Eusebio, is *en situation* in an existential sense, and must react to her given situation.[5]

Doña Angela's life is one of mere appearances. She says to don Manuel,

---

[5] *En situation* is a term frequently used by Sartre to express the idea that an individual is confronted with circumstances that force him to make a choice. Sartre's characters are always *en situation*. So are Calderón's. Faced with the requirements of the honor code, doña Angela is free either to accept them or to rebel against them.

si hoy a aquesta luz me veis,
y por eso me estimáis,
cuando a otra luz me veáis,
quizá me aborreceréis.

(Tercera jornada, (147-150)

These lines are more than a comment on the lack on con-
stancy of men or on the relationship between doña Angela
and don Juan and don Luis. They reveal that doña Angela's
entire life is a deceit. Life is a dream, a projection of the
imagination, Calderón tells us in his more "serious" plays.
Terrestrial life is *engaño;* it is reality seen under a distorting
light. Men's values are mere inventions. Doña Angela echoes
this philosophy in her lamentations.

This scene between doña Angela and don Manuel has a
definite function in terms of Calderonian philosophy. And it
has an important function in terms of the structure of the play
as well. We have seen that the play revolves partially around
the problem of awareness or knowledge of the situation, of
conocimiento. In this scene don Manuel is in the same room
as doña Angela without knowing her identity, and doña
Angela, in order to continue the game and assure her freedom
of movement inside the house, is obligated to keep it from
him. If we look at this scene in terms of the structure of the
play, we see doña Angela, always with maximun awareness
of the situation, protecting desperately her position of
superiority, while Manuel comes nearer and nearer to
mastery of the enigma, and while don Luis and don Juan
remain in their initial ignorance.

While Segismundo and Eusebio react violently to their
respective situations and openly rebel, doña Angela maintains
her decorum and manipulates her destiny through cunning.
Doña Angela, as a woman, must maintain appearances, and,
therefore, secrecy. But secrecy, rather than being a hindrance,
becomes her trump. Secrecy is precisely what permits her to
manipulate the action of the drama. Don Juan and don Luis

do not even suspect what their sister is up to. For this reason, when don Juan surprises doña Angela in her apartments shortly after she has received don Manuel, he is completely amazed to find her dressed in her finery. And when doña Angela explains to him that she has dressed up merely to amuse herself, don Juan becomes angry, not because he suspects that a man may have entered the room, but because it is improper for a widow to dress in such frills. Don Juan, who, like don Luis, spies on his sister, functions as the father figure in the play. In this scene, don Juan is still far from the truth, for he judges from appearance; he believes in what he sees.

Don Juan and don Luis remain in the dark until the very end of the play. When doña Angela at last discloses her secret, they are totally surprised by their sister's revelations.

If Calderón offers Segismundo and Eusebio salvation when at last they discover themselves and master their will, to doña Angela, protagonist of *La dama duende* in which salvation is precluded as a solution by the very nature of the play —a comedy— he offers a relatively unsatisfactory solution. The play ends in the conventional way: with arrangements for the wedding of the protagonists. But the solution is an unsatisfactory one for several reasons.

Doña Angela's first obsession was liberty, not love. When at the end of the play Angela explains her situation and the reason for her actions, she returns to the question of freedom, which she had replaced with a fascination for don Manuel. Her house has been a prision, when one's home should be a port of refuge:

> Sola, triste y turbada,
> llego de mi discurso mal guida
> al umbral de una esfera,
> que fué mi cárcel, cuando ser debiera
> mi puerto o mi sagrado.

> (Tercera jornada, 691-695)

Angela says that her lot improved with don Manuel's arrival.

> Entré donde los cielos
> mejoraron, con verte, mis desvelos.
>
> (Tercera jornada, 745-746)

But she admits that her love for don Manuel was only a way
to achieve her original goal. Her relationship with don
Manuel has never been much more than a game. And she is
hardly convincing when she says,

> Por haberte querido,
> fingida sombra de mi casa he sido;
> por haberte estimado,
> sepulcro vivo fui de mi cuidado;
> por que no te quisiera,
> quien el respeto a tu valor perdiera;
> por que no te estimara,
> quien su pasión dijera cara a cara.
> Mi intento fué el quererte,
> mi fin amarte, mi temor perderte,
> mi miedo asegurarte,
> mi vida obedecerte, mi alma hallarte,
> mi deseo servirte,
> y mi llanto, en efecto, persuadirte
> que mi daño repares,
> que me valgas, me ayudes y me ampares.
>
> (Tercera jornada, 747-762)

Doña Angela, nevertheless, was a *fingida sombra* even
before don Manuel's arrival. Besides, being a determined and
rebellious woman, her goal was never to "obey" or to "serve"
anyone. What she wanted all along was the aid *(la ayuda)*
and the protection *(el amparo)* of don Manuel, much more
than his love. The real problem —doña Angela's liberty—
remains unsolved.[6]

[6] Edwin Honig's assertion that at the end of the play "the rites of love have
superseded the bleak honor formula" seems an over-simplification. (Introduction to *Four Plays)* Freedom, more than love, is the question involved. Love is simply the means through which freedom is realized in the
play.

Marriage seems more a convenient way of ending the play then a real solution. It provides simply a conventional means of permitting the characters to exit from the stage. But one can hardly help asking if the lively and rebellious doña Angela will be happy once she is married, or if don Manuel will replace don Luis and don Juan as the guardian of the prision of the Dama Duende. In short, will doña Angela once again crave freedom once she is married and the flirtation has ended?

On the other hand, what is her alternative? Outside of marriage —or, perhaps, the convent— she has no options. Seventeenth-century society, with its rigid honor code, offers young upper-class women few choices.

The alternative to the confinement of the parental home is the equally stiffling confinement of marriage. The latter is no less restrictive than the former, for the laws of honor give the husband complete dominion over the life and death of his wife. The only real alternative is a continued life of deceit —an unsatisfactory solution at best.

Don Luis: A Study in Frustration

The obstruction to doña Angela's self-realization is the honor code, implemented with perfection by her two brothers. Don Luis and don Juan are both obsessed with honor. For don Luis, honor is so fragile that it is to be compared with glass which can be broken at any moment:

> pues ya dices
> que no ha puesto por defensa
> de su honor más que unos vidrios,
> que al primer golpe se quiebran.
> (Primera jornada, 365-368)

Here don Luis is referring to the glass which separates don Manuel's room from doña Angela's. The passage reveals that

105

don Luis is expecting the worst. He is anxiously awaiting the insult that will force him to defend his honor. He is obsessed with the idea that the honor of his household could be blemished and, blinded by this obsession, he will search for the insult that will at last obligate him to draw his sword.

When don Luis enters doña Angela's room after having dueled with don Manuel in the first act, his first words are:

> Harto tengo, tengo honor
>
> (Primera jornada, 448)

His honor occupies his thoughts constantly. And at the end of the play, he at last discovers what he believes to be a betrayal on the part of don Manuel. Don Luis lights a candle on entering doña Angela's room precisely because he is serching for —he is actually hoping to find— some indication that his honor is in danger.[7]

> Luz tomaré, aunque imprudente,
> pues todo se halla con luz,
> y el honor con luz se pierde.
>
> (Tercera jornada, 466-468)

Don Luis is ready to take vengeance on someone, to terminate his light —that is, his life. And when he surprises don Manuel, whom he believed to be absent, in his own room, he at last has an excuse to draw his sword. The events of the last part of the drama are comical because there is so much confusion, and because don Luis, always anxious to duel, vacillates from one moment to the next between being friend or foe to don Manuel. Don Luis never understands exactly

---

[7] Fyodor Dostoyevsky describes the craving of the jealous man for a rival in *The Brothers Karamazov:* "For, even if the rival did disappear next day, he would invent another one and would be jealous of him. And one might wonder what there was in a love that has to be so watched over, what a love could be worth that needed such strenuous guarding. But that the jealous will never understand." tr. by Constance Garnett (New York: Random House Modern Library, 1950) p. 462.

what is going on. When he comes back to don Manuel's room, after having gone out in search of a sword with which to duel with don Manuel, he discovers doña Angela in the room. And don Luis, always ready to see treachery in every deed, is stunned.

> Ya vuelvo. —Pero ¿qué miro?
> ¡Traidora!...

(Tercera jornada, 799-800)

But don Manuel explains that he has every intention of returning doña Angela safely to her room, leaving poor don Luis totally confused. He now sees himself obligated to let don Manuel leave, since don Manuel permitted him to exit to look for a sword. Nevertheless, he sees an affront in the presence of doña Angela in the room. With courteous words, which emphasize the ridiculousness of his dilemma, don Luis gives don Manuel permission to escort doña Angela to her own quarters and then to return to the serious affair of honor. But don Manuel cheats don Luis out of the much desired duel by asking for doña Angela's hand and thereby terminating the drama. Poor don Luis would like to take vengeance, but he no longer has anything to avenge. He is in a thoroughly absurd situation.

This obsession with honor is tinged with subtle overtones of incest. Don Luis is obsessed with his sister. He spies on her; he is jealous of her; he tries to control her. If don Juan's attitude toward doña Angela approximates that of a father, don Luis's is that of a domineering husband. The fact that in the first act don Luis hurries from the Court in pursuit of doña Angela —without, of course, knowing her identity— is not only an indication of the possibility of incest which exists in any family, but also an indication of a very real situation. It is no wonder that doña Angela complains,

107

> encerrada
> sin libertad he vivido,
> porque envidué de un marido,
> con dos hermanos casada.

(Primera jornada, 389-392)

Don Luis's obsession with his sister is due in part to another frustration: that of the hopelessness of his love for his cousin. Don Luis feels totally defeated in his own amorous pursuits, for Beatriz is in love with don Juan.

According to the seventeenth-century concept, the honor of a household is the responsibility of the male members. Any failure to protect the family honor reflects a lack of virility.[8] Don Luis's obsession with honor is at least partially a manifestation of his sexual insecurity. In his relations with Beatriz, he is constantly confronted with his failure as a suitor. He is jealous of Beatriz and obsessed with the idea of punishing her. Like all of Calderón's noblemen of honor, he desires vengeance. Don Luis wants to take vengeance not only on don Manuel for his apparent betrayal of his sister's honor, but on everyone. He searches for reasons to take vengeance:

> Ya sé que mi loco amor
> en tus desprecios no alcanza
> un átomo de esperanza:
> pero yo, viendo tan fuerte
> rigor, tengo que quererte
> por sólo tomar venganza.

(Segunda jornada, 223-228)

Don Luis feels condemned to misfortune by the stars and by the rigorousness of doña Beatriz. He sees his situation as imposed by incombatable external forces and therefore, he relinquishes his will to what he accepts as his Fate. Don Luis

---

[8] See Pitt-Rivers, p. 42.

108

lives enclosed in the circle of his passions; he lives, like Calderón's other men of honor, in complete ignorance that the reason for his misfortunes is his own attitude, his own lack of compassion and flexibility. Like other Calderonian honor heroes, don Luis is incapable of seeing a woman —in this case, doña Angela— as a human being. He considers her only as a symbol of his own honor or dishonor.[9] He does not see beyond the narrow limits of the world which he himself has constructed with the aid of certain social values. He does not conspire against this false world as doña Angela does. He does not exert his will against Fate, as she does. He relinquishes his will to Fate.

Don Luis lives in a world of paranoia in which everything and everyone conspire against him:

> cada dia
> mis hermanos a porfia
> se conjuran contra mi.
>> (Segunda jornada, 290-292)

He feels alone and defeated:

> sin estrella y sin ventura.
>> (Segunda jornada, 355)

Don Luis is so obsessed that the moment he sees doña Angela and doña Beatriz talking secretively, he concludes immediately that they are plotting against him. In reality the two women are discussing a plan to hide Beatriz in the house

---

[9] In other words, don Luis is a total egotist. Montesquieu emphasized the egotistical quality of honor, which he deplored. Juan Luis Vives describes the psychology of the egotist in his *Tratado del alma:* "Y así acontece que quienes se aman a sí mismos, aman a los demás con frialdad y todo lo refieren a sí mismos y a lo que ellos consideran como bienes, verbigracia, placeres, regalos, honores, dignidades, poderio. Verás que hay algunos que no tienen miramientos para con su mujer ni para con sus hijos y para otros afectos merecedores de todo respeto y consideración, por servir a su egoísmo." (p. 1262).

so she may be there when doña Angela receives don Manuel. Basing himself on appearances, don Luis collects circumstantial evidence with the hope that it will give him a reason for taking vengeance. Don Luis is convinced that doña Beatriz plans to receive don Juan in secret. He is so blinded by his jealousy and by his vindictive spirit that he never even suspects the real objectives of the tête-à-tête.

Don Luis directs the jealousy which he feels for doña Beatriz toward his sister. This does not mean that don Luis is in love with his sister in a romantic sense, but rather that he watches over and spies on her as though he were her lover. Calderón's men of honor typically are not in love with their wives. Don Gutierre, in *El médico de su honra,* demonstrates no preoccupation at all with his wife's well-being; he never seriously considers the possibility of her innocence, and he never demonstrates any real understanding and compassion toward her. What he does show is selfish preoccupation with his own honor. Rather than give his wife the benefit of the doubt or display a willingness to forgive her if she is guilty, he viciously seeks reasons to condemn her. Similarly, don Luis's attitude is not that of a man truly in love with his sister, as in the case of Eusebio in *La devoción de la Cruz,* but that of a husband, like don Gutierre, pathologically obsessed with honor.

If don Luis cannot satisfy his feelings for his cousin, he can control, or at least try to control, his sister's actions. Until the last act of the play, don Luis is so intent on finding a betrayal of his honor and so obsessed with jealousy and desire for vengeance that he remains unaware of his sister's scheme. He seeks with such intensity that he destroys his capacity to see and so he remains ignorant until the last minute.

If the exaggerated courtesy, the confusion and the clumsiness of don Luis make us laugh, this frustrated gentleman of honor is nonetheless an essentially tragic character. Like *Le Misan-*

thrope, Le Bourgeois Gentilhomme and so many other characters who evoke laughter by their distorted views and their mad and perverse obsessions, don Luis is a man whose frustrations and manias deprive him of his will and leave him empty, alone, and incapacitated, without any solution to his predicament, as we see him at the end of *La dama duende.*

Cosme and Don Manuel: Superstition vs. Reason

Just as don Luis is obsessed by honor, Cosme is obsessed by supernatural beings. No sooner do he and don Manuel enter don Juan's house, then Cosme begins to complain about the amount of baggage he has to carry and to insist that he would rather be the victim of "doscientos mil demonios" than have to live at Court, where so much paraphernalia is needed (Primera jornada, 697-707). Later, when doña Angela enters don Manuel's room with her maid, Isabel exchanges the money in Cosme's pocket for a piece of coal. Cosme automatically assumes a *duende* has been playing tricks on him, even though doña Angela has not yet identified herself as the Dama Duende (Primera jornada, 916-917). References to *duendes* are constantly on Cosme's lips. When doña Angela does finally identify herself as a *duende,* he does not for a moment question the veracity of the appellation.

Don Manuel, in contrast, doubts the intervention of supernatural beings, even though the mysterious visits to his room have no apparent explanation. Rather than attribute the odd goings-on in don Juan's household to *duendes,* he attempts to postulate possible explanations and then to subject them to careful scrutiny. He assumes that there exists behind the strange events he and Cosme have witnessed a cause-effect relationship totally within the natural limits of the universe. [10] He suggests, for example, that the person who

[10] The difficulty of deciphering cause-effect relationships is one of Calderón's favorite themes. In a number of plays, one cause is responsible

left the note in his room may be don Luis's *dama,* who could
freely enter and leave the house. Cosme offers several valid
objections to this hypothesis. Don Manuel then suggests that
a servant may have left the note, but Cosme points out flaws
in this theory as well. Even when don Manuel finally runs out
of plausible explanations, he refuses to believe a supernatural
power is involved, and vows to explore the situation further.
Cosme, on the other hand, latches on to the ready-made explanation which coincides with his superstition. Throughout
the play don Manuel and Cosme engage in an intellectual
tug-of-war as each tries to win the other over to his own way
of thinking. The conflict reaches a climax at the end of Act I:

    Don Manuel. Que ingenio y arte
                      hay para entrar y salir,
                      para cerrar, para abrir,
                       y que el cuarto tiene parte
                      por dónde. Y en duda tal,
                      el juicio podré perder;
                      pero no, Cosme, creer
                      cosa sobrenatural.
    Cosme.   ¿No hay duendes?
    Don Manuel.   Nadie los vió.
    Cosme.   ¿Familiares?

for various —and sometimes contradictory— effects. In *Saber del mal y
del bien* Doña Hipólita says:

        Luego, Don Alvaro, pueden
        verse en una misma causa
        dos efectos diferentes (Vol. I, p. 228)

In *En la vida todo es verdad y todo mentira,* Heraclio asks:

          ¿cómo, di, de una causa
          nacen contrarios efectos...? (Vo. I, 228)

In *De una causa, dos efectos,* Diana says:

        Igualmente de los dos
        convencida y obligada
        estoy, viendo dos efectos
        tan opuestos, de una causa. (Vol. II, p. 491)

Don Manuel.	Son quimeras.
Cosme.	¿Brujas?
Don Manuel.	Menos.
Cosme.	¿Hechiceras?
Don Manuel.	¿Qué error?
Cosme.	¿Hay sýcubos?
Don manuel.	No.
Cosme.	¿Encantadoras?
Don Manuel.	Tampoco.
Cosme.	¿Mágicas?
Don Manuel.	Es necedad.
Cosme.	¿Nigromantes?
Don Manuel.	Liviandad.
Cosme.	¿Energúmenos?
Don Manuel.	¡Qué loco!
Cosme.	¡Vive Dios que te cogi!
	¿Diablos?
Don Manuel.	Sin poder notorio.
Cosme.	¿Hay almas del purgatorio?
Don Manuel.	¿Que me enamoren a mí?

(Primera jornada, 1071-1090)

Cosme's last two questions are obviously a trap, since he asks in essence if don Manuel believes in the Devil and in God, and don Manuel cannot supply a negative answer to these questions as he has to the others.

Cosme picks up this theme again in the second act, when doña Angela leaves don Manuel a note that closes, *"Dios os guarde"*. Cosme comments that there really is such a thing as a "duende religioso", bringing up once again the question of religious apparitions (Segunda jornada, 553). The remark points up a potential danger of rationalism as seen from a Christian point of view. Cosme implies that to reject supernatural beings is to reject those accepted by the Church as well, while to accept them is to accept even those declared inexistent by the Church. For don Manuel there is no such conflict; for him, reason stops short of interpreting dogma.

Cosme interprets all appearances in accordance with his belief

113

in *duendes*. Once he is convinced a *duende* is teasing him and don Manuel, no amount of rational explanation can persuade him otherwise. When, in the second act, Cosme enters the room with a light, Isabel, who is there, risks being discovered. But she can count on Cosme's fear to prevent him from trying to follow her, so she puts out his candle and heads for the door. In the midst of the confusion she bumps into don Manuel, who grabs the handle of the basket she has in her hand. By the time Cosme lights the room again, Isabel has escaped, leaving don Manuel holding the basket. For Cosme, the disappearance of whatever was in the room is proof of its supernatural nature. Reason might tell him that the person who was there left through a secret door, but judging simply from appearances, he concludes that the being disappeared into thin air. And since he did not really get a good look at Isabel, he describes her as a Capuchine monk, for that is the form *duendes* traditionally take (Segunda jornada, 533-537). Cosme's imagination, embellishing the material provided by his senses, forms a figure quite in keeping with his preconceived notions. The contrast between Isabel's real appearance and the form Cosme assigns to her is a source of much of the hilarity of the scene.

Cosme's reactions are mechanical and predictable. Given the premise that *duendes* exist, he attributes every unexplained occurrence to their intervention. And it is his very predictability that allows others to manipulate him to their own ends, just as Isabel does in this scene.

Cosme is prisoner of his will, for he interprets everything he sees and hears in accordance with those ready-made ideas he chooses to believe:

> Pues déjame que lo crea;
> que se apura el sufrimiento,
> queriendo negarle a un hombre
> lo que está pasando y viendo.
>
> (Segunda jornada, 608-611)

Cosme trusts his senses because he wants to trust them.

The debate that highlights the end of the first act is reiterated dramatically at the end of the second, when Cosme almost wins his master over to his way of thinking. Don Manuel and his servant return to their room unexpectedly just after doña Angela has entered. Cosme, unaware of her presence, mutters about the need for light at the very moment when doña Angela lights her candle. The fortuitous sequence of events suggests an apparent causality that stuns don Manuel. For a moment he is convinced that their room really is haunted by *duendes* (Segunda jornada, 911-914). As both he and Cosme gaze at doña Angela, he sees an angel, while Cosme sees a devil, or fallen angel, complete with hooves and luminous eyes. Doña Angela is, as her name implies, an angel to both, but what kind of angel depends on the particular point of view of each. Don Manuel is influenced by chivalrous idealism, while Cosme is not. The ambiguity of appearances is, of course, implicit here, but so is the matter of religious apparitions. Both don Manuel and Cosme see supernatural beings admitted by Church dogma. At the end of the act Cosme reminds don Manuel that the Devil —who can assume any form— can easily appear as a woman, to which don Manuel gives no answer. Cosme has once again cornered his master.

Doña Angela is used to playing the role expected of her in order to achieve her ends. Just as she plays the virtuous widow for her two brothers, she now plays the *duende*. She hopes to frighten don Manuel and Cosme so that she can manipulate the situation in such a way as to permit her to exit. But don Manuel's superstitiousness is short-lived. A rationalist at heart, he doubts that doña Angela is really a supernatural being:

> Mujer, quien quiera que seas
> (que no tengo de creer
> que eres otra cosa nunca,)
> ¡vive Dios!, que ha de saber
> quién eres, cómo has entrado
> aquí, con qué fin, y a qué.
>
> (Segunda jornada, 1021-1026)

Having hypothesized that doña Angela is mortal, don Manuel experiments. He draws his sword, and she corroborates his suspicions by showing fear. Finally, she admits she is not a *duende* at all.

But the minute don Manuel and Cosme turn their backs, doña Angela slips out once again. Cosme, who was almost convinced that doña Angela is human, sees proof in her mysterious disappearance that she is a *duende* after all. Once again, don Manuel demonstrates a spirit of investigation. He makes ready to search the room. Cosme, on the other hand, is not at all anxious to investigate. He would prefer not to search. Don Manuel admits he is confused, for neither his own theory nor Cosme's seems to be fool-proof. Doña Angela seems to be both *duende* and *dama* at the same time:

> Como sombra se mostró
> fantástica su luz fué;
> pero como cosa humana
> se dejó tocar y ver.
> Como mortal se temió;
> receló como mujer;
> como ilusión se deshizo;
> como fantasma se fué.
> Si doy rienda al discurso,
> no sé, ¡vive Dios! no sé,
> ni qué tengo de dudar,
> ni qué tengo de creer.
>
> (Segunda jornada, 1123-1134)

At the end of the second act, don Manuel wavers dangerously

116

on the brink of considering seriously Cosme's irrational explanations.

Don Manuel is still in a state of confusion at the beginning of the third *jornada,* when doña Angela has him brought before her without his being aware he is still in don Juan's house. Convinced upon seeing her that she is a mortal woman, he interrogates her as much as he is able, but the scene is interrupted by don Juan's appearance.

Don Manuel is returned to his room through the glass closet. Believing himself to be elsewhere, he is amazed to find himself face to face with Cosme, and even more amazed to find himself in his own room. Since Cosme cannot explain his master's unexpected appearance, he has recourse to his usual catch-all: it must be the work of the *duende.* But don Manuel has just seen doña Angela and knows her to be a real woman. When he returns to the room again after a brief absence, he finds Cosme gone. Don Manuel postulates the existence of a secret entrance and vows to hide in the room until the Dama Duende appears through it and the mystery is cleared up.

At the end of the play, don Manuel does not in fact discover the door by cornering doña Angela. It is revealed when don Luis opens it and finds Cosme in the glass closet. Don Luis explains the system of entry from doña Angela's room to don Manuel's, and doña Angela herself explains her reasons for undertaking the amorous adventure. Reason and investigation guide don Manuel to the discovery that someone in the house is playing a prank, but they do not lead him to the discovery of the mechanics of that prank. The mystery is solved not only through reason and investigation, but also through a twist of fortune. This solution is somewhat ambiguous. It suggests that even the most reasonable of individuals may be mislead by appearances, especially when those appearances are being manipulated.

Structure and Content of *La dama duende*

La dama duende develops around two conflicts: the struggle between convention and personal liberty that is implicit in the battle of wits between doña Angela and her brothers, and the struggle between reason and superstition encompassed in the dissension between don Manuel and Cosme. These two conflicts are somewhat similar. Both pit a sense of freedom —social, in the case of doña Angela and intellectual, in the case of don Manuel— against a spirit of closed-mindedness and inflexibility.

The adversaries of doña Angela and don Manuel share a number of traits. They have in common their trust in appearances and the pertinacity with which they interpret them in accordance with their respective "systems". Doña Angela's brothers, especially don Luis, explain every unusual occurrence in terms of their honor; Cosme explains every unusual occurrence in terms of supernatural beings. Because of their particular outlooks, both doña Angela's brothers and Cosme are obsessed by irrational fears: the honor characters fear to the point of paranoia for their dishonor; Cosme fears the tricks of *duendes*. Because they are obsessed by one determining force, their reactions are predictable and manipulable. These characters are easily kept in the dark as to the real goings-on in the household because they are easily fooled by appearances. At the end of the play they are all proven wrong: the brothers have not in fact been dishonored by don Manuel and Cosme has not been the victim of *duendes*.

The two separate conflicts are joined by the congenial yet anonymous relationship established between doña Angela and don Manuel. These two characters have in common their willingness to defy closed-minded convention while maintaining the proper decorum. As doña Angela plays her game, she invites don Manuel to play along. Because he is not inhibited either by the fear of *duendes* or by preoccupation for his own dishonor (since doña Angela's flirtations are a threat to her brothers' good name, not his), he is able to enter into the game with an open mind. While doña Angela can hold her brothers and Cosme in check by manipulating appearances, she cannot do so with don Manuel. Step by step he approaches her vantage point until the riddle of the Dama Duende is solved. At the end of the play, he is the only one of the male characters who receives a certain amount of satisfaction.

The separate conflicts between doña Angela and her brothers and don Manuel and Cosme are also joined by cross-conflicts between don Manuel and don Luis and doña Angela and Cosme. The play both begins and ends with and attempted duel between don Manuel and don Luis. In both cases the duel is interrupted and the outward animosity dissolves into a strained, mechanical ceremoniousness. The basis of both attempted duels is doña Angela. In both cases don Luis places himself in the position of her tormentor and persecutor, while don Manuel occupies that of her protector. In both cases doña Angela is unidentified. In the first, don Luis takes her to be an exotic courtesan; in the second, he mistakes her for doña Beatriz. In neither case is don Manuel aware of her identity.

The conflict between Cosme and doña Angela is a humorous one. She and Isabel tease him repeatedly, causing him to feel truly persecuted by some malicious supernatural being. The point of all this mockery is of course doña Angela's flirtation with don Manuel.

Thus, the two major conflicts are related dramatically on several levels.

The polarity between the conflicting characters is reinforced visually. The entire play is constructed around the metaphor

119

of light and darkness.[11] The action takes place principally
in two rooms, one illuminated and the other dark, lit
periodically by doña Angela and her servant or don Manuel
and his. Darkness represents ignorance and superstition,
while light represents reason or truth, and also love, which is,
in platonic Christian terms, the source of all knowledge.
When don Luis first shows don Manuel his room, it is dark,
illuminated by a valet carrying a candle. This scene simply introduces the audience to the place of the action. The game of
the Dama Duende has not yet begun. In the scene in which
Isabel steals Cosme's money, there is no mention of light. The
flame of love has not yet been ignited in doña Angela. She is
still searching for her freedom, groping blindly for the key to
her personal emancipation. Shortly afterwards, don Manuel
and Cosme enter. They do not illuminate the room until don
Manuel finds doña Angela's note. Now don Manuel is on the
track of knowledge; this is his first clue to the mystery of the
Dama Duende. It is at this point that the says:

>   Alumbra,
> Cosme.   (Primera jornada, 983-984)

It is in this scene that don Manuel establishes himself as a
seeker of truth. The scene ends in the argument between him
and Cosme over the existence of supernatural beings.

In the second act, don Manuel and Cosme again enter the
darkened room. Don Manuel tells Cosme to get the light
ready, to which the latter replies somewhat mockingly. He is
ready to serve the *duende* with light, for he would like to see
the mystery solved once and for all:

> Luz al duende llevaré,
> que es hora que sea servido,
> y que no esté a oscuras.
>   (Segunda Jornada, 418-420)

[11] I wish to express my thanks to Professor Antonio Regalado for his help
in developing this section.

120

On the other hand, he trembles with fear, for he is blinded by superstition. No sooner does Cosme enter the room, then Isabel puts out the light. Before the apparition, Cosme remains in the dark, both literally and symbolically. The light that guides don Manuel does not guide his servant. When the former enters the room again, he exclaims:

¡Cosme! ¿Cómo estás sin luz? (Segunda jornada, 485)

The room will not be properly illuminated until don Manuel enters. Unlike Cosme, don Manuel is not afraid, for the rational mind does not fear.

At the end of the second act, don Manuel and Cosme return to their room for some papers. Just as they enter, doña Angela lights her lamp. The situation is "enlightening" for don Manuel in the sense he sees doña Angela face to face and finds out she fears death and therefore must be mortal. In order to make her getaway, doña Angela asks him and Cosme to close the doors so that others cannot see the light—that is, so that they will not gain knowledge of what she has been up to. She escapes, and don Manuel, now holding the light, makes ready to search the room, for, guided by the light of reason, he wishes to investigate.

At the beginning of the third *jornada,* don Manuel is ushered in the dark to doña Angela's room. Before he enters, Isabel brings him a light, and as he waits to enter, he sees the light emanating from the room:

Pero ya veo
Luz   (Tercera jornada, 31-32)

Don Manuel has been in the dark regarding the identity of the Dama Duende, but he is approaching the truth. Shortly after he is brought into doña Angela's illuminated room, don Luis threatens to enter and he is returned to the darkness of his own room by way of the glass closet. There, he and Cosme, unaware of each other's identity, converse in the

121

dark. They are "in the dark" not only about the Dama Duende but also about each other. When Isabel enters to bring don Manuel back to doña Angela's room, it is Cosme she grabs —precisely because he is literally in the dark.

At the end of the third act, don Luis enters the dark room with a candle. He is looking for the knowledge that will give him reason to take vengeance. But his flame has another meaning: throughout the play don Luis associates flame with passion. In the second act, speaking of his jealousy for doña Beatriz, he says:

> Yo me abrase
>
> (Segunda jornada, 710)

Soon afterwards he speaks of

> el fuego que me abrasa
>
> (Segunda jornada, 720)

And then he says:

> abrasado de amor, muero de celos.
>
> (Segunda jornada, 724)

Now, searching for the man whom he believes to be Beatriz's suitor but who in reality is the object of doña Angela's affections, he enters the darkened room, still inflamed with passion and seething with jealousy. With his light, he seeks reason to vent his passion:

> todo se halla con luz,
> y el honor con luz se pierde.
>
> (Tercera jornada, 467-468)

And the light of passion reveals unexpected threats lurking in the darkness; don Luis is amazed to find don Manuel in the room where he expected to find don Juan:

> ¿qué haces aquí encerrado
> sin luz?

122

At last, doña Angela enters, the mystery is cleared up, and light is shed on the entire situation.

Throughout the play the characters enter and leave the two rooms. As Angela schemes with Beatriz and Isabel in her own room, she is periodically and rythmically interrupted by her brothers, whose apparent motive is their interest in their cousin, but whose actions show them to be overcome with jealousy of their own sister. Don Luis and don Juan are always "in the dark" with regard to doña Angela's activities when they enter the illuminated room. The same is true of don Manuel, although to a lesser extent, for, although he is ignorant of doña Angela's identity, he is somewhat more aware of her activities. Conversely, the room of darkness is repeatedly entered by characters carrying light. This series of entries and interruptions builds up dramatic tension and culminates in the resolution of the mystery.

The metaphors of light and darkness are also developed linguistically. At the beginning of the second act don Manuel equates light to life and truth when he refers to God as "dador de la luz" in his note to doña Angela. Don Luis uses Platonist symbolism in the *décimas* he dedicates to doña Beatriz, in which he refers to her as light and to himself as darkness:

> La luz más hermosa y pura,
> de quién el sol la aprendió,
> ¿huye porque llego yo?
> ¿Soy la noche por ventura?
>
> (Segunda jornada, 209-212)

Here light represents human beauty, purity and truth, reflections of Divine perfection. Don Luis uses the same symbolism later on when he tells don Manuel of his love for doña Beatriz:

123

> huye esta beldad de mí
> como de la noche el velo
> de la hermosa luz del día
>
> (Segunda jornada, 359-361)

The most dramatic use of platonic symbolism comes at the beginning of the third act, when don Manuel faces doña Angela in her own room. His address is filled with terms referring to light and darkness: *aurora, sombras, noche oscura, día, sol, arrebol, tornasol de la noche, amanece, alba, ilumina, rayos y luz, dora, abrasa, brilla, lucir, amanecer* (Tercera jornada, 52-90). But doña Angela deflates his Platonist idealism when she says:

> no soy sol, pues no divisa
> mi luz la verdad que adoro
> y así, lo que soy ignoro
>
> (Tercera jornada, 105-107)

She is not the light of truth, for she is forced to live a life of deceit; she possesses the light of life imperfectly, for she is unable to achieve self-realization.

Furthermore, human light, insomuch as it represents truth and reason, is imperfect, for it relies on the senses, which are misleading. Our perception of reality varies according to the light in which reality is examined:

> Pincel que lo muerto informa
> tal vez un cuadro previene,
> que una forma a una luz tiene,
> y a otra luz tiene otra forma.
>
> (Tercera jornada, 141-144)

Here doña Angela returns to the message conveyed in the scene at the end of the second act in which Cosme and don Manuel see her as a devil and an angel respectively: what one sees depends on one's perspective.

The use of light and darkness is essential, then, not only to the mechanics of *La dama duende,* but also to the symbolism, expressed both visually and linguistically.

Conclusion

In spite of the Church's stand against superstition in the seventeenth century, the majority of people —including clergymen— continued to believe in supernatural beings, including those not accepted by Catholic dogma.[12] The ideas presented in *La dama duende* place Calderón among a very small intellectual elite that rejected all such heretical beliefs.

---

[12] Fascination with ghosts, *duendes,* haunted houses and other such phenomena existed well into the eighteenth century. In 1565 Francisco de Vitoria published *Relectiones Theologicae* in which he asserts that most of the wondrous acts attributed to necromancers are false, but that black magic can be worked. He denies that magicians can perform real miracles, but affirms that they do have certain power over demons.

In 1539 Pedro Ciruelo published *Reprobación de las supersticiones y hechicerías. Libro muy útil y necesario a todos los buenos cristianos.* In it he indicates the exorcisms necessary to cleanse those houses possessed by the Devil. He also makes a distinction between false and true astrology, comparing the latter to such legitimate sciences as medicine.

Another work of this type was written by the Jesuit Benito Pereiro. It is a treatise entitled *Adversus fallaces et superstitiosas artes, id est, de Magia, de observatione somniorum et de divinatione astrologica,* published in 1603. The author distinguishes among different types of magic and asserts that much of what is said of magicians is false. He makes an exception in the case of miracles recounted in the Holy Scriptures and in certain other religious books. He barely admits the existence of witches and denies outright the appearance of ghosts or agonizing souls *(almas en pena).* He also denies astrology as a science and dreams as a source of revelation.

Another Jesuit who was concerned with superstition was Martín Antoine del Río, who wrote *Disquisitionum Magicarum, Libri Fex In Tres Tomas Partiti,* published in 1604. Del Río was a good deal more credulous than Pereiro. He accepts alchemy, although he condemns astrology. He believes in black magic and describes the ceremonies by which pacts with the Devil are made and the powers of the Devil, who cannot, he asserts, stop or change the movement of the planets or the stars, or tear the moon from the

125

La dama duende is one of three plays whose aim it is to attack belief in those supernatural beings not admitted by the Church. The other two are *El encanto sin encanto* (1629) and *El galán fantasma* (1635). As in *La dama duende*, the allegedly supernatural goings-on in these plays are eventually explained in terms of purely rational causes and effects and the supposed ghosts and phantoms are found out to be real people.

In *El encanto sin encanto*, a rift between master and servant similar to the one in *La dama duende* occurs. Don Enrique and his servant Franchipán have been stranded in Marseilles. Don Enrique saves the life of a lady, Serafina, in an accident,

---

sky as the ancients believed, but who can move the earth, leash the winds, start and stop storms, control lightning, dry up fountains and sources, divide bodies of water, cover the earth with darkness, produce minerals in his bowels, remove his servants from prison and secure all kinds of honors for them.

In 1629, Martyn de Castañeda wrote *Tratado muy sotil y bien fundado de las supersticiones y hechizerías y vanos conjuros y abusiones, y otras cosas al caso tocantes de la posibilidad y remedio de ellas.* (Menéndez Pelayo cites Fr. Martín de Castañega, author of *Tratado de las supersticiones, hechicerías y varios conjuros y abusiones y de la posibilidad y remedio de ellos* in his *Historia de los heterodoxos españoles.* Note discrepancies.) Castañeda, like others who wrote on the subject, did a poor job of convincing his readers of the ineffectiveness of supernatural powers because he himself was not convinced. Castañeda maintains that since the Devil is authorized to tempt men and women, he can make use of supernatural powers and make pacts with individuals who then become his *familiares.* Castañeda discusses different types of witches and sorcerers, and maintains that witches can, in effect, fly through the air.

Two other significant studies are that of Father Antonio de Fuente la Peña and that of Father Lebrun, of the Paris Oratory. The first, published in 1676, is entitled *El ente dilucidado. Discurso único novísimo que muestra ay en naturaleza Animales irracionales invisibles, y quales sean.* The author maintains that *duendes, tragos* and *phantasmas* do exist. Father Lebrun's book is entitled *Historia crítica de las supersticiones prácticas que han engañado a los pueblos y embarazado a los sabios.* Published in 1702 it shows that superstition was rampant throughout Europe, not only in Spain.

then becomes involved in a duel and consequently with the law. Serafina, indebted to don Enrique, has him kidnapped and hidden in a tower. There, he and Franchipán hear all kinds of inexplicable comings and goings. Franchipán immediately assumes supernatural intervention, but don Enrique rejects this idea. Step by step the mystery is unraveled, although at times the events don Enrique and Franchipán witness almost leave them both convinced that some enchantress is at work. However, don Enrique always snaps back to a rational perspective, while Franchipán is always ready to give credence to the Devil and his staff.

In *El galán fantasma,* Astolfo, a young *galán,* pretends to be dead in order to escape the wrath of his rival, the Duke, who, like himself, is in love with Julia. Those who catch sight of Astolfo, who comes out of hiding at night, are convinced they have seen his ghost. One exception is Candil, an opportunistic, picaresque-type valet who steadfastly refuses to believe in ghosts:

> Ya prosigo,
> que en materia de fantasmas
> nada en mi vida he creído
>
> (Vol. II, p. 660)

The message of the play is summed up at the end by Julia:

> si se llega a descubrir
> será risa; que así todas
> las fantasmas son en fin.
>
> (Vol. II, p. 663)

Calderón's stand on supernatural beings makes him a precur-

Torres Villarroel mentions superstitious beliefs of which he himself does not deny the truth in his *Vida,* published in the late eighteenth century. For an extensive discussion of superstition in Spain see Marcelino Menéndez Pelayo, *Historia de los heterodoxos españoles,* Vol. IV (Madrid: Consejo superior de investigaciones científicas, 1963), pp. 365-370

sor of Father Feijóo, who attacked the still prevalent belief in *duendes* in the eighteenth century. [13]

It is not only the kind of closed-mindedness represented by Cosme that Calderón ridicules in *La dama duende,* but also the kind represented by don Luis and don Juan. These two characters, obsessed as they are by honor, box themselves into a system that prevents them from seeking truth beyond appearances and fills them with irrational fears. Honor is, for them, a kind of superstition. Just as Cosme feels himself to be persecuted by *duendes,* the honor characters feel persecuted by the possibility of their own dishonor. *Duendes,* by definition, are supernatural beings over which the individual has no control. Don Luis and don Juan see honor and dishonor as fate, over which they have no control. In his discussion of the two-fold nature of reason in *Reason and Existenz,* Karl Jaspers writes: "Without infinite reflection we should fall into the quiet of the settled and established which, as something permanent in the world, would become absolute; that is, we should become superstitious. An atmosphere of bondage arises with such a settlement. Infinite reflection, therefore, is, precisely through its endlessly active dialectic, the condition of freedom." [14] Don Luis and don Juan are precisely the kinds of characters who accept social convention as something "settled and established"', as something "permanent" which has thereby become "absolute". Their unquestioning faith in honor makes them narrow and superstitious. They are so concerned with their honor that they

[13] Father Benito Jerónimo Feijóo (1676-1764) attacked superstition in numerous articles. In *Voz del pueblo* he speaks of the "extravagantísimas supersticiones de varios pueblos" as proof that the voice of the masses does not always spout the truth. In *Vara divinatoria* he attempts to prove that there is no truth to the legend of the divining rod. In *Astrología judiciaria y almanaques* he attacks astrology, arguing that future events depend on innumerable factors to which the astrologer does not have access. In his *Cartas* he attacks popular belief in vampires and other supernatural beings.
[14] P. 32.

128

become slaves to it, seeking in every crook and cranny indications of its imperfection to be rectified. The "atmosphere of bondage" that pervades don Juan's household is a direct result of this attitude. Freedom is impossible for characters such as these, for they are so much on the look-out for signs of their dishonor that all their thoughts and actions are determined by this one overriding preoccupation.

To assume a premise without putting it to the test and then to base an entire series of conclusions on it is to misapply reason. Characters such as doña Angela's brothers and Cosme do not reason, they *rationalize*. They first form a notion of how things are, and then grasp at every piece of information that may be construed as evidence to sustain their untenable premise. Reason is then reduced to the subservient role of backing up a preconceived notion. Through Cosme, don Luis and don Juan, Calderón mocks not merely belief in supernatural beings and fanatic obsession with the honor code, but a whole way of thinking dependent on appearances.

The proper use of reason, as presented in *La dama duende*, is not to impose answers, but to ask questions, not to box in, but to open up. By postulating and investigating, don Manuel eventually arrives close to a plausible solution to the mystery of the Dama Duende... Even though reason alone does not supply the answer and at times appearances are so misleading as to confuse even him, in the end, it is his open-mindedness and willingness to propose, investigate and discard solutions that brings him closer to truth than any of the other male characters of the play.

The attitude adopted by don Manuel is at the disposal of every individual; that is, every human being is free to accept the guidance of reason. The fact that it is he who is open-minded and Cosme who is superstitious does not imply any kind of social determinism on the part of Calderón. After all, in *El galán fantasma* it is the valet who rejects superstition and the aristocrat who does not.

129

Although Calderón's treatment of superstition places him in the intellectual avant-guard of seventeenth-century Spain, it would be a mistake to consider him a precursor of the eighteenth-century French Illuminists. Unlike them, he does not exalt reason to the point of viewing it as the answer to all human ills, but rather emphasizes the difficulty in applying reason in a world diffused throughout by misleading appearances. Furthermore, for Calderón, there is never a conflict between reason and religion, for he does not view dogma as subject to human reason. That is why there is no contradition between the ideas presented in *La dama duende* and, for example, the miracle that highlights the end of *La devoción de la Cruz* or the appearance of the Devil in *El mágico prodigioso*. Calderón's orthodoxy is not unusual, but characteristic of seventeenth-century intellectuals, not only in Spain, but throughout Europe.[15]

[15] Unquestioning faith in God characterized widely different facets of seventeenth-century thought. The skeptics argued that since reason was imperfect and all human knowledge uncertain, our only means of attaining truth was through divine revelation. Religious truth, therefore, had to be accepted on faith. Reason could be used to second faith, argued the skeptic Montaigne, but is insufficient to reveal divine truth. Faith alone must be the cornerstone of religion: "C'est à elle seule (à la majesté divine) qu'apartient la science et la sapience; elle seule qui peut estimer de soy quelque chose, et à qui nous desrobons ce que nous nous contons et ce que nous nous prisons." (Michel de Montaigne, p. 160) Montaigne goes on to debase man's pretentions to understand the cosmos unaided by Divine Light. He finds in keeping with Christianity the Pyrrhonian attitude of maintaining complete doubt and suspending judgment regarding all matters but religion, which must be accepted on faith: "Cette-cy présente l'homme nud et vide, recognoissant sa faiblesse naturelle, propre à recevoir d'en haut quelque force estrangère, desgarni d'humaine science et d'autant plus apte à loger en soy la divine, anéantissant son jugement pour faire plus de place à la foy..." (p. 238).
The skeptic Sánchez also maintains that religion must be accepted on faith: "Tampoco me pidas autoridades ni falsos acatamientos a la opinión ajena, porque ello más bien sería indicio de ánimo servil e indocto que de un espíritu libre y amante de la verdad. Yo sólo seguiré con la razón a sola naturaleza. La autoridad manda creer; la razón demuestra las cosas; aquélla es apta para la fe; ésta para la ciencia." (p. 47).

La dama duende is a comedy, but although at some moments it borders on slapstick, it is not a farce, for it has an important philosophical message to convey. The comic genre, as much as the tragic, is well suited to Calderón's purposes. In comedy, traditional views can be mocked in a way they cannot in tragedy. In comedy, social conventions can be challenged and the culprit go unpunished. The genre of *La dama duende* leaves Calderón ample room to poke fun at the closed-mindedness of Cosme and don Luis, and through them, of man. It permits him to guide the sympathies of the audience to the clever and charming doña Angela, as she defies the code of honor and teases and provokes Cosme for her own ends. In *El galán fantasma,* Julia is equally

The advocates of the "new science," who constantly found themselves at odds with the skeptics did not question religion. Johannes Kepler (1571-1630), for example, saw the hand of God in the rational harmony of the universe. In Book Four of his *Epitome of Copernican Astronomy,* Kepler explains how God and man are reflected in geometrical truths: "Geometrical reasons are co-eternal with God —and in them there is first the difference between the curved and the straight line." (Chicago: Britannica, 1952, p. 863) "...the curved somehow bears a likeness to God; the staight line represents the creatures. And first the adornment of the world, the farthest region of the fixed stars has been made spherical, in that geometrical likeness of God, because as a corporeal God —worshipped by the gentiles under the name of Jupiter— it had to contain all the remaining things in itself." (p. 864) God, says Kepler, did nothing gratuitously. He followed a rational plan. He gave special importance to Earth, for Earth was meant to be the home of man, image of God. (See p. 869 and p. 873) Throughout this and other works (for example, *Harmonies of the World),* Kepler reiterates his basic idea that all things in the universe are the result of God's master plan.

Gottfried Whilhelm Leibniz (1646-1716) developed ideas of universal harmony along totally unique lines. The universe, according to Leibniz's system as presented in the *Theodicy* (1710) and the *Monadology* (1714) is made up of monads. These are the simplest of substances of which all things are composed. They cannot be dissolved or composed since they are without parts. Since they cannot interact, apparent interaction of monads can be explained in terms of preestablished harmony. God sets the monads working and each one functions in accordance with His plan. That is why it seems that all are working together while in fact each is working independently with God. Arthur O. Lovejoy summarizes Leibniz's view of the

131

disrespectful of the honor code. Comedy gives Calderón the opportunity to satirize social convention.

In Calderonian tragedy, the characters are inevitably so caught up in their obsessions that they bring destruction upon themselves. They are responsible for their own unhappiness, yet they view themselves as victims. Their confusion and suffering cannot help but awaken the compassion of the viewer. Guilt and innocence are so diffused as to cause the spectator ambivalent feelings toward the characters. But in Calderonian comedy, issues are more clearly defined. Characters such as Cosme and don Luis are clearly shown to be wrong at the end of the play.

universe as follows: "The essential characteristics of the universe are for him plentitude, continuity, and linear gradation. The chain consists of the totality of monads, ranging in hierarchical sequence from God to the lowest grade of sentient life, no two alike, but each differing from those just below and just above it in a scale of least possible difference..." (See Arthur O. Lovejoy, *The Great Chain of Being: A Study of the History of an Idea*, The William James Lectures delivered at Harvard University, 1933, Cambridge, Mass.: Harvad University Press, 1936, p. 144) God is, then, the primary cause behind all phenomena.

For Isaac Newton (1642-1727), a contemporary of Leibniz, the existence of God was perfectly reconcilable with the rational make-up of the universe, He being the primary cause behind the mathematical relationships of all things. In Book III of his *Mathematical Principles* Newton asserts: "This most beautiful system of the sun, planets, and comets, could only proceed from the counsel and dominion of an intelligent and powerful Being. And if the fixed stars are the centres of other like systems, these, being formed by the like wise counsel, must be all subject to the dominion of One... (Chicago: Britannica, 1952) pp. 369-370 He then goes on to state: "This Being governs all things, not as the soul of the world, but as Lord over all..." (p. 370) Newton explains the meaning of the word God, and His significance in terms of duration and space. He reiterates his belief that God is a necessary part of the system, the primary cause, as the ancients believed: "In him are all things contained and moved; yet neither affects the other: God suffers nothing from the motion of bodies; bodies find no resistance from the omnipresence of God. It is allowed by all that the Supreme God exists necessarily; and by the same necessity he exists *always* and everywhere." (p. 371) Newton ventures no theories on the nature of God. That is a supreme mystery: "As a blind man has no idea of colors, so

132

In comedy, there is no spiritual uplift. *La dama duende* does not end with a conversion, as does *La vida es sueño*. Don Luis and Cosme, although they recognize themselves to be mistaken in this one instance, do not forsake the beliefs that have mislead them. Don Luis remains preoccupied with honor and Cosme remains a heretic. Both are potentially tragic characters. Eric Bentley has written, "...comedy, like tragedy, is a way of trying to cope with despair, mental suffering, guilt and anxiety... Just as the satisfactions of tragedy transcend those of melodrama, so those of comedy transcend those of farce... The comic dramatist's starting point is misery; the joy at his destination is a superb and thrilling transcendence."[16] If Aureliano *(La gran Cenobia)* and don Lope de Almeida *(A secreto agravio, secreta venganza,* to be analyzed in the next chapter) demonstrate the tragic consequences of intellectual rigidity, don Luis and Cosme demostrate their comical consequences. But the similarity that exists among all these characters is proof that comedy and tragedy are irrevocably intertwined.

have we no idea of manner by which the all-wise God perceives and understands all things." (p. 371) Yet, it is not necessary for the believer to accept this mysterious being in spite of his reason, as it was for nineteenth and twentieth-century existencialists concerned with the existence of God, such as Kierkegaard and Unanumo, but rather it is precisely reason which leads us to the knowledge of the existence of God.

[16] *The Life of the Drama* (New York: Atheneum, 1964) p. 302.

CHAPTER III

ABSURDITY AND ALIENATION:
A SECRETO AGRAVIO, SECRETA VENGANZA

The Court of Honor

The plot of *A secreto agravio, secreta venganza* is similar to the plots of Calderón's other honor plays: Don Lope de Almeida, a Portuguese gentleman, suspects his wife Leonor of infidelity and takes vengeance on her and her alleged lover by drowning the latter and causing the former to perish in a fire. In spite of the conventionality of the plot, don Lope stands out as one of Calderón's most successful dramatic creations. He is a character of great complexity. He is, in a sense, both guilty and innocent, for while he is most definitely a murderer and the creator of his own misfortune, he is, at the same time, a victim of circumstances. Although typical of his century in his obsession with sexual honor, he is appealing to the twentieth-century reader, for his awareness of the absurdity of the social conventions which bind him and his consequent sense of alienation liken him to many creations of modern fiction.

The honor which binds don Lope is a complex social code that obligates a man to consider as an affront any real or suspected sexual transgression on the part of his wife or any other woman for whom he feels responsible. The defense of honor is an exclusively masculine duty, and the man, as protector of honor, must punish by death not only the offender of his honor but also the woman, regardless of whether she is innocent or guilty.[1]

From the very beginning of *A secreto agravio, secreta*

[1] In the context of Spanish seventeenth-century society and consequently, drama, honor is linked irrevocably with virility. Julian Pitt-Rivers writes, "The natural qualities of sexual potency or purity and the moral qualities associated with them provide the conceptual framework on which the (honor) system is constructed," p. 45. While for men honor becomes associated with sexual potency, for women it becomes associated with sexual purity. One of the natural qualities Pitt-Rivers refers to is physical strength, and one of the moral qualities is courage. The man of the family is, then, supposed to be its strength and courage, its means of defense. The honor of the entire family is deposited in his keeping. "The manliness of a husband must be exerted above all in the defence of the honour of his wife on which his own depends. Therefore her adultery represents not only an infringement of his rights but the demonstration of his failure in his duty." Pitt-Rivers, p. 46. The question at stake in matters of honor is not the guilt or innocence of the wife, but the reputation of the husband.
This concept of honor is a degeneration of a medieval ideal which envisages the honorable man as both virtuous and valorous. The hierarchic conception of society made a distinct division between the lower classes, whose duty it was to toil and to produce, and the nobles, whose duty it was to protect virtue. Chivalry was primarily an ethical concept, second in importance only to religion. The fact that noblemen ordinarily did not live up to the moral excellence expected of them did not tarnish the ideal any more than the debauchery of the clergy weakened faith in the Church.
Manly perfection was to be achieved through war; the ideals of the Church and State were to be defended by force. The early crusades provided the nobility with a military function. The honor of the knight depended greatly on his serving his king's religious-military expeditions.
But it was not only the ethical and combative aspects of chivalry that gave it its framework, but also the erotic. Compassion, fidelity, justice, sacrifice were inspired not primarily by religion, but by a woman. The knight performed deeds of heroism for his lady —to win her attention, her esteem, her favor. The lady was not necessarily his wife, for in an age when marriage was conceived of primarily as a political and economic convenience, pure and impassioned love was reserved for a woman who

136

venganza, we are given some insight as to the phychological complexity of the honor code. King Sebastian has just given don Lope permission to join the bride he has wed by proxy. Don Lope is so anxious to reach the side of his promised doña Leonor, that when his manservant Manrique compares him with the wind, he insists he would rather have wings of fire in order to arrive at his bride's side all the more rapidly:

> el viento
> es perezoso elemento.
> Diérame el amor sus alas,
> volara abrasado y ciego;
> pues quien al viento se entrega,
> (olas) de viento navega,
> y las de amor son de fuego.
>
> (Primera jornada, 24-28)

might be perceived as an ideal, often a virgin, a queen, or the wife of a noble of higher rank. An important motif of chivalrous literature is the defense of the imperiled virgin, or, as J. Huizinga has put it, "the ousting of the rival."

Chivalry, like religion, touched every aspect of life of the nobility. The cultivation of courtesy, the search for refinement, the obsession with ceremony were part of the chivalric outlook. War games, jousts and tournaments in which rival knights fought each other to the death in the name of their respective ladies were a manifestation of the chivalric military ideal. The novels of chivalry, such as *Amadís de Gaula* and *Tirante lo Blanco,* which were popular well into the Renaissance, were spectacular portrayals of the most fantastic exaggerations of the ideals of knight-erantry. The Church was openly hostile to the cultivation of courtly love, to the jousts, and to the novels of chivalry which idealized them.

By the time the novels of chivalry were written, the world they depicted was rapidly declining. In reality, it had never been very much as they described it. Wars had been fought for political, economic or personal motives far more than for lofty ethical ideals. Courtly love was frequently a masquerade for licentiousness. Honor was often used, in practice, as a banner for wars of vengeance and retaliation.

Pride and reputation had always been important elements in the concept of honor. Ideally, one performed good deeds out of a sense of duty and self-esteem, and one who performed acts of valor in defense of virtue would achieve a reputation that would bring honors. By the sixteenth century, chivalry was outmoded as a way of life, yet honor, in a degenerated form, continued to be an issue. The military emphasis was somewhat diluted and

Throughout the play the elements reflect important truths about de characters.[2] If don Lope is not anxious to give himself over to that "sloughful element", it is because he is anxious to reach the joy that is waiting for him at home. But Manrique's observation is more relevant than is immediately obvious. Don Lope *is* carried by the wind; that is, throughout the action of the drama he is whisked along by circumstances and events over which he feels he has no control. Manrique, as is often the case with Calderón's buffoon-servant characters, speaks the truth.

But the alternative don Lope has chosen for himself is also significant. He would rather ride on wings of fire than on the waves of the wind. The second metaphor alludes to the passionate, vengeful aspect of don Lope. Honor ignites in him a thirst for vengeance. He will proceed, burning and blind ("abrasado y ciego") until vengeance has been taken. Thus, from the very beginning of the play, we have a notion of the

the ethical aspect had all but disappeared. What remained were the violent, egotistical and erotic elements coupled with a keen sense of rivalry. The erotic inspiration was no longer an inaccessible virgin to whom one owed homage, but one's own wife, daughters and sisters, for whose sexual purity one was responsible. Infidelity became a point of *desafío*. Noblemen in seventeenth-century literature are portrayed as sensitive to the point of paranoia regarding the sexual purity of their women, although in real life the situation was undoubtedly less exaggerated.
See J. Huizinga, *The Waning of the Middle Ages,* (Garden City: Doubleday and Company, 1954), pp. 56-84; Denis de Rougemont, *L'Amor en l'Occident* (Paris: Plon, 1939), pp. 18-20, 227-256; and Julio Caro Baroja, "Honour and Shame." On the role of honor in Spanish literature and life in the seventeenth century, see C. A. Jones, "Honor in Spanish Golden Age Drama: Its Relation to Real Life and to Morals," *Bulletin of Hispanic Studies,* 35 (1958), pp. 199-210; C.A. Jones, "Spanish Honor as Historical Phenomenon," *Hispanic Review,* 33 (1965), pp. 32-39; and Melveena McKendrick, *Woman and Society in the Spanish Drama of the Golden Age,* (London and New York: Cambridge University Press, 1974).
[2] E. M. Wilson discusses the use of the elements in Calderón's work in "The Four Elements in the Imagery of Calderón" in *The Modern Language Review,* XXXI, No. 1 (1936), pp. 34-47. He does not, however, speak of the use of the elements to reveal psychological truths.

double aspect of don Lope's predicament: on the one hand, he is victim of uncontrollable forces which catch him unawares; on the other, he is author of his own destruction, for he yields to passionate and blind drives.

Don Lope's system of values becomes evident in an encounter between him and his long lost friend, don Juan, who had been his intimate companion in India. Don Lope had had to return to Portugal because of the death of his father. Don Juan stayed on, comfortable in a position of respect and esteem. His choice of words is significant; he had gone to India not in search of riches, but in search of honor:

> No codicia de riqueza,
> sino codicia de honor...
> (Primera jornada, 90-91)

The key word is *codicia,* which might be rendered in English as "covetousness," "cupidity," or "greed." Don Juan's insistence on honor is not merely a desire for self-respect, but a kind of vice. Don Juan is fanatical concerning the question of his reputation. He reiterates that after don Lope left,

> me quedé yo,
> bien sabéis con cuánta fama
> de amigos y de opinión,
> que ahora perdido hacen
> el sentimiento mayor
> (Primera jornada, 114-118)

For don Juan, honor is primarily a question of reputation.[3] It is not necessarily achieved through the performance of vir-

[3] Pitt-Rivers writes: "Honour is the value of a person in his own eyes, but also in the eyes of his society. It is his estimation of his own worth, his *claim* to pride, but it is also the acknowledgement of that claim, his excellence recognized by society, his *right* to pride." Pitt-Rivers, p. 21 Honor, as it applies to seventeenth-century Spanish society, is not virtue or personal value, although it may include those concepts as well, but is primarily the individual's reputation and his ability to live up to that

tuous acts, but depends rather on the esteem one commands of others through means of force, social position, wealth and other factors.[4]

Don Juan had been forced to leave India as the result of an affair of honor involving a woman two men had qualified as "cruel." One challenge hurled by an adversary —the word *mentis*— was sufficient to require him to draw his sword. What was at stake was not the truth or falsity of the allegation, but the challenge itself. Upon hearing it, don Juan is overcome by a kind of cold rage:

> "Mentis", dijo. Aquí no puedo
> proseguir, porque la voz
> muda, la lengua turbada,
> frío el cuerpo, el corazón
> palpitante, los sentidos
> muertos y vivo el dolor,
> quedan repitiendo aquella
> afrenta.
> (Primera jornada, 197-204)

reputation: "the validation of the image which they (people) cherish of themselves." Pitt-Rivers, p. 22.

Honor-reputation is not an exclusively seventeenth-century Spanish concept. In 1651 the English philosopher Thomas Hobbes (1588-1679) published his controversial work, the *Leviathan,* in which he discusses honor: "The manifestation of the value we set on one another is that which is commonly called *honouring* and *dishonouring.* To value a man at a high rate is to *honour* him; at a low rate is to *dishonour* him. But high and low, in this case, is to be understood by comparison to the rate that each man setteth on himself." (Chicago: Encyclopedia Britannica, 1952) p. 73. Montesquieu discusses the role of honor-reputation in the monarchy in *De l'Esprit des lois* and Pascal speaks of it in his *Pensées.* Beaumarchais' *Le Mariage de Figaro* is concerned with changing concepts of honor. Dostoevsky's *The Brothers Karamazov* contains a heated discussion about honor between Russians and Poles and Dmitri Karamazov insists constantly during his trial that he is a man of honor. Thomas Mann mentions duels of honor in *The Magic Mountain.* In Jorge Amado's *Tereza Batista cansada de guerra,* the brutal rapist Justiano Duarte da Rosa brags of being a man of honor.

[4] Pitt-Rivers emphasizes that honor and honors are not necessarily bestowed on those who are most virtuous. Reputation and favor are

Don Juan's reaction to the verbal affront is not intellectual but physical. His vocal chords, tongue, body, heart and senses are shaken and momentarily immobilized, a phenomenon which is repeated each time he relives the moment in his mind.

But at the same time, he recognizes the situation as absurd:

¡Oh vil ley
del mundo! ¡Que una razón,
o que una sinrazón pueda
manchar el altivo honor
tantos años adquirido,
y que la antigua opinión
de honrado quede postrada
a lo fácil de una voz!

bestowed on those who claim them and, "just as possession is said to be nine-tenths of the law, so the de facto achievement of honour depends upon the ability to silence anyone who would dispute the title... On the field of honour might is right." Pitt-Rivers, pp. 24-25.

The discrepancy between honor and virtue was of concern to seventeenth and eighteenth-century moralists, who wrote extensively on the subject. Hobbes commented: "Nor does it alter the case of honour whether an action (so it be great and difficult, and consequently a sign of much power) be just or unjust: for honor consisteth only in the opinion of much power." p. 75 Pascal wrote: "Nous ne nous contentons pas de la vie que nous avons en nous et en notre propre être: nous voulons vivre dans l'idée des autres d'une vie imaginaire, et nous efforçons pour cela de paraître. Nous travaillons incessament à embellir et conserver notre être imaginaire et négligeons le véritable. Et si nous avons ou la tranquillité, ou la générosité, ou la fidélité, nous nous empressons de le faire savoir, afin d'attacher ces vertus-là à notre autre être, et les détacherions plutôt de nous pour les joindre à l'autre; nous serons de bon coeur poltrons pour en acquérir la réputation d'être vaillants. Grande marque du néant de nostre propre être, de n'être pas satisfait de l'un sans l'autre, et d'échanger souvant l'un pour l'autre! Car qui ne mourrait pour conserver son honneur, celui-là serait infâme." Blaise Pascal, *Pensées sur la Religion et sur quelques autres sujets* (Paris: J. Delmas et Cie, 1960) p. 149 This extremely relevant analysis not only separates honor from virtue and establishes it as reputation, but also categorizes it within the realm of imagination, much as Calderón does. For don Lope, just as for Aureliano, the issue involved is

Don Juan recognizes that it is illogical that an accusation
—perhaps a false one, a *sinrazón*— can topple a reputation
acquired over a period of many years. Yet one single utterance
constituting a provocation caused him to return to Portugal,
poor and miserable, the victim of an insult he had provoked
out of a sense of obligation and which society required him to
punish.

Honor is an absolute for men like don Juan; that is, it is a
reality with which there can be no compromise. It resembles
the diamond, not only in its purity, but also in its fragility, for
like the diamond it can be soiled by only a breath. Likewise,
it resembles the sun, which for all its splendor can be hidden
by a lowly cloud:

> ¡Que el honor, siendo un diamante,
> pueda un frágil soplo (¡ay Dios!)
> abrasarle y consumirle,
> y que siendo su esplendor
> más que 'el sol puro, un aliento
> sirva de nube a este sol!
>
> (Primera Jornada, 213-219)

self-image. The imaginary self becomes so much more important than the
real self that all virtues are sacrificed to it. Pascal continues: "Nous avons
une si grande idée de l'âme de l'homme que nous ne pouvons souffrir d'en
être méprisés et de n'être pas dans l'estime d'une âme; et toute la félicité des
hommes consiste dans cette estime." Montesquieu also comments on the
false virtues one learns in the school of honor: "Les vertus qu'on nous y
montre sont toujours moins ce que l'on doit aux autres, que ce que l'on se
doit à soi-même: elles ne sont pas tant ce qui nous appelle vers nos con-
citoyens, que ce qui nous en distingue. On n'y juge pas les actions des
hommes comme bonnes, mais comme belles; comme justes, mais comme
grandes; comme raisonnables, mais comme extraordinaires." Charles de
Montesquieru, *De l'Esprit des lois, Oeuvres completes,* (Paris: Seuil,
1964) p. 540 Montesquieu emphasizes even more than Pascal the
egotistical quality of honor, which requires that one think first of oneself
and one's reputation. Both authors point out the "unreasonable" quality of
honor.

Don Juan kills his offender in a duel, then takes refuge in a church, where he is obliged to remain in hiding for three days. He has behaved honorably —that is, he has behaved according to the dictates of the honor code— and yet, he is forced to hide like a common criminal. He has complied with his duties, and yet he is punished, not rewarded. Finally, he returns to Portugal, a poor and broken man. Had he failed to take vengeance, don Juan would have been dishonored as a coward. Having taken vengeance, he is forced into exile.

Don Juan reiterates the absurdity of his situation:

> ¡Injusto engaño
> de la vida! O su pasión
> no dé por infame al hombre
> que sufre su deshonor,
> o le dé por disculpado,
> si se venga; que es error
> dar a la afrenta castigo,
> y no al castigo perdón.
>
> (Primera jornada, 255-262)

He seems to be before a high court whose workings are totally illogical, for it condemns both those who comply with its rules and those who do not. Don Juan sought to be acquitted —disculpado. But, although he avenged himself, the acquittal was not granted.

The passage is an important one, for it introduces the metaphor of the court of honor, which tries and condemns but never exonerates. This metaphor, carried throughout the play, is far from gratuitous.[5] Through it Calderón makes the point that honor has its own laws, procedures and punishments, divorced from those which make up the legitimate legal system. The point he makes linguistically in *A secreto agravio, secreta venganza* he makes dramatically in

---

[5] Calderón uses the metaphor of the legal system which accuses, judges and convicts without motive in a number of other plays. In *El médico de su honra,* don Gutierre says:

another play, *Luis Pérez, el gallego,* in which there is an explosive confrontation between the honor hero and a corrupt judge.

Like Aureliano in *La gran Cenobia,* don Lope is confronted early in the play with an example. Yet he, like Aureliano, is none the wiser for it. He continues to believe naively that once a man's honor has been defended, his name remains cleansed forever:

> ¿Quién se libra, quién se excepta
> de una intención mal segura,
> de un pecho doble, que alienta
> la ponzoña de una mano
> y el veneno de una lengua?
> Ninguno. Sólo dichoso
> puede llamarse el que deja,
> como vos, limpio su honor
> y castigada su ofensa;
> honrado 'estáis: negras sombras
> no deslustren, no escurezcan
> vuestro honor antiguo.
>
> (Primera jornada, 286-297)

> ¿Qué injusta ley condena,
> que muera el inocente y que padezca?
> (Segunda jornada, 641-642)

Don Juan Roca uses the legal metaphor in *El pintor de su deshonra:*

> ¡Mal haya el primero, amén,
> que hizo ley tan rigurosa!
> Poco del honor sabía
> el legislador tirano,
> que puso en ajena mano
> mi opinión, y no en la mía.
> (Tercera jornada, 487-492)

In *La devoción de la cruz,* Curcio, the honor figure, says:

> ¿Qué ley culpa a un inocente?
> ¿Qué opinión a un libre agravia?
> Miente otra vez; que no es
> deshonra, sino desgracia.
> (Primera jornada, 681-684)

It is not until he himself has been accused by the honor court that he will begin to appreciate the complexity of the system. And that moment is not far off.

Doña Leonor, his new bride, married him by proxy under unfavorable circumstances. She is in love with don Luis de Benavides, whom she believes to be dead. Even before the unexpected arrival of don Luis, she speaks passionately of the unhappiness she feels, now married to a man whom she hardly knows and whom she does not love. Once again the elements participate in the passions of the character. A "violent fire' consumes doña Leonor; her voice is "fire and wind," her tears, "fire and sobs."

> Abrasen, cuando navego
> tanto mar y viento tanto,
> mi vida y mi fuego cuanto
> consume el fuego violento
> pues mi voz es fuego y viento,
> mis lágrimas fuego y llanto.
>
> (Primera jornada, 233-438)

And, as a reaction against the great passion she feels, Sirena, her maid, who functions in the traditional role of the servant as alter-ego of her mistress, reminds her of her obligations to her honor.

This preoccupation with honor above all and in spite of one's own desires is characteristic of Calderón's men and women of honor. Love and desire are no longer —or should no longer be— factors in determining one's behavior. A past love must be forgotten and present actions must be decided in terms of that overwhelming absolute: one's honor.[6]

[6] In *El médico de su honra* Mencía must conquer her feelings for don Enrique, her former love:

> y solamente me huelgo
> de tener hoy que sentir,
> por tener en mis deseos
> que vencer;
>
> (Primera jornada, 140-144)

Doña Leonor is determined to remain firm in her commitment to her husband, not out of love, but out of honor:

> Hasta las aras, amor,
> te acompañé; aquí te quedas,
> porque atreverte no puedas
> a las aras del honor.
>
> (Primera jornada, 505-508)

The *aras del honor* —the holy communion table of honor— has sanctified her marriage.

The appearance of don Luis is the force that sets the action of the play moving. He comes disguised as a diamond merchant —the diamond being a symbol of honor[7] —and his very presence constitutes a threat to don Lope's honor. The roguish don Luis, an impetuous and violent Castillian, whom Calderón opposes to the calm and deliberate Portuguese don Lope, desires doña Leonor and will eventually feel a truly sadistic pleasure in robbing don Lope of his honor. Don Luis comes upon doña Leonor with his hopes —symbolized by the

Love is preterit; Mencía's present preoccupation must be honor:

> tuve amor, y tengo honor.
> (Primera jornada, 573)

In *El pintor de su deshonra* Serafina must reject her former love Don Alvaro, for honor requires her to remain loyal to Don Juan Roca:

> Cuando me acuerdo quién (fuí),
> el corazón las tributa;
> cuando me acuerdo quién soy,
> él mismo me las rehusa:
> (Primera jornada, 1040-1043)

[7] Valbuena Briones notes: "Generalmente el honor es comparado al cristal por la fragilidad que éste posee... Calderón, que compara el honor al cristal numerosas veces, como todos los dramaturgos de la época, va más allá esta vez al establecer la comparación con el cristal más precioso, el diamante." Pedro Calderón de la Barca, *A secreto agravio, secreta venganza,* ed. Angel Valbuena Briones (Madrid: Espasa Calpe, 1956), p. 11.

green emerald— totally destroyed, for he has heard of her marriage, and with his jealousy —symbolized by the blue sapphire— ignited.

> Estaba con un záfiro;
> mas la esmeralda llevaron
> solamente, y me dejaron
> esta azul piedra que miro;
> y así dije en mis desvelos:
> "¿Cómo con tanta venganza
> me llevasteis la esperanza
> para dejarme los celos?"
>
> (Primera Jornada, 657-644)

The purification of honor requires vengeance. Doña Leonor, feeling dishonored by don Luis's disappearance, took vengeance the only way possible for a woman to do so: by marrying another man.[8] Earlier in the play she states:

> me casé
> sólo por vengarme en mí
>
> (Primera Jornada, 501-502)

Now don Luis complains that out·of vengeance she has robbed him of his hope and left him with nothing but jealousy. Like don Juan, doña Leonor is the victim of her vengeance, for now it is impossible for her and don Luis to realize their love.

Once again the language of the tribunal is used. The question arises as to who is guilty. Through a series of *doubles entendres,* doña Leonor speaks both to the diamond merchant, who has arrived too late to make a sale and to her lover, who has arrived too late to marry her.

---

[8] Since the defense of honor is a masculine duty, women have little recourse once they have been dishonored. In seventeenth-century works in which women do actively seek to avenge their honor, they dress as men. Rosaura in Calderón's *La vida es sueño* is one example.

> No culpéis la condición
> que en mí tan esquiva hallasteis;
> culpaos a vos, que llegasteis
> sin tiempo y sin ocasión.
>
> (Primera Jornada, 967-700)

She uses the same technique of *doubles entendres* in the next scene in which she defines more explicitly her feelings for don Luis in a sonnet meant for him but addressed to don Lope, her husband:

> Disculpa tengo, cuando, temeroso
> y cobarde mi amor, llego a miraros,
> si no pago un amor tan generoso.
>
> De vos, y no de mí, podéis quejaros,
> pues, aunque yo os estime como a esposo,
> es imposible, como sois, amaros.
>
> (Primera Jornada, 765-770)

The ambiguous language reflects doña Leonor's ambiguous feelings, for she is torn between desire and duty.

The metaphor of society as a courtroom has been widely used in modern literature. Dostoevsky uses it in *The Brothers Karamasov;* Camus, in *L'Etranger;* Kafka, in *The Trial*[9] and in a number of short stories. The courtroom of Calderón's *A secreto agravio, secreta venganza* is a sexually closed society, suspicious, vengeful, and paranoid. For the man who lives and functions within this system, honor is an obsession, and the fear that his honor may be blemished and his valor and virility thereby cast into doubt —since the man who fails to maintain his honor pure has failed in his masculine duties —gives rise to a feeling of guilt.

[9] See my article, *Calderón's Don Lope de Almeida: A Kafkian Character,* from which some of the material in this chapter has been taken. *Colección Scholar* (New York: Plaza Mayor, 1971).

The Trial

It is during the second *jornada* of the play that the accusation is made that will bring don Lope de Almeida before the High Court of Honor. The court is the society of which don Lope is a part. And, as a representative of his society, he will accuse himself, judge himself, and finally condemn himself. As in the case of Kafka's characters, the individual will be destroyed by his feelings of guilt.[10]

When don Lope asks doña Leonor for her permission to accompany King Sebastian on his African campaign, he is surprised that she gives it so readily, while his friend don Juan advises him not to go. Don Lope immediately feels accused and obliged to defend himself. If a friend advises him not to leave his wife alone, it must be that his honor is in danger.

But why and by whom has don Lope been accused? He has always lived honorably. Like Joseph K in *The Trial*[11] and K in *The Castle*[12] don Lope is ignorant of the nature of his crime and of his accuser. But of one thing he is certain: he has been accused.

> Ahora bien: fuerza es quejarme;
> mas no sé por dónde empiece;
> que, como en guerra y en paz
> viví tan honrado siempre,
> para quejarme ofendido,
> no es mucho que no aprendiese
> razones; porque ninguno
> previno lo que no teme.
>
> (Segunda Jornada, 225-232)

[10] Edwin Honig points out the "dehumanized absurdity" of Don Lope's situation and the Kafkesque quality of *A secreto agravio, secreta venganza* in his introduction to *Calderón, Four Plays*, pp. xvii-xviii. He also compares the honor code to a machine in "Dehumanizing Honor," *Calderón and the Seizures of Honor* (Cambridge: Harvard University Press, 1972), p. 50.
[11] Franz Kafka, *The Trial* (New York: Alfred A. Knopf, 1965).
[12] Franz Kafka, *The Castle* (New York: Alfred A. Knopf, 1966).

Don Lope's crime is to be without honor and his accuser is his own sense of guilt:

> ¿Osará decir la lengua
> qué tengo?... Lengua, detente,
> no pronuncies, no articules
> mi afrenta; que si me ofendes,
> podrá ser que castigada,
> con mi vida o con mi muerte,
> siendo ofensor y ofendido,
> yo me agravie y yo me vengue.
> No digas que tengo celos...
> Ya lo dije, ya no puede
> volverse al pecho la voz.
>
> (Segunda Jornada, 233-243)

The very admission that he is jealous constitutes an accusation that his honor has been offended, and such an accusation requires vengeance.

By admitting the threat presented by the presence of don Luis, the accused explains the attitude of doña Leonor, who consents to his going with the King, and that of don Juan, who admonishes him not to go.

But don Lope vacillates and finally rebels against the accusation. He reasons, like Joseph K in *The Trial*, that it must be false, for he knows himself to be innocent.

> Pero ya que el cargo es éste,
> hablemos en el descargo:
> Leonor es quien es y yo
> soy quien soy (y) nadie puede
> borrar fama tan segura
> ni opinión tan excelente.
>
> (Segunda Jornada, 315-319)

Yet, his very insistence betrays his feelings of guilt. Calderón's men and women of honor most often affirm "I am who I am" precisely in those situations in which they are no

150

longer sure who they are. For them, one is one's reputation; they cling to the famous formula of self-identification precisely when their reputations are in danger.

Although don Lope struggles to cast aside the accusation, in the end he yields to it. But not without first condemning the horrors of the honor system:

> ¿Hay, honor, más sutilezas
> que decirme y proponerme?
> ¿Más tormentos que me aflijan,
> más penas que me atormenten,
> más sospechas que me maten,
> más temores que me cerquen,
> más agravios que me ahoguen
> y más celos que me afrenten?
>
> (Segunda Jornada, 325-332)

Don Lope's anger only affirms his belief in the law of honor. One does not rebel against that which has no meaning for one. Although he knows the honor code to be unjust, don Lope nevertheless respects and abides by the obligations of honor. Little by little, he relinquishes his free will to a sense of fatality.

All that matters now is to cleanse his tarnished honor. He may feel that he has been unjustly accused, but he must nevertheless try to defend himself. And, by resolving to undertake his defense, he in a sense surrenders. Like Joseph K, who at last stops denying the importance of his accusation and begins the battle for his acquittal, don Lope at last stops trying to convince himself that there has been an error and undertakes the vengeance of his honor. He fights for his acquittal, for the social salvation that is for him as real and as important as religious salvation is for a man of God.[13]

---

[13] The choice of the word "salvation" is not gratuitous. As P. N. Dunn has pointed out, honor is a kind of religion for characters such as don Lope. As such, it has rites and requires sacrifice and bloodshed. It is conferred by Grace, not by right. Dunn demonstrates that the honor-religion is not com-

His trial and the necessity of obtaining an acquittal become, for don Lope as for Joseph K, an obsession. Don Lope feels guilty of not having complied with society's obligations, of not having protected the honor of his house. Only by taking vengeance on don Luis can don Lope be worthy of acquittal, according to the law of honor.

It is important to note that during the trial (until this moment a merely psychological process, since don Lope has never been openly accused by anyone) the facts connected with the case have never been explicitly stated, and it has never been clearly explained of exactly what crime don Lope is guilty. Don Lope feels guilty of not having complied with certain obligations, but in the long soliloquy in which he accuses himself, he never defines the nature of his crime and he never explicitly states what those social obligations are with which he has not complied. He himself could never analyze the nature of his own guilt; the accused man faces an absolute which he is incapable of understanding. In the tribunals of *The Trial* the law books, which it is supposed the judges study carefully, appear to be blank to Joseph K. All that he can find in those that he succeeds in examining are some empty pages and a few pornographic drawings. The rationale according to which the Absolute functions is incomprehensible to the accused. And therefore, don Lope must surrender blindly to the circumstances without understanding the logic of its workings, just as Joseph K does.

patible with Christianity because it assumes that the world is unredeemed. Honor's passion requires bloodshed without redemption, while Christ's passion signifies precisely redemption. For the religion of honor, vengeance is the end, while for Christianity, the end is love. See P. N. Dunn, "Honour and the Christian Background in Calderón," In *Critical Essays on the Theatre of Calderón,* ed. Bruce W. Wardropper, (New York: New York University Press, 1965), pp. 24-60. In "La discreción de don Lope de Almeida," E. M. Wilson also points out this religious quality of the honor plays. He sees *A secreto agravio, secreta venganza* as a kind of "disfrazada comedia de santos" and don Lope as a "místico del honor." *Clavileño,* 2, No. 9 (1951), pp. 1-10.

And once don Lope has surrendered, it no longer matters whether or not doña Leonor is guilty. According to the rules of honor that don Lope acccepts, any sexual transgression, *real or merely suspected,* must be avenged. Don Lope feels accused; he feels he must take vengeance, because for a man like don Lope, dishonor is worse than death.

Since a man's honor depends on public opinion, any implication of dishonor puts his good name in danger. Consequently, don Lope, in order to defend his honor before society —though there has never been a formal, open accusation— must take the lives of don Luis and doña Leonor. It is enough that he feels guilty to make vengeance a necessity.

As in the case of Joseph K, the evidence that could be produced in defense of the accused seems unimportant. Don Lope no longer considers the facts. The vital question is no longer the guilt or innocence of his wife, but the impeccable state of his honor. But the fact is that while don Lope is going through the mental process that constitutes his accusation, doña Leonor is battling with her own conscience.

Until this moment doña Leonor is innocent. When her maid Sirena arrives with an amorous note from don Luis, doña Leonor experiences tremendous confusion. Should she read it or not? Doña Leonor secretly wishes Sirena to insist that she read it. Doña Leonor wants to read the message yet she dares not, for to yield to her whim would be the first step toward yielding to don Luis. Doña Leonor argues with herself —or with Sirena, her alter-ego— and finally reads the note, fully aware of the possible consequences.

In spite of the danger involved, doña Leonor surrenders easily to Sirena's suggestion that she admit don Luis into her house in order to explain to him that he must return to Castille. In this act of the play it is always Sirena who advances the action regarding the relations between doña Leonor and don Luis. It is she, functioning as Leonor's alter-ego, who urgés and convinces her mistress to do what the latter, consciously or unconsciously, desires to do. Sirena is the antithesis of doña Leonor's conscience, that is, of her good judgment. As soon as doña Leonor gives her maid license to call don Luis, an act which in itself is a transgression, she assures herself that she will be able to control her passions:

> Amor,
> aunque en la ocasión esté
> soy quien soy, vencerme puedo,
> no es liviandad, honra es
> la que a esta ocasión me puso;
> ella me ha de defender;
> que cuando ella me faltara,
> quedara yo, que también
> supiera darme la muerte,
> si no supiera vencer.
>
> (Segunda Jornada, 546-555)

Once again an honor character has recourse to the familiar "I am who I am." But doña Leonor is slipping. She has already yielded to don Luis by sending for him and she already foresees the possibility of her failing her husband.

Don Luis's entry into Leonor's house symbolically represents the lovers' fall. While she waits for don Luis, doña Leonor trembles with the fear that at any moment her husband may return. Her fears are those of a guilty woman. She receives don Luis in dark quarters; the implication is obvious.

When don Juan arrives on the scene and discovers the presence of don Luis, he draws his sword in defense of the honor of his friend. Seconds later, don Lope arrives and discovers don Juan. The first reaction of the anxious husband is to dissimulate. To show himself perturbed before don Juan would be to confess his guilt; that is, to confess that he believes his honor to be in danger. Don Lope has already

154

passed the stage in which he believes his accusation to be an error, and also the stage of rebellion. He is now in another stage of the development of his trial: he feels the need to dissimulate, to appear innocent in spite of the circumstancial, evidence collecting around him.[14]

Don Lope convinces himself that he must dissimulate until he has verified the facts. He does not know what circumstances are behind the scene he has just witnessed, and until he does, he must pretend that nothing is wrong. Like Joseph K, who tries to keep secret everything concerning his trial, and whose greatest fear is that the other employees of the bank where he works will find out about it, don Lope proceeds with discretion.

> ([Ap.] Hoy seré cuerdamente,
> si es que ofendido soy, el más prudente,
> y en la venganza mía
> tendrá ejemplos el mundo,
> porque en callar la fundo.)
>
> (Segunda Jornada, 726-730)

"If I've been offended," says don Lope. He still clings to the feeble hope that he has not been offended, that he is really innocent, even though his innocence would not alter his need to take vengeance. The accused man is in a paradoxical situation. On the one hand he must defend himself against the accusation, whether or not it is justified; on the other, he feels the need to convince himself of his own innocence.[15] Don

---

[14] Compare: "You will see that you are nothing but a rat's nest of miserable dissimulations. The most trifling of your acts will not be untainted by these dissimulations." Franz Kafka, *Diaries: 1914-1923* (New York: Alfred A. Knopf, 1965), p. 114.

[15] Compare: "... to achieve anything, it was essential that he should banish from his mind once and for all the idea of possible guilt. There was no such guilt. This legal action was nothing more than a business deal such as he had often concluded to the advantage of the Bank, a deal within which, as always happened, lurked various dangers which must simply be obviated.

155

Lope must take vengeance in defense of the honor of his household. At the same time, he desperately grasps at the possibility that there has been no dishonor.

The accused must keep his trial a secret because publicity of any kind, both in the case of don Lope and in the case of Joseph K, would mean public humiliation. For this reason don Lope dispatches even Manrique, his servant, when he confronts don Luis. Any witness is dangerous. Don Lope cannot trust anyone.

It is now that don Lope begins to feel the isolation that every accused man experiences during his trial. The horrible isolation that K· feels in *The Castle* at not being able to communicate with the citizens of the village; the exasperating isolation that Joseph K experiences before his superiors at the bank and before everyone else, and the terrifying fear that someone will find out about his trial: these are the same feelings that don Lope experiences. No one must know; no one can possibly understand. Dissimulate. Proceed, like Joseph K, in silence.

When don Luis reveals himself, don Lope exercises complete self control. He listens to don Luis's explanation and lets him leave, although he experiences at the same time a tremendous sense of confusion. The accused man suffers constantly; he tortures himself; is he innocent or guilty? Don Lope is now at the stage of his trial in which he himself no longer knows.

> ¿Pueden juntarse en un hombre
> confusiones más extrañas?
> ¿Tantos asombros y miedos,
> penas y desdichas tantas?
> (Segunda Jornada, 808-811)

The right tactics were to avoid letting one's thoughts stray to one's own possible shortcomings, and to cling as firmly as one could to the thought of one's advantage. ...Yet, even though K. believed he could manage all this, the difficulty of drawing up the petition seemed overwhelming." *The Trial*, pp. 158-60.

Basta, basta, pensamiento,
sufrimiento, basta
que verdad puede ser todo,
                    (Segunda Jornada, 816-818)

Don Lope wants to believe that his honor is unblemished,
but on the other hand, he knows he must defend that honor,
regardless of its state, always suffering, dissimulating, and
remaining silent:

y cuando no, aquí no hay causa
para mayores extremos:
sufre, disimula y calla.
                    (Segunda Jornada, 819-821)

And he does not fail to let don Luis know that he will not
hesitate to take vengeance, should he feel it necessary.

¿qué es mi honor?
en mi opinión y en mi fama,
y en la voz tan solamente
de una criada, una esclava,
no tuviera, ¡vive Dios!,
vida que no le quitara,
almas que no le sacara;
y éstas rompiera después
a ser visibles las almas.
                    (Segunda Jornada, 860-869)

The discretion which don Lope is obliged to maintain isolates
him more and more from his wife and from his friend, don
Juan. In the same way that K's struggle for acceptance by the
Castle isolates him from the marital fulfillment that could
have been his road to salvation, don Lope's struggle for
honor and the silence which he must keep, isolates him from
conjugal happiness and from honor itself. It alienates him
from those who might help him.

Until now Leonor's crime has been implied, and even realized
on a psychological or symbolic plane. But in reality, she is

157

still innocent. However, don Lope has so totally isolated himself that he has lost contact with his wife and therewith any possibility of saving his marriage. He has lost all flexibility. He has engulfed himself in a self-imposed blanket of silence and is no longer capable of communicating with anyone.

The Judgment

By the beginning of the third *jornada* don Lope has lost all sense of rebelliousness; all that matters now is vengeance. His obsession with honor has taken control of his mind and of his acts; it dominates his every step. He is totally resigned to the necessity of murdering don Luis and doña Leonor. He has lost all sense of compassion. A vicious sense of vengeance now controls him.

Don Lope is no longer a rational man. He feels himself to be on the margin of society, incapable of sharing his pain even with his best friend, don Juan. He feels condemned to a horrible lack of communication. The condemned man feels alone. His trial is totally personal.

The terrible lack of communication that the accused suffers combines with another feeling, more terrifying still: the feeling that *other* men know his secret.

Like Joseph K, who does everything possible to keep his trial clandestine and who feels that with every movement, with every word, he reveals to his superiors and even to his inferiors at the bank the circumstances which engulf him, don Lope is confronted with the exasperating feeling that don Juan knows his secret. And one man is not only incapable of understanding another's trial, he is without any right to know about that trial.

The friendship which don Juan feels for don Lope puts him in the difficult position of suspecting a blemish on his friend's honor, but of feeling the necessity to keep silent. In some cases, according to the unwritten code of honor that governed the period, it was acceptable for a friend or a relative to defend the honor of a man physically unable to do so himself. But in the case of don Lope, although don Juan knows that the town is gossiping about don Luis's constant presence before don Lope's house, the circumstances do not permit him to avenge his friend's honor.[16] The accused is alone before the Absolute. Don Lope must avenge himself alone. Like Joseph K, who finds that neither the official painter of the judicial courts, nor the lawyer, nor the maid who works in the tribunals can help him, although they may sincerely want to, don Lope will have to take vengeance without assistance from anyone. He cannot trust even don Juan. The struggle of a man for the Absolute is a personal battle that divorces him from all other men.

Like Joseph K, don Lope will take the initiative in closing all lines of communication between himself and others. Joseph K decides to take up his own defense, without the aid of a lawyer; don Lope decides not to confide in don Juan. Don Juan and don Lope maintain a discreet and strained Portuguese decorum when don Juan tells his friend the story of two *hidalgos*, one of whose honor is in danger. Don Juan gives his friend the option of accepting or rejecting him as a confidant, without obliging him to speak overtly about the question at hand. And don Lope chooses to reject him because to reveal the circumstances of his trial and the possibility of his guilt —even to such a dear friend— would force don Lope to break the silence he feels obligated to maintain.

Don Lope now feels that he has been accused by his friend

---

[16] See Pitt-Rivers, p. 28.

of being without honor, and therefore, his vengeance must be immediate and open.

> Pues el que supo mi afrenta,
> sabrá la venganza mía.
> Y el mundo la ha de saber.
> Basta, honor: no hay que esperar;
>
> (Tercera Jornada, 149-152)

When don Lope feels that he has been accused by the King, he will feel even more acutely the need for immediate action. The King is the symbol of highest social authority, of Society itself. The fear that the King may have heard about the supposed affront to his honor fills don Lope with terror.

> ¿No fuera mejor castigo,
> ¡cielos!, desatar un rayo,
> que con mortal precipicio
> me abrasará, viendo antes
> el incendio que el aviso,
> que la palabra del rey,
> que grave y severo dijo
> que yo haré falta en mi casa?
> ¿Pero qué rayo más vivo,
> si fénix de las desdichas,
> fuí ceniza de mí mismo?
>
> (Tercera Jornada, 210-220)

Once he feels accused by the King, don Lope is overcome by a sense of defeat. Like Georg Bendemann in Kafka's "The Judgment",[17] who, accused and condemned to death by his own father without any apparent reason, runs to the river and throws himself into the water, don Lope feels condemned to die and obligated to execute his own sentence.

Don Lope's third soliloquy reveals the despair experienced by the man who feels himself to be unjustly accused. Honor is an

---

[17] Franz Kafka, "The Judgment", *The Penal Colony* (New York: Alfred A. Knopf, 1948), pp. 49-69.

incomprehensible fatalism which accuses, tortures, and condemns certain men, and concedes an apparently unwarranted and totally inexplicable grace to others.

> ¡Ay honor, mucho me debes!
> Júntate a cuentas conmigo.
> ¿Qué quejas tienes de mí?
> ¿En qué, dime, te he ofendido?
> Al heredado valor,
> ¿no he juntado al adquirido,
> haciendo la vida en mí
> desprecio del mayor peligro?
>
> (Tercera Jornada, 229-236)

> Casado, ¡ay de mí! casado,
> ¿en qué he faltado?, ¿en qué he sido
> culpado?
>
> (Tercera Jornada, 243-245)

> ¿En qué tribunal se ha visto
> condenar al inocente?
> ¿Sentencias hay sin delito?
> ¿Informaciones sin cargo?
> Y sin culpas ¿hay castigo?
> ¡Oh locas leyes del mundo!
> ¡Que un hombre, que por (sí) hizo
> cuanto pudo para honrado,
> no sepa si está ofendido!
>
> (Tercera Jornada, 254-262)

The accused man, "sentenced without crime," feels impotent before the fate that condemns him.[18] And so don Lope, like so many other men of honor produced by seventeenth-century Spanish literature, resigns himself to commit the act of vengeance which, according to the social code, will cleanse his honor.

---

[18] Compare: "...the important thing was that he suddenly realized the futility of resistence. There would be nothing heroic in it were he to resist... to snatch at the last appearance of life by struggling" *The Trial*, p. 288.

But don Lope has still another lesson to learn. Like Joseph K and like don Juan, don Lope must learn that there are few cases of "definite acquittal."[19] The accused has no hope of being cleared. The only possibilities really open to him are what Kafka calls "ostensible acquittal" and "postponement."[20] "Ostensible acquittal" is provisional; the man to whom this type of acquittal is conceded may be accused again at any time, even after his acquittal —in this case, even after avenging his honor. He is never free of his accusation; he will never have the right to consider himself avenged. Don Juan, who publicly slays the man who accuses him, is nevertheless accused again of the same crime by others. His acquittal is only provisional:

> "¡Este es aquel desmentido",
> dijo, no "aquel satisfecho!"
> ¿Quién en el mundo previno
> su desdicha? ¿No hizo harto
> aquel que la satisfizo?
> (Tercera Jornada, 362-366)

The other possibility, postponement, requires that the accused not let his trial ever go beyond its first stages; that is, he must never let his sense of guilt overwhelm him. But it is too late for don Lope, already consumed by his sense of guilt, even to consider this solution.

Don Lope learns from don Juan's experience that acquittal is always provisional. The only means of trying to avoid being newly accused is to take vengeance secretly. The affront was secret; the vengeance must also be secret, for a public act of

[19] Compare: "I have listened to countless cases in their most crucial stages, and followed them as far as they could be followed, and yet —I must admit it— I have never encountered one case of definite acquittal." *The Trial*, p. 192.
[20] "Ostensible acquittal and postponement. These are the only possibilities." *The Trial*, p. 194.

162

vengeance would reveal the victim's dishonor, thereby facilitating the possibility of another accusation.

Don Lope is persecuted by a terrifying sense of guilt, by a strange paranoia. He sees signs of his dishonor everywhere:

> Nada escucho, nada veo
> que ser mi pena no creo.
>> (Tercera Jornada, 443-444)

With deliberate steps, he plans don Luis's murder; with ambiguous words, he warns his victim of his intentions. But don Luis, impetuous and confident, pays no attention to don Lope's carefully worded invitation when he agrees to accompany the latter by boat to his home. Don Luis thinks only of enjoying Leonor, and of mocking the husband who brings a lover to his own wife.

But to murder don Luis is not enough. Doña Leonor, who has commited a tangible act of adultery by writing to don Luis and asking him to come to her while her husband is away, must also die, although her sentence would be the same even if she were innocent.[21] By a culminating act of violence, accompanied by the violence of the elements, don Lope sets fire to his own house.[22] Don Lope makes use of each of the

---

[21] In *El médico se su honra* Mencia performs no act of infidelity, yet is murdered by her honor-obsessed husband, who suspects her of having an affair with Don Enrique. Mencía's dream in which she sees Don Enrique cannot be considered an act of infidelity, since an act can only be considered a punishable sin if it is perfomed knowingly and deliberately. Calderón suggests in *El mágico prodigioso* that the individual is not responsible for the images projected by his imagination, buy only for the acts he performs. See Chapter 5.

[22] As F. M. Wilson points out, the Christian position is that the elements are man's servants, the instruments for his salvation. p. 34 P. N. Dunn shows how Calderón makes use of Christian symbolism, including the elements, in the context of honor. "The Four Elements" Don Lope uses the elements to achieve his social salvation, but, as Dunn shows, there is

elements —sea, wind, earth and fire— to achieve total annihilation of his wife and her lover, and of his own life, for he destroys all that is dear to him. His world has become violence, horror and despair. The elements —the totality of his world— have become tools of destruction.

How differently King Sebastian sees those same elements as he approaches don Lope's house:

> las aguas
> tan dulces y lisonjeras,
> que el cielo, Narciso azul,
> se vió contemplando en ellas,
>
> (Tercera Jornada, 846-849)

> Entre la tierra y el mar
> deleitosa vista es ésta;
>
> (Tercera Jornada, 860-861)

The contrast between the King's view of the elements and don Lope's is significant. Don Lope's world is one of violence and destruction.

The accused has been found definitively guilty, and has been condemned to death. Like Joseph K and other Kafkian characters such as the officer of *The Penal Colony* and Georg Bendamenn of "The Judgment", don Lope must now execute his death sentence with his own hand.[23] He will go to Africa with the King —symbol of authority and of the social values of the society he rules, symbol of Honor itself— where he and his King will die. Don Lope accuses himself, judges himself, and condemns himself.

no redemption. From a religious point of view, he achieves not his salvation but his perdition. "Honour and the Christian Background".
[23] "K now perceived clearly that he was supposed to seize the knife himself... and plunge it into his own breast." *The Trial*, p. 285.

The man of honor is accused and condemned precisely because he fails to comply with his masculine duties. No to succeed in protecting the honor of one's household reflects a lack of virility. In *The Castle,* K never achieves his ideal of a happy married life. For him, as for don Lope, the solution is conjugal happiness. The marriage between Frieda and K would have assured K of the right to remain in the village; for don Lope, conjugal fulfillment would have been a protection against the dishonor he so desperately fears. But neither he nor K succeeds satisfactorily in the role of husband. They both manifest flaws. The guilt feelings of the accused are due to his feelings of inadequacy. The death sentence is imposed on the accused because he is guilty.

Don Lope, like K, feels an acute sense of failure, although he argues that he believes himself to be a worthy husband. Like the man in the story "The Night Watchman" in *The Trial,* who leaves his family to wait anxiously at the door of the tribunal, who responds to a distant and incomprehensible call in the night and waits all his life to be able to enter the Court of Justice without ever being granted admittance, don Lope waits at the door of the Court of Honor.

But, from a Christian point of view, that is not the way to achieve salvation. Salvation is achieved by living a tranquil family life. It is those who live *dans le vrai*[24] so to speak, those who do not seek salvation, who live tranquilly at home with their wives and children that actually belong to the Castle. It is the man who is not a part of this tranquil everyday existence to whom entrance is denied.[25] And to the men of honor,

[24] "'Ils sont dans le vrai'... (Commanville explains) en faisant allusion à cet intéieur de famille honnête et bon."... Kafka often .quoted this sentence." Brod, p. 96.

[25] "I do not envy any particular married couple, I simply envy all married couples together; and even when I do envy one couple only, it is the happiness of married life in general, in all its infinite variety that I envy —the happiness to be found in any one marriage, even in the likeliest case. would probably plunge me into despair." *Diaries 1914-1923,* pp. 194-195.

who seek and frantically defend their honor, the only salvation they desire, the door is also closed.[26] Don Lope might have lived happily and even honorably with his wife had he known how to see after his marriage, if he had known how to establish a stable marriage and been concerned about the well-being of his wife *before* she became involved for a second time with her former admirer, if he had really known how to love.[27] For, in reality, don Lope never really gives don Luis any competition as a lover. It is by failing to comply with the requirements of everyday life that K and Joseph K lose their salvation. It is by neglecting his obligation as a husband that don Lope loses his honor. It is by not knowing how to be truly loving and compassionate.

Don Lope's death is one befitting a man of honor. In the service of his king, he joins a military expedition which constitutes one final pursuit of glory. But the seventeenth-century audience knew that Sebastian of Portugal represented fanaticism and failure. Weak and sickly, he was a religious zealot determined to win glory by waging war against the Moslem infidels. Having procured money from his uncle, Felipe II of Spain, he spent vast sums in preparation for an expedition that met with total failure. Four years later, in 1578, he undertook another expedition —the one on which don Lope supposedly accompanied him— and was wiped out in a far-from-glorious defeat at Alcazarquivir. As T. E. May has pointed out, don Lope was destroyed, like don Luis and doña Leonor, by water and fire, for the Spanish troops were

[26] "It is astounding how I have systematically destroyed myself in the course of the years, it was like a slowly widening breach in a dam, a purposeful action." *Diaries 1914-1923*, p. 195.

[27] It is entirely conceivable that life's splendor forever lies in wait about each one of us in all its fullness, but veiled from view, deep down, invisible, far off. It *is* there, though, not hostile, not reluctant, not deaf. If you summon it by the right word, by its right name, it will come. This is the essence of magic, which does not create but summons." *Diaries 1914-1923*. p. 195.

caught up between the Moslem fire and a river. Perhaps, suggests May, the final vengeance was God's against don Lope.[28]

King Sebastian was succeeded by his uncle Henry, after whose reign Felipe II took control of the Portuguese crown and the period of Spanish control of Portugal began. The significance of these events, which were such recent history that they undoubtedly took place in the lifetime of some of Calderón's spectators, is symbolic. King Sebastian was known to be headstrong, fanatical, and doomed. His reign was associated with the waning and decay of the Portuguese crown. Don Lope's esteem for and blind trust in his king are indicative of his adherence to an empty, decaying system that he himself recognizes as absurd.

Conclusion

The historical drama *La gran Cenobia*, the comedy *La dama duende*, and the honor tragedy *A secreto agravio, secreta venganza* are plays of different genres and periods, yet all illustrate Calderón's view of the human psyche and its power to distort and misrepresent. Don Lope, like Aureliano and Cosme, has a fixed notion of the world and interprets appearances in accordance with his particular view of reality. In all three plays, the character in question starts out with a premise and by misapplying logic comes to faulty conclusions. In each case, his preconceived notions and his reluctance to examine his premise lead to a deterministic view of the world in which the human being is seen as inferior to some stronger outside force other than God. Such a view necessarily inhibits the freedom of those who hold it and renders their wills ineffective.

[28] T. E. May, "The Folly and Wit of Secret Vengeance: Calderón's *A secreto agravio, secreta venganza*" *Forum for Modern Language Studies* II. 2. (April, 1966) pp. 114-122.

Aureliano, Cosme and don Lope are what we have defined as men of "bad faith", for all are determinists. But while Aureliano is best described as a *salud,* don Lope is more accurately described as a *lâche,* for he hides behind his rigoristic views in order to avoid confronting a given situation head-on. Brave in battle, he is a coward before the court of public opinion. Don Lope never recognizes his own freedom. Once the question of his personal honor has been raised, he feels *obligated* to seek vengeance. He may vacillate over the accuracy of the accusation he feels has been brought against him, but never over what needs to be done once he has decided that accusation has been made. For men like don Lope, there is no alternative, and herein lies the tragedy of their situation from both a Christian and an existential point of view. [29]

[29] This lack of lucidity characterizes the individual of bad faith. Sartre writes: "Entendons bien qu'il ne s'agit pas d'une décision réfléchie et volontaire, d'une détermination spontanée de notre être. On *se met* de mauvaise foi comme on s'endort et on est de mauvaise foi comme on rêve..." Jean-Paul Sartre, *L'être et le néant,* p. 109. The comparison with dreaming, is significant. Characters of bad faith live in a dream world of images and appearances. They are like Segismundo before his *desengaño.* They, like he, exist in a world of fabrications of which they are not entirely conscious but which guide their lives. All of Calderón's *engañados* —Aureliano, Cosme, don Lope, Basilio— are *soñadores* of this type.

Characters such as these become trapped in their own dream world. They become more and more involved in their own self-justifying net of lies. They become alienated. Sartre describes the phenomenon as follows: "Dans la négation interne, le pour-soi est écrasé sur ce qu'il nie. Les qualités niées son précisément ce qu'il y a de plus présent au pour-soi, c'est d'elles qu'il tire sa force négative et qu'il la renouvelles perpétuellement. En ce sens, il faut les voir comme un facteur constitutif de son être, car il doit être là-bas hors de lui sur elles, il doit être *elles* pour nier qu'il les soit. En un mot, le terme-origine de la négation interne, c'est l'en-soi, la chose qui *est là;* et en dehors d'elle il n'y a rien, sinon pure négation dont *cette* chose fournit le contenu même." *L'Etre et le néant,* p. 225. Characters such as don Lope are examples of individuals of bad faith, "smashed on what they deny," (i.e. their own dishonor) and who in the process suffer total alienation due to their intense feelings of guilt.

Don Lope is bound by the codes and obligations of his social class. For him, honor is not the *patrimonio del alma* as it is for the wealthy peasant Pedro Crespo, in *El alcalde de Zalamea*. For don Lope, honor is the patrimony of public opinion, and he is unable to consider any alternative to his own way of thinking. As H. Huizinga points out, most members of the ruling classes were oblivious to the sense of honor that prevailed in the lower estates.[30]

The sense of honor of rich peasants was a topic of many Spanish plays, among them *El Villano en su rincón, Peribáñez* and *El alcalde de Zalamea*. Even within the framework of *A secreto agravio, secreta venganza*, Calderón offers a striking contrast, not between the ethics of the nobility and the peasantry, but between those of the nobility and the servant class. Toward the beginning of the second act don Lope speaks of his obligations to fight in King Sebastian's African campaignes. Of course, it is his reputation he is concerned with. He must go to Africa because all the nobles are going (Segunda Jornada, 61-65). Manrique, in contrast, shows a pragmatic disinterest in such matters. His attitude represents, to some extent, the characteristic cowardice of the *gracioso* —and yet, there is more to it than that. Manrique founds his objetions on moral grounds:

> Podrá ser
> que vaya; mas será a ver
> por tener más que decir;
> no a matar, quebrando en vano
> la ley en que vivo y creo;
> pues allí explicar no veo
> que sea moro ni cristiano.
> No matar, dice. Y los dos
> eso me veréis guardar;
> que yo no he de interpretar
> los mandamientos de Dios.
>
> (Segunda Jornada, 70-80)

---

[30] *The Waning of the Middle Ages*, p. 60.

As Manrique's comment makes clear, the principles that guide the nobility are decidedly un-Christian, for they disregard the Commandment "Thou shalt not kill."

Manrique's contempt for the customs of the upper class is a recurrent topic in the play. In the second act he mocks courtly love, creating a grotesque verbal image of a noble dame crying syrup out of one eye and oil out of the other (Segunda Jornada, 423-424). In the midst of the trauma of the third act he recites a humorous and rather vulgar sonnet in which there is a play on the words *cinta* and *encinta*. Manrique's cynical attitude toward the values of the aristocracy accentuates the absurdity of don Lope's self-imposed situation and the senselessness of his violence.

For don Lope's situation *is* self-imposed. Just as Aureliano has a self-image from which he is unwilling to deviate, so does don Lope. Don Lope's, like Lucien's in Sartre's *L'Enfance d'un chef*, is a creation of society that he constantly revalidates for himself. When an honor character maintains, "Yo soy quien soy," he is saying he must act in a certain way because his social position demands it. He must defend his honor because that is what is expected of him. As Alexander A. Parker has pointed out, Calderón's view of the human predicament "is not a heroic but a sad one. It is the predicament of man individualized from all other men yet in intimate solidarity with them caught in circumstances that are the responsibility of all, whose ramifications the individual cannot see, prisoner as he is of the partial perspectives of a limited time and space, yet both the sufferer of acts that come in from outside the partial perspectives and the agent of acts that have their repercussions beyond them."[31] Don Lope is both victim and perpetuator of the code. He is guilty, but he shares his guilt with the society of which he is a part.

[31] Toward a Definition of Calderonian Tragedy, *Bulletin of Hispanic Studies*, (Liverpool, 1962). p. 236.

The honor system is inflexible. Just as the word *rigor* is frequently used in *La gran Cenobia* to refer to Aureliano's unbending view of the world and his position in it, it is used in *A secreto agravio, secreta venganza* to refer to the honor code. Doña Leonor, confirming her intentions to remain loyal to don Lope, says:

> declárese mi *rigor*
> porque mi vida y mi honor
> ya no es mío, es de mi esposo. (Segunda Jornada, 30-32)

Don Luis writes to her:

> Mi muerte injusta tu *rigor* me advierte
> (Segunda Jornada, 496)

Don Lope speaks of the obligations of honor:

> *Rigor,*
> disimulemos (Tercera Jornada, 445-446)

The honor code is "rigorous" in the sense it permits no deviations, no clemency. The man who is bound by the honor code cannot forgive, for the code requires vengeance; magnanimity is outside the system, for to forgive is to remain dishonored. And yet clemency is the key to Christian salvation.

Honor is a closed system. No questions need be asked, for suspicion alone is enough to justify vengeance. There is no sense in an open confrontation between doña Leonor and don Lope, for explanations would change nothing. There can be no solution because neither will expose the problem. Reason has no rôle to play here.[32] The second meeting between don

[32] Don Lope misapplies reason when he rationalizes his murder of doña Leonor and her lover, for he begins with a false premise and fails to give adequate consideration to alternative solutions. The skeptic Sánchez saw that reason could be manipulated through logic and rhetoric and warned against considering valid hypotheses which could be demonstrated only through words: "Cada cual tiene en su favor razones y argumentos en apariencia inexpugnables, y no hay agur sentencia posible sin riesgo de la verdad y del propio juez." *Que nada se sabe*, p. 185.

171

Lope and don Luis takes place in symbolic darkness signifying both sin and ignorance.[33]

And yet, honor is an absolute for characters such as don Lope only insofar as they accept it as such. Spanish drama does offer examples of characters who reject the honor code, and while most of these are either servants[34] or protagonists of comedies,[35] not all of them are. In *El médico de su honra*

Suárez describes the process by which the will may put reason to its service in the eleventh *Disputación:* "el mal de culpa formalmente y en cuanto tal... no sólo no requiere la causa final, sino que ni siquiera puede tenerla recta y ordenadamente, porque no puede pretenderlo directamente más que una voluntad depravada, ya que ni puede ser buscado como fin, puesto que bajo tal aspecto no tiene bondad, no como medio, porque no se pueden hacer males para que vengan bienes; pero la voluntad desordenada puede buscar ese mal, más aún, incluso la malicia misma, al menos como medio y *bajo alguna aparente y falsa razón de bien* (italics mine) como, por ejemplo, *para tomar venganza de alguien* (italics mine) or para inferir una injuria a aquél a quien se tiene odio, o cosas parecidas." Vol. II, p. 302.

[33] In *El médico de su honra,* don Gutierre puts out the light as he comes upon the sleeping Mencía:

Mato la luz, y llego,
sin luz y sin razón, dos veces ciego.
                    (Segunda jornada, 895-96)

In *La dama duende,* don Luis says:

pues todo se halla con luz,
y el honor con luz se pierde.
                    (Tercera jornada, 467-68).

[34] In *El médico de su honra,* Coquín classifies honor as an upperclass value:

el honor de esa ley
no se entiende en el criado.
                    (Segunda jornada, 257-258).

It is he who, in opposition to the honor code, begs the king to prevent Mencía's murder. (Tercera jornada, 711-716).

[35] In *El galán fantasma,* Astolfo opts against taking vengeance:

Será la mayor fineza
volver la espalda, pues nadie
es más valiente que aquel
que con celos es cobarde. (Vol. II, p. 639).

172

the noble don Arias adheres to a moral rather than a social concept of honor. He warns that heaven punishes noblemen who are over-zealous in questions of honor:

> En mi vida he conocido
> galán necio, escrupuloso
> y con extremo celoso,
> que en llegando a ser marido
> no le castiguen los cielos.
>
> (Segunda jornada, 793-797).

But don Lope does not share don Arias' insight. Although he questions the logic of the honor code, he never examines the validity of its authority to justify murder. Acting on inconclusive evidence, he carries out the exigencies of honor without ever stopping to consider an alternative. He surrenders his will to the dictates of the code without ever comprehending that his very acceptance of it represents a choice on his part. He negates his own freedom. He becomes resigned, impotent. He acts mechanically. He becomes the pawn of what Edwin Honig has called a situation of "dehumanized absurdity."[36]

The mechanical acceptance of authority was very much an issue during the sixteenth and early seventeenth centuries, both in the contexts of scientific investigation and theological discussion. It divided Catholics from Protestants and Catholics and Protestants among themselves. It divided the scholastics from the reformers, the scientists who accepted the teachings of Aristotle as infallible from those who rejected

---

[36] "Introduction" to Calderón: Four Plays, p. xviii. Honig also discusses the mechanized quality of honor in "Dehumanizing Honor," in Calderón and the Seizures of Honor, (Crambridge, Mass.: Harvard University Press, 1972), pp. 37-52.

them in favor of original experimentation. The skeptic Sánchez disallowed all scientific information taken on the authority of teachers and textbooks in favor of individual free investigation.[37] Suárez maintained that the individual is responsible for all his acts —sinful or otherwise— even if such acts are performed on the authority of another, for since men possess both judgment and free will, they are capable of discerning false authority or authority improperly administered and of refusing to abide by it.[38] Likewise, the individual who acts, like don Lope, on inconclusive or false evidence is nevertheless responsible for sins performed as a consequence, for he is capable of judging such evidence invalid and discarding it.[39] Probabilists, such as Suárez, held that moral decisions must be made through an examination of the conscience and that such decisions were justifiable whether or not they coincided with the modes of action prescribed by temporal authorities. Calderón artfully creates characters who are responsible for despicable crimes, yet remain oblivious to that responsibility, blinded as they are by the overpowering authority of social convention. Characters such as don Lope

---

[37] *Que nada se sabe*, p. 176.

[38] "Cuando el juicio es... basado únicamente en la autoridad del expositor, resulta fácil encontrar en él la raíz de la falsedad, pues en cuanto a su especificación —por así decirlo— procede de una imperfección del que dice o enseña... En cambio, en cuanto al ejercicio, la causa propia es *la voluntad del hombre mismo que juzga,* y esto tiene validez universal para todo juicio falso, (talics mine) (Suárez, *Disputaciones,* Vol. III, p. 196).

[39] Suárez grants that evidence may sometimes be misleading: "hay ocasiones en que la misma evidencia es sólo aparente; luego en tales casos puede versar sobre lo falso y, sin embargo, no ejercer sobre el entendimiento menor fuerza obligatoria que si fuera verdadero." (Vol. III, p. 194). Suárez does not exonerate the individual who is victim of false evidence, for he is not obligated to draw false conclusions simply because he has before him false evidence. Rather, he is obliged to judge such evidence as false. In other words, false evidence is simply no evidence at all: "... la evidencia puede decirse aparente en dos sentidos. Primero, porque en ningún orden natural es efectivamente una evidencia suficiente, aunque de intervenir algún influjo sobrenatural pueda apartarse de la verdad. (Vol. III, p. 196). Barring Su-

de Almeida confront us with the nebluous area between guilt and innocence that has so fascinated modern writers such as Dostoevsky.

What are don Lope's options? After all, he cannot simply pretend that honor does not exist. Honor is a social reality. *Entes de razón* such as honor are psychological realities.[40]

But man's freedom consists not in his denial of such realities but in his reaction to them.[41] To stand up to honor, to recognize it and reject it or to work around it and manipulate it are ways of confronting the issue. But don Lope does not challenge the code. He does not examine his conscience. He has no awareness of having made a choice. He has no notion of his own responsibility.

pernatural intervention, there is really no such thing as false evidence, but only information which the judgment erroneously interprets as evidence. Don Lope, by admitting three facts as evidence (doña Leonor's urging him to leave, don Juan's urging him to stay and don Luis's presence on his property) is guided by his will to vengeance, not by reason.

[40] Suárez specifically mentions honor as an *"ente de razón"*: "A su vez en la cualidad parece que hay una gran serie de entes de razón; porque, por ejemplo concebimos la fama y el honor como una disposición que conviene a la persona honrada o de buena fama, siendo así que en ésta no se trata más que de un ente de razón." (*Disputaciones*, Vo. VII, p. 422). These *"entes de razón"* have the power to attract the will, as does any other good because"... (la voluntad) no tiende al ente en cuanto ente, sino en cuanto bueno." Although the good may be fictitious, the attraction is real: "Y aunque a veces la voluntad humana tienda a lo que no es realmente bueno como si fuese bueno, sin embargo ella no finge ese bien, sino que lo supone captado y representado por el entendimiento; por eso, aunque se lo cuente entre los entes de razón, no ha sido elaborado por la voluntad, sino por el entendimiento. Y por más que la voluntad, igual que lo hace el sentido, denomine a su objecto amado y deseado, con una denominación real extrínseca, por la referencia de su acto a tal objecto, sin embargo la voluntad misma no reflexiona ulteriormente ni investiga en qué consiste en tal objecto el ser amado o deseado, ni finge en él una relación de razón, sino que esto corresponde al entendimiento." (Vol. VII, p. 409).

[41] "Freedom and will consist not in the abnegation of determinism but in our *relationship* to it. 'Freedom,' wrote Spinoza, 'is the recognition of ne-

Once don Lope has taken vengeance, he has little left to live for. His wife is dead; his honor, tarnished by accusation. The future can bring only repeated accusations and repeated acts of vengeance. There can be no happiness, no personal fulfillment for don Lope. He is face to face with the void. Like Aureliano, he remains victim of an insatiable passion to the end. There is nothing left for him to desire but his own death —a glorious, heroic death in the service of the king. His decision to go to Africa with don Sebastian— where he will meet an ironically unheroic death— is, in effect, a suicide.

Many modern writers have explored the themes of absurdity, alienation and guilt through the metaphor of the trial. In Dostoevsky's *The Brothers Karamasov,* all three brothers are indirectly guilty of the death of their father. Dimitri is condemned by a jury ignorant of the facts of which he too is ignorant, while Ivan is left to battle with the demon of his reason and plot his brother's escape with Allyosha. In *The Trial,* Franz Kafka's K is challenged by the incomprehensible bureaucracy of a court which accuses and condemns him of an unknown crime. Overcome by a sense of guilt, he succumbs to the accusation and dies. In Camus' *L'Etranger,* Mersault is condemned by a court that neither understands nor seeks to understand the circumstances of his crime but judges him guilty because he has failed to conform to the norms of society. But for Mersault, this noncomformity is given meaning by his death, which becomes an act of liberation. Don Lope never experiences the joy of liberation; he remains a man of honor until the end.

cessity.' Man is distinguished by his capacity to know that he is determined, and to choose his relationship to what determines him. He can and must, unless he abdicates his consciousness, choose how he will relate to necessity, such as death, old age, limitations of intelligence, and the conditioning inescapable in his own background. Will he accept his necessity, deny it, fight it, affirm it, consent to it? All these words have an element of volition in them. And it should, by now, be clear that man does not simply 'stand outside' in his subjectiviy, like a critic at the theater, and look at necessity and decide what he thinks of it." Rollo May, *Love and Will*, p. 269.

In *Antigone,* the author Jean Anouilh does not use the metaphor of the trial but a classic Greek tragedy for the framework of his drama. Crion is, like don Lope, bound by his self image and by laws which he himself has created. These, which he is forced to recognize as absurd, cause him to put to death his niece, an act which results in the subsequent deaht of his son and his wife. Because he refuses to rebel against his own system, Crion is left, at the end of the play, alone and empty. He has destroyed everything. He has nothing left to look forward to but eternal staff meetings and an empty death. Antigone, in contrast, defies the rules and her death becomes an exalted act of self-liberation.[42]

Don Lope is strikingly like Crion, and yet, as an artistic creation he is much more subtle and sophisticated, for while Crion is alone responsible for the laws he abides by, don Lope is the product of a system against which he dare not rebel. He is less lucid than Crion. The line of demarcation between guilt and innocence is more subtle. He is guilty, yet he shares his guilt with society. As king, Crion has only to change the law, while for don Lope the solution is less clearly defined. It is don Lope's, not Crion's, predicament that ressembles more closely that of twentieth-century man in a complex, mechanized, bureaucratic society.

[42] For the existentialists, the concept of absurdity stems from the sense of a world without finality, for in such a world all is gratuitous. Social convention and social values which rest on the assumption that certain procedures are right and others wrong are absurd because, since nothing was "meant to be," no form of human behavior can be considered reprehensible simply on the grounds that it does not comply with some universal design. Sartre pokes fun at the presumptions of the bourgeoisie in a number of works. For example, in *Les Mots* he mocks the game-like quality of gratuitously assigning certain values to certain actions. In Simone de Beauvoir's *Mémoires d'une jeune fille rangée,* the author describes the law of "il faut... il ne faut pas." For example, one does ("il faut") peel a peach before eating it, but one does not ("il ne faut pas") peel a plum.

In Calderón's honor plays the sense of absurdity does not stem from a belief in the lack of finality but rather in the gratuitous, illogical and un-Cristian quality of a social custom which deprives the individual of choice and conscience, coercing him into robot-like obedience.

CHAPTER IV

FREEDOM, POWER, AND SELF-ASSERTION: *LA VIDA ES SUEÑO*

Segismundo: Man in Potential

La vida es sueño constitutes one of Calderón's strongest attacks against astrology. His position is in complete accordance with the prevailing Church doctrine. In 1585 Pope Sixtus V officially condemned astrology in a papal bull and in 1631 Urban VIII seconded his stand with another bull.[1] Important religious thinkers of the period, including Francisco Suárez, criticized the belief in astrology.[2] Yet, the practice of astrology continued well into the nineteenth century. In the eighteenth, Feijóo attacked astrology along with other superstitions,[3] and toward the end of the same century Torres Villarroel still hesitated to dispute its validity as a science.[4]

---

[1] A principal source for the attacks against astrology was Saint Augustine, who writes in *The City of God:* "... those who are of the opinion that, apart from the will of God, the stars determine what we shall do, or what good things we shall possess, or what evils we shall suffer, must be refused a hearing by all..." Vol. 1 (Chicago: Encyclopedia Britannica, 1952), p. 208.

[2] See *Disputaciones,* III, pp. 433-434.

[3] See, for example, "Astrología judiciaria y almanaques," in *Discursos y cartas,* ed. J. M. Alda Tesan (Zaragoza: Ebro, 1958) pp. 45-46.

[4] Torres maintains his own ineffacy as an astrologer is due only to his insuffcent training. See *Vida,* ed. Federico de Onís (Madrid: Espasa-Calpe, 1954) pp. 76-79.

La vida es sueño is constructed around two separate but interrelated plots. The main plot concerns the conversion of Prince Segismundo of Poland, imprisoned shortly after birth by his father, King Basilio, as a consequence of what the latter assumes to be dire astrological omens regarding his son's future. The subplot revolves around Rosaura, who has been dishonored by Astolfo, a pretender to the throne, and has come to Poland to seek redress. The plots are interwoven as Segismundo and Rosaura meet and he is intensely attracted toward her, first in the craggy mountains where he is imprisoned, then at King Basilio's Court, and finally on the battlefield, during a political insurrection.

Segismundo is, as we see him in the first act, a man only in potential. Encarcerated in a womb-like tower in a state of prenatal helplessness, Segismundo displays all the qualities, good and bad, which will characterize him when he is at last "born" into the world.

It is not the brutish, willful aspect of Segismundo's character which is immediately obvious, but rather, his immense suffering, his capacity to reason, and his yearning for freedom. He is intensely aware of his unnatural state. Although he is not yet fully a man, neither is he a beast, for he questions and analyzes his situation:

> ¡Ay mísero de mí! ¡Ay infelice!
>   Apurar, cielos, pretendo,
> ya que me tratáis así,
> qué delito cometí
> contra vosotros naciendo.
>
> (Primera jornada, 102-106)

In the confines of his tower Segismundo displays not the arrogance and certainty which characterize his behavior at Court, but doubt. Did he bring such anguish upon himself or is suffering inevitable? He seeks an explanation first in his own failings, then turns to the facile solution of original sin

180

(Primera jornada, 109-112). But Segismundo immediately notes the flaw in his own logic: all others were born out of sin and yet only he is enchained.[5] Why do they enjoy freedom while he does not? He recognizes himself as intrinsically superior to those beings which seem to enjoy control over their own destinies, for he has a soul, superior inclination, free will and the gift of life:

> y teniendo yo más alma
> ¿tengo menos libertad?
>> (Primera jornada, 131-132)

> ¿y yo con mejor instinto
> tengo menos libertad?
>> (Primera jornada, 141-142)

> ¿y yo con más albedrío
> tengo menos libertad?
>> (Primera jornada, 151-152)

> y teniendo yo más vida
> ¿tengo menos libertad?
>> (Primera jornada, 161-162)

His own mental powers are sufficient to permit him to see the unreasonableness —and hence, unnaturalness— of his state.

Faced with the intolerability, injustice and illogic of his encarceration, Segismundo gives vent to his anger (Primera jornada, 163-172). Here, as elsewhere in Calderón's plays, feelings of impotence give way to an impulse toward self-destruction. Segismundo speaks of violently tearing his heart forth from his breast. But there is an important difference between the Polish prince and characters such as Aureliano

---

[5] Suárez denies that man is doomed to err by original sin: "...el pecado original no introdujo en el hombre ninguna entidad positiva que lo lleve al error o entenebrezca sus sentidos o su entendimiento." *Disputaciones*, II, p. 192. Also, "...el mal que nace de la causa libre, que es propiamente el mal moral o de culpa, no supone necesariamente en la causa otro mal semejante; de lo contrario, no podríamos detenernos en un primer mal de culpa proveniente de tal causa, lo cual es imposible." p. 311.

(La gran Cenobia), don Lope *(A secreto agravio, secreta venganza),* and Focas *(En la vida todo es verdad y todo mentira):* while the latter do not lucidly analyze their situations, Segismundo bursts into rage as an expression of his frustration before an apparently reason-defying problem. Furthermore, while they are at least partially responsible for the predicaments in which they find themselves, Segismundo is entirely a victim of Basilio. Rosaura, who accidentally discovers his hiding place and overhears his lament, feels not only fear but also pity.

Segismundo's soliloquy is characterized not only by intense emotion and skillful reasoning, but also by refined language and magnificent imagery. The first eight lines of the first *décima* of the series in which he compares himself with the beasts are exemplary:

> Nace el ave, y con las galas
> que le dan belleza suma,
> apenas es flor de pluma
> o ramillete con alas,
> cuando las etéreas salas
> corta con velocidad,
> negándose a la piedad
> del nido que deja en calma:
>
> (Primera jornada, 123-130)

The magnificent finery and the sumptuous colors of the bird are suggested by the word *galas.* Its lightness, delicateness and varying hues are evoked through the metaphor of the flower. The immensity of the space spanned by the bird is suggested by *salas,* "halls," —but not ordinary halls; the noun is qualified by the adjective "ethereal," which suggests lightness or airiness. The vigor and strength of the bird are connoted by the image of it "cutting" across the halls of air, distaining the calm of the nest. The complete image is one of a thing of great delicacy and beauty, yet master of its own destiny.

182

But it is not only in imagery, but also in form and structure that Segismundo's monologue reflects extraordinary intellect. There is a calculated progression from the description of the most significant to the least, from the magnificent bird to the lowly stream. The first three descriptions refer to the skies (bird), the earth (animal) and the seas (fish) —that is, to the totality of man's environment— while the last functions as a unifying element: the stream flows through the earth into the sea, evaporates into the skies and falls again to earth. Segismundo considers himself within the entirety of the universe and concludes that something is drastically amiss; he not only feels it, but reasons it to be so.[6]

The exquisite language and masterful structure of Segismundo's monologue emphasize that within the beast-like exterior there beats the heart of a rational, educable man.

But the as yet unformed Segismundo is ambivalent.[7] He is both rational and irrational, sublime and animalistic. Upon seeing Rosaura and her servant Clarín, he turns against them in fury:

> Pues muerte aquí te daré
> por que no sepas que sé (A'sela.)
> que sabes flaquezas mías.
> Sólo porque me has oído,
> entre mis membrudos brazos
> te tengo de hacer pedazos.

> (Primera jornada, 180-185)

Segismundo's immediate concern is for his self-image: *"por que no sepas que sé / que sabes flaquezas mías."* Image,

---

[6] See also A. E. Sloman's introduction to *La vida es sueño* (Manchester: Manchester University Press, 1961).

[7] Both Marcelino Menéndez Pelayo and Milton A. Buchanan have seen this duality in Segismundo's nature as a flaw in the play. See *Calderón y su teatro*, p. 275 and The Presidential Address: Calderón *Life is a Dream"*, PMLA, XLVII (1932), p. 1315.

we have said elsewhere, is a projection of the will. For an individual acutely aware of his own lack of freedom and consequent inability to act, image is immensely important, for it is the only means by which he can manifest his will. Image is Segismundo's only source of self-respect.[8] Domination of the will —and also the ability to recognize and reject one's own images— requires the exercise of power or control over the self. But power cannot be exercised by an enslaved individual. Segismundo does not demonstrate power but brute force. Violence and force are not manifestations of power, but of impotence.[9] They are the lashing out of the individual who feels himself to be vulnerable. Segismundo has recourse to his "membrudos brazos" —to beast-like violence— because he cannot protect his image any other way and because he has not the confidence and sense of control of his own destiny that come with freedom and that liberate the individual from the cult of the image.

Yet once again the ambivalence of Segismundo's nature becomes apparent. His impulsive violence is halted when he is confronted by Rosaura's beauty (Primera jornada, 219-222). Beauty, as we pointed out in the analysis of *La gran Cenobia,* is an elevating force. Beauty provides man with a goal, something for which to strive, a reality above and beyond his own creative forces. While Aureliano supresses his momentary attraction toward Cenobia, Segismundo's

[8] In his discussion of violence in contemporary society Rollo May writes: "Deeds of violence in our society are performed largely by those trying to establish their self-esteem, to defend their self-image, and to demonstrate that they, too, are significant. Regardless of how derailed or wrongly used these motivations may be or how destructive their expression, they are still the manifestations of positive interpersonal needs." *Power and Innocence: A Search for the Sources of Violence* (New York: W. W. Norton & Co., 197) p. 23. May's observations might easily be applied to Segismundo, or even to honor characters such as Don Lope de Almeida, who resort to violence precisely when their self-image is thrown into question.
[9] "For violence has its breeding ground in impotence and apathy... violence is the expression of impotence." May, *Power and Innocence,* p. 23.

erotic awakening is far more meaningful. Rather than rejecting his emotions, he yields to them. He is overcome with desire:

> Con cada vez que te veo
> nueva admiración me das
> y cuando te miro más
> aun más mirarte deseo.
> Ojos hidrópicos creo
> que mis ojos deben ser:
> pues cuando es muerte el beber,
> beben más, y desta suerte,
> viendo que el ver me da muerte,
> estoy muriendo por ver.
>
> (Primera jornada, 223-232)

Segismundo describes himself as insatiable, "hydropic." This
is a term Calderón frequently uses to refer to characters
dragged mindlessly on by their own uncontrolled wills, such
as Aureliano *(La gran Cenobia)*, Focas *(En la vida todo es
verdad y todo mentira)*, Baltasar *(La cena de Baltasar)*.[10]
Segismundo shares with these characters their willfulness, but
he differs from them with regard to the role played by eros in
his development.

Segismundo desires Rosaura. There can be no doubt that his
attraction is at least partially sexual.[11] From Greek
mythology to Freudian psychology the themes of death and
copulation are interwoven. The constant repetition of the

[10] See Note 40, Chapter 1.
[11] Sloman denies the existence of this sexual attraction owing to the fact
that Rosaura is dressed as a man. "Introduction," p. xvi. Other critics,
such as Francisco Ayala and Gisele and Carlos Feal do maintain that
Segismundo intuits Rosaura's real sex, although the Feals, developing
Wardropper's idea that the first scenes of the play represent a symbolic
parturition, assert that Segismundo sees in Rosaura a mother image. See
Francisco Ayala, *Realidad y ensueño* (Madrid: Gredos, 1968), p. 28; Gisele and Carlos Feal, *"La vida es sueño:* De la psicología al mito," *Reflexión* 2, I, i, (1972); and Bruce W. Wardropper, "Apenas llega cuando llega a penas," *Modern Philology,* 57 (1960), p. 244.

word "morir" and its derivatives make it clear that Segismundo throbs with desire. Yet, while sex and eros are different —the former being a biological function and the latter a psychological attraction— the two, of course, are not mutually exclusive. Eros is precisely the source of human tenderness, the pull toward union with another individual. It is an uplifting force. Segismundo is not overcome with lust, but with love. He does not wish to harm Rosaura, but to stand back and look at her, to drink in her beauty. He does not wish to overpower her, but to surrender:

> Pero véate yo y muera;
> que no sé, rendido ya,
> si el verte muerte me da,
> el no verte qué me diera.
> Fuera más que muerte fiera,
> ira, rabia y dolor fuerte;
> fuera muerte, desta suerte
> su rigor he ponderado,
> pues dar vida a un desdichado
> es dar a un dichoso muerte.
>
> (Primera jornada, 233-242)

He describes himself as incapacitated, *"rendido"*. While sex alone is characterized by a desire for self-gratification, love is characterized by the giving of oneself, by giving in and giving up. While Aureliano's death wish was the culmination of his road toward self-destruction, Segismundo's —as expressed here— is an impulse toward union and surrender; not toward destruction but toward procreation. It does not heighten his animal instincts, but pacifies them, for while to be with Rosaura signifies "death", to be without her signifies "ire, anger and intense pain". Death, as a metaphor for erotic love, is "rigorous" in that it permits no compromise; eros is an unbending ideal, but one worth striving for. The "death" Segismundo seeks is "life-giving"; it is love in the highest sense, the source of creativity and procreativity, union and sublimation.

186

As E. M. Wilson explains in his analysis of the term "sueño", it is Segismundo's confrontation with death at the end of *La vida es sueño* that makes him aware of the vanity of the world and of the desirability of striving for something beyond the temporal.[12] This first confrontation with eros is in a sense a preliminary confrontation with death. It results in Segismundo's first step toward maturity, his first sign of willingness to abandon his self-image and stand *"rendido"* before his loved one. The episode with Rosaura illustrates Segismundo's ability to exercise restraint.

Here, as before, the action in mirrored by the language. The subtlety of the concepts *(dar vida a un desdichado / es dar a un dichoso muerte)*, the plays on words *(desdichado, dichoso; muerte, vida);* the assonance (muerte, fuerte, suerte) and the alliteration (fiera, fuerte, fuera) reflect refinement, control.

Segismundo's meeting with Rosaura is a first step, but it is incomplete, for love requires more than surrender. It requires self-confidence, power over the self. As Rollo May explains, "A person must have something to give in order not to be completely taken over or absorbed as a nonentity."[13] Love cannot exist in a healthy form if one partner simply relinquishes his will to the other, but only if both partners maintain their will intact. Then, and only then, can each will what the other wills in order to insure a harmonious relationship. Eros requires not abandonment of the will, but control of it. Eros requires that the will be directed. But one can only direct one's will if one is free. It is in this sense, as May points out, that love "introduces the elements of personal responsibility and freedom"[14] into the life of the individual.

---

[12] See "On *La vida es sueño*", in *Critical Essays on the Theatre of Calderón*," ed. by Bruce W. Wardropper (New York: New York University Press, 1965).
[13] *Love and Will*, p. 114.
[14] *Love and Will*, p. 94.

Segismundo cannot love completely because he possesses neither the freedom nor the control of the will that love requires. He can stand back in awe but he cannot offer himself. His love, therefore, is imperfect.[15]

Segismundo's guardian, Clotaldo, has orders to put to death anyone who discovers Segismundo's hiding place. But when Clotaldo threatens Rosaura, Segismundo becomes violent once again. If love has been a liberating force for Segismundo —albeit an imperfect one— Rosaura's capture threatens the only sense of freedom he has ever known. Rosaura triggers in him a sense of rebellion; his reaction constitutes an act of self-assertion which is positive in spite of its destructiveness.

To accept enslavement is to resign oneself to apathy, impotence, death. To rebel against it is a positive gesture, an affirmation of life. Segismundo's violence is a step toward self-assertion, a part of his struggle toward birth and self-realization.

The first act of *La vida es sueño* reveals a man who is, more than anything, a mass of possibilities, capable of developing in one direction or another, capable of both good and evil. He tells Rosaura:

> soy un hombre de las fieras
> y una fiera de los hombres;
>
> (Primera jornada, 211-212)

Later on, at Court, he tells Basilio:

> sé que soy
> un compuesto del hombre y fiera.
>
> (Segunda jornada, 560-561)

[15] Edwin Honig offers another explanation why the potential love between Rosaura and Segismundo is not fully realized: he sees a kind of incest barrier established between them due to the "similarity and common urgency of their grievances." "The Magnanious Prince and the Price of Consciousness: *Life is a Dream,*" in *Calderón and the Seizures of Honor,* p. 160.

This is not the monolithic vision of man depicted by the seventeenth-century French playwrights such as Racine, but an infinitely more complex projection comparable with that of Dostoevsky. Segismundo is archetypal. He is every man. His possibilities for development are infinite.[16] His future depends on the choices he makes. But before he can choose one mode of action or another, Segismundo must be "born"; he must be released from the womb-tower and granted his freedom.

The ambivalence of Segismundo's character is reflected by the setting itself. The environment is rough and unfriendly. Rosaura describes the "aspereza enmarañada" of the countryside; the crude, tangled landscape reflects the tortured confusion that characterize both her and Segismundo. The prince's tower is scarcely distinguishable from the craggy surroundings (Primera jornada, 56-64). The tower is so obscured that the sun —symbol of the light of reason— penetrates with difficulty.[17] Here lives Segismundo, surrounded by animals. He himself resembles an animal, for he is dressed in skins. His attire is symbolic of the beast-like aspect of his character, of his brutish willfulness and impulsiveness.

Segismundo first appears in chains. He is enslaved both literally and symbolically. He is Basilio's prisoner and he is also prisoner of the passions he has not yet learned to control.

[16] Milton A. Buchanan has expressed the opposite point of view. According to him, Segismundo's conversion illustrates the influence of inheritance or *la fuerza de la sangre;* that is, "a prince, even when living in unfavorable surroundings, reveals his royal blood." "Presidential Address," p. 1314.

[17] Sloman discusses the symbolism of light and darkness in *La vida es sueño* in his introduction to the critical edution, p. xxxii. Honig discusses the same subject in "The Magnanimous Prince," p. 160. Both emphasize Rosaura's role as a symbol of light.

But the skins and chains reflect only one aspect of Segismundo's potential. There is a light in the tower. The rude, forbidding surroundings are illuminated. And from the outside the sun is steadfast in its attempts to penetrate. As the scene opens on Segidmundo's carefully structured, linguistically ornate monologue, we have the impression of a priceless jewel enclosed in a crude, earthen box. The coarse rustic setting hides within it beauty and light.

Rosaura and Segismundo

Rosaura, like Segismundo, is, on the one hand, sensitive and compassionate, on the other, headstrong and violent. Like him, she has been wronged by another and seeks to rectify an unjust situation. Like him, she craves self-respect. But while Segismundo is entirely the victim of the will of his father, Rosaura is at least partially the victim of her own passion. Segismundo is brought to the mountains by Basilio; Rosaura stumbles into the mountains unwittingly, just as she unwittingly fell into a state of dishonor. She is carried into the unfriendly mountains by her horse, the horse being a traditional symbol of passion. The play opens with her fall from her mount, symbolic of her moral fall. In the first scene of the play, Rosaura is carried into an area of primitive emotion —reflected by the primitive landscape— by the unrestrained feelings that were responsible for her dishonor and by the passion for redress that moves her throughout the rest of the play.

The primitive nature of Rosaura's sentiments is disguised, just as she herself is disguised. It is obscured by exaggeratedly refined and ornate language. Yet, each of the images she uses to describe her horse connotes passion and violence:

190

Hipogrifo violento
que corriste parejas con el viento,
¿dónde, rayo sin llama,
pájaro sin matiz, pez sin escama
y bruto sin instinto
natural, al confuso laberinto
destas desnudas peñas
te desbocas, arrastras y despeñas?

(Primera jornada, 1-8)

The hipogriff itself symbolizes irrationality, for it is a conglomeration of unrelated parts. It connotes wrecklessness, for it soars at great speed on the wings of an eagle, and violence, for it has the beak of an eagle and the claws of a lion. Rosaura's passion is a magnificent yet monstrous and highly destructive force. Rosaura compares the speed of her horse with that of the wind, yet another metaphor stressing irrationality, for what is borne by the wind has no control over its own direction. *"Rayo sin llama," "pájaro sin matiz"* and *"pez sin escama"* likewise connote speed and irrationality; lightning strikes unpredictibly and must strike at tremendous velocity in order to appear "without flame"; a bird rides the winds and a fish the ocean currents, both of which move with great speed and violence. Furthermore, in order for a bird to appear to be without shades of color and a fish to appear to be without scales, they must be moving swiftly. Lastly, *"bruto sin instinto"* connotes not only irrationality, but also primitive sensuality.

The horse leads Rosaura into a *"confuso laberinto,"* a mass of contradictions and beguiling appearances, reflections of her own jumbled, tortured state of mind. She, like Segismundo, is confronted with reason-defying confusion. Yet, while he seeks to analyze and understand, she is carried further and further into the labyrinth by her unrestrained passion for vengeance.

191

Basilio's Experiment

Toward the end of the first act of *La vida es sueño* the scene shifts abruptly to King Basilio's court. The court is permeated by a preoccupation with the stars, just as in the honor plays the aristocracy is permeated with a preoccupation with honor. References to astrology and astrologers are on everybody's lips. Astolfo's and Estrella's discussion of the succession of the throne is riddled with allusions to astrological signs (Primera jornada, 475-564). When Segismundo comes to court and misbehaves, Astolfo points out the inevitability of the circumstances, given the predictions of the stars. Yet, he also points out a weakness of the system when he says:

> ¡Qué buen astrólogo fuera,
> si siempre casos crueles
> anunciara; pues no hay duda
> que ellos fueran verdad siempre!
> (Primera jornada, 738-745)

In a complex society with an unstable government, constant vying for power, violence, bitterness and individual misfortunes are inevitable. Therefore, it is easy to second-guess the stars simply by always predicting calamity. Furthermore, adds Astolfo, the stars can be wrong, for although good fortune, honor and glory were predicted for him, the prediction has not been fulfilled.

Astolfo's allusions to astrology recur not only in his political observations, but also in his amorous intrigues. Wooing Rosaura, he refers to the traditional Renaissance love theme of celestial music (Segunda jornada, 928-930).

Rosaura, too, alludes constantly to astrology. She sees her unfortunate situation as determined by an unfavorable horoscope (Segunda jornada, 834-837).

Even the names of the two principal female characters,

192

Estrella and Astrea —the name Rosaura takes when she comes to Court— reflect a preoccupation with the stars.

Basilio is the foremost representative of this mentality. When he appears for the first time, he is immediately identified as a king who governs by the stars, a sage comparable to Thales and Euclid. To his subjects, his most salient achievement is mastering the intricacies of astrology (Primera jornada, 579-584). Basilio is proud of his learning. He boasts that "en el ámbito del orbe/ me aclaman el gran Basilio" (Primera jornada, 604-612). Basilio's self-assuredness stems from his having reduced the world to a science that he presumes to comprehend.

Astrology, in *La vida es sueño,* is an established, generally accepted system that interprets all human acts and conditions as consequences of cosmological relationships. When, in the fourth scene of the first act of *La vida es sueño,* Calderón introduces Basilio's court, he abruptly switches from *romance* to *quintillas,* that is, from the familiar narrative form to refined verse. The Court, in violent contrast with the rugged mountain setting of the preceding scenes, is the epitome of civilization, of acquired mannerisms and polished systems.

One of the most important pieces of information Basilio believes the stars to have imparted to him is the nature and future of his son Segismundo. He bases this supposed knowledge on three signs: 1.) while she was still carrying him her womb, Segismundo's mother dreamed that a monster burst forth from her body, killing her; 2.) Segismundo's horoscope was particularly unfavorable, for the boy was born on the day of a frightening eclipse; 3.) Segismundo's mother died in childbirth. These three ocurrences —a nightmare, an eclipse and death in childbirth— all fairly common phenomena, were sufficient to convince Basilio his son would become a dangerous tyrant if allowed to grow up and take his

193

place upon the throne. He therefore determined to banish Segismundo from the Court and have him raised by Clotaldo in a tower far from civilization.

Many years after this initial decision is made, Basilio vacillates and decides to test the predictions. But Basilio does not experiment in good faith, for he has already undermined his experiment by operating from the beginning from a false premise. Until now he has assumed not only that the stars determine, but also that man can know what the stars determine. In so doing, he has bound himself to a whole system of logic that made it necessary for him —according to his own way of thinking— to encarcerate his son. When, at last, he does release Segismundo, substantial damage has already been done. Segismundo is a young man whose upbringing in uncivilized surroundings has prevented him from developing an adequate sense of moderation and self-control. Basilio has unconsciously subverted his own experiment.

Segismundo at Court: Power as Self-assertion

Once at Court, Segismundo displays an overwhelming thirst for power. Even in the tower, this tendency is evident. In a conversation with him, Clotaldo compares Segismundo with the eagle, sovereign among birds. The prince immediately picks up the metaphor to convey his personal ambition:

> en tocando esta materia
> de la majestad, discurre
> con ambición y soberbia;
>
> (Segunda jornada, 64-66)

Segismundo seeks power. But power must be comprehended in a more ample sense than mere competitive striving. Power is not solely a negative, destructive force. For example, power as Nietzsche understood it was the means of self-realization

194

or self-actualization. Segismundo's ambition is precisely a manifestation of his feeling of powerlessness, of his refusal to accept his state of enslavement:

> "...si estoy
> sujeto, lo estoy por fuerza;
> porque voluntariamente
> a otro hombre no me rindiera."
>
> (Segunda jornada, 75-78)

It is the rejection of the concept that another other than he should be sovereign over his own destiny.

Released from his prison, Segismundo is thrown into a state of confusion. He is confronted with things never before seen or heard. He is granted what seems to be unlimited power. At first he doubts:

> ¡Válgame el cielo, qué veo!
> ¡Válgame el cielo, qué miro!
> Con poco espanto lo admiro,
> con mucha duda lo creo.
>
> (Segunda jornada, 238-241)

From his first moment at Court, Segismundo is in a position to choose. Whether he adopts a skeptical attitude with regard to the information imparted by the senses or whether he admits it as truth is his own decision, and represents his first act of power over his own destiny. Segismundo chooses to reject doubt:

> Decir que sueño es engaño:
> bien sé que despierto estoy.
> ¿Yo Segismundo no soy?
> Dadme, cielos, desengaño.
>
> (Segunda jornada, 251-254)

In the analysis of *La gran Cenobia* we showed that words such as *imagen, fantasía, apariencia, representación* frequently occur together and that all refer to projections of the

195

will. Sense perception is repeatedly linked with these words. *Sueño*, too, forms part of this list of synonyms.[18] Aureliano sees himself crowned king "entre sueños". Segismundo now sees himself king in a situation he is warned may well be a dream. But what Segismundo sees coincides with what he wills. He therefore opts to accept the image conveyed by the senses as true. He seeks intellectual certainty and allows his will to impose it by accepting the images before him. That is, Segismundo hands himself over to his will.

Until now, Segismundo's will had been ineffective. At Court, assertion of the will becomes vitally important. Like the honor characters, Segismundo asserts his identity at the very moment he is plagued by doubt. *"¿Yo Segismundo no soy?"* he asks. By reconfirming his identity he both casts away doubt and asserts his will as an active force that others must take into consideration. Segismundo, like Basilio, wills a system —a system in which he commands and all others are his vassals. His means of assertion of the will is the flaunting of power. Segismundo's abuse of power is his way of making his presence felt. It is his way of demanding the esteem of which he has for so long been deprived. It is not surprising that his violence is coupled with repeated affirmations of identity:

> ¿qué tengo más que saber
> después de saber quién soy,
> para mostrar desde hoy
> mi soberbia y mi poder?
>
> (Segunda jornada, 311-314)

The flaunting of power *(poder)* and the display of arrogance *(soberbia)* are clearly the means by which Segismundo attempts to make his identity *(quién soy)* felt.

---

[18] The relationship of dreams, fantasy, and imagination to sense perception was understood in the sixteenth and seventeenth centuries and discussed entensively by a number of philosophers. See, for example, Vives, *Tratado*, pp. 1223-1224 and Suárez, *Disputación* 9, Sección 1.

Naturally, it is within Segismundo's power to control himself, to dominate the will and not be swept away by it, but in order to do that he must first become aware of his freedom —of his own power over himself. The tragedy of characters such as don Lope, Aureliano and Basilio is that they *do* have a choice, they *can* rebel against or alter what seems to be their fate, but they remain unaware of their own power. Segismundo's violence is his first step toward awareness of the will.

Segismundo's wrath turns first against Clotaldo, whom he identifies as his former jailer. Vengeance is a means of rejecting the past, of denying one's own responsibility for past failures. Clotaldo's presence reminds Segismundo of his former imprisonment. He is an obvious scapegoat for the prince's sense of failure. Segismundo wants and needs to deny his feelings of impotence. He identifies his enslavement with Clotaldo, and has no need of going beyond immediate appearances in order to find a means of venting his anger. Again, appearances second the will. Segismundo wants to find someone on whom he can blame his enslavement and Clotaldo appears to be responsible.

Segismundo turns next against Astolfo. Astolfo's claims to the throne, his insistence on equality and mutual respect between himself and Segismundo, and his refusal to honor Segismundo as future king, illustrated in the episode in which he dons his hat in the prince's presence, threaten Segismundo's system. Segismundo needs to feel unique and powerful. He needs to maintain the newly created image of himself as sovereign. Astolfo's presence and apparent disrespect menace his self-image. In order to protect it, he asserts himself by turning violently against his rival.

Estrella provides Segismundo with another means of self-assertion. The prince is at once taken with her beauty. Yet, he does not react as he did when he saw Rosaura in the first act.

In the tower Segismundo still felt enslaved, will-less. Now, he is obsessed with the assertion of his power. One of the most common means of imposing manipulative power is through sex. Overpowering a weaker individual physically enables one to define himself in his own mind as strong —thus, Segismundo's disrespectful advances toward Estrella.

These three examples of Segismundo's aggressiveness illustrate his attempt to mold the world into a system in which he is supreme. They are illustrative of his intense desire for self-assertion. Every piece of evidence, every indication that the world is not as he would have it must be disposed of. His violence is a savage attempt to adjust the universe to his will:

> Nada me parece justo
> en siendo contra mi gusto.
>
> (Segunda jornada, 431-432)

Yet, Segismundo is unsuccessful. Clotaldo and Astolfo stand up to him. Estrella does not yield to his advances. It is now against the Servant whom Segismundo turns. The Servant is socially and physically inferior. He provides Segismundo with a means of proving his strength. The Servant's moralizing and chastizing challenge Segismundo, and here at last is a challenge he can meet:

> Criado 2:   Con los hombres como yo
> no puede hacerse eso.
> Segismundo: ¿No?
> ¡Por Dios que lo he de probar!
>
> (Segunda jornada, 439-441)

This necessity for "proving himself" has motivated Segismundo's arrogance not only in this but also in the previous confrontations.

In the confrontation between Basilio and Segismundo, the prince is pitted against an adversary as willful as he. Basilio

198

and Segismundo have in common their arrogance, their insistence on intellectual certainty, their tendency to systematize, their unwillingness to see beyond appearances. Basilio, judging appearances from his own point of view, blames the stars for Segismundo's outrageous behavior. Segismundo, more perceptive and less corrupted by courtly refinements, blames his willfulness on his father. However, both fail to see the fundamental reality of the situation: Segismundo's actions, while influenced by outside forces such as his upbringing, depend solely upon himself. While Basilio is wrong to maintain the stars have determined Segismundo, Segismundo is wrong to place the blame for his lack of self-control entirely on Basilio.[19] Basilio cannot determine Segismundo's actions; he can only offer him the kind of guidance which will enable him to determine them intelligently for himself. This, of course, is a parental responsibility with which Basilio has failed to comply.

Basilio and Segismundo have yet another thing in common: a craving for self-assertion. Just as Segismundo felt the necessity to prove his strength before Clotaldo, Astolfo, Estrella and the Servant, Basilio feels he must assert his

[19] Alexander Parker discusses this point at length in "The Father-Son Conflict in the Drama of Calderón". Conjecturing that *La vida es sueño* was probably written after *La devoción de la Cruz* and *Las tres justicias en una,* Parker sees Segismundo's conversion as an answer to the question implicit in the two earlier dramas: "If one man leads another indirectly but inevitably to sin, how far is the latter man predetermined to sin and so deprived of free-will and responsibility for his own actions?" Parker concludes that, "The influence of a father's cruelty can predispose his son to rebellion but it cannot force him to consummate it in the ultimate criminal act..." *Forum of Modern Language Studies,* Vol. II, No. 2, University of St. Andrews (April, 1966), pp. 108-109. See also Peter N. Dunn, "The Horoscope Motif in *La vida es sueño", Atlante I (1953), pp. 187-201 and R.D. F. Pring-Mill, "Los Calderonistas de habla inglesa y La vida es sueño":* Método del análisis temático-estructural", *Litterae hispanae et Lusitanae,* Munich, 1968, pp. 369-413.

authority before Segismundo. He meets his son's defiance
with arrogance. Segismundo has thrown into question
Basilio's system; he has disputed his knowledge; he has
challenged his image of astrologer-sage. The king is indignant. He manifests his anger first by reminding
Segismundo that he alone is responsible for the youth's rise
from prisoner to prince (Segunda jornada, 514-516).
Basilio's contention is ill received by Segismundo, who
argues that the kingship is his by natural right (Segunda jornada, 516-525).

Segismundo understands that for one individual to attempt to
determine another's role is a presumptuous usurpation of the
divine prerogative. What he does not understand is that once
one occupies the place duly assigned to him, he has the
responsibility to perform righteously. Segismundo correctly
alleges that by depriving him of his freedom, Basilio has
deprived him of life and honor —honor understood here as
self-respect— which are the natural rights of all men:

> y pedirte cuentas puedo
> del tiempo que me has quitado
> libertad, vida y honor.
>
> (Segunda jornada, 528-530)

Segismundo knows that it is his natural right to be free and to
be king.[20] But he does not yet grasp the nature of freedom.
He does not yet know that freedom entails responsibility.

[20] There is a similar confrontation between Julia and Curcio in *La devoción de la Cruz*. Curcio declares that his daughter must enter a convent
solely because it is his wish. She replies that she has a right to her freedom,
and that no predetermination or "fate" —including the one her father
wishes to impose on her— can deprive her of it:

> Sólo tiene libertad
>   un hijo para escoger
> estado; que el hado impío
> no fuerza el libre albedrío.
>
> (I, 588-591)

Basilio is angered by Segismundo's challenge to his authority. He lashes out against the defiant prince just as Segismundo lashed out against those who threatened his self-image. Basilio resorts to vengeance; he menaces his son with the tower (Segunda jornada, 542-545). By returning Segismundo to the prison Basilio will set things right again. He will remove the constant reminder of his own failure as a father —a failure Segismundo has made perfectly clear by his accusations— and will restore his system, his self-image and his self-assurance.

In this violent battle of two wills seeking self-assertion, Segismundo refuses to yield. He rejects Basilio's warning as an empty threat (Segunda jornada, 546-549). For Segismundo to recognize that appearances are wrong, as Basilio suggests, would be to relinquish his dream and consequently his will. Segismundo needs his dream of power in order to assert himself as an independent human being. His rejection of Basilio's warning is followed by still another declaration of identity:

> sé quién soy, y no podrás
> aunque suspires y sientas,
> quitarme el haber nacido
> desta corona heredero;
> (Segunda jornada, 553-555)

When Crucio threatens to take her life in punishment for her display of disrespect, Julia answers:

> La libertad te defiendo,
> señor, pero no la vida.
> Acaba su curso triste,
> y acabará tu pesar;
> que mal te puedo negar
> la vida que tú me diste:
> la libertad que me dió
> el cielo, es la que te niego.
> (I, 607-614)

But like the honor characters who insist "soy quién soy", Segismundo does not really understand his own identity. He confuses the self with the role. He knows himself to be "Prince" without grasping the notion that political position is merely a temporal status. There are many who play the role of prince, but there is only one Segismundo. The man Segismundo can be defined not by his title but by his acts. It is not by flaunting power in the name of authority but by performing justly that one merits the respect of others. Segismundo has been turned loose with no guidance, with no understanding of his own freedom. For him, freedom is to give free reign to the will. He does not truly understand his own power for he does not comprehend that it is within his power to control his will. He will only be truly free when he governs his will and is not governed by it.

Segismundo "discovers" himself a second time through Rosaura. Upon seeing her he exclaims:

> (Ya hallé mi vida.)
> (Segunda jornada. 596)

His remark reveals that she triggers in him the memory of what he has known all along, but what now lies buried deep in his potential: the possibility ' of self-restraint, the recognition of something beyond the self and its images.

But the memory is repressed. Segismundo's will cannot tolerate the menace of compromise. To show restraint toward Rosaura imperils his self-image ot all-powerful prince. To reject his natural tendency now becomes a new challenge.

> Sólo por ver si puedo
> harás que pierda a tu hermosura el miedo,
> que soy muy inclinado
> a vencer lo imposible...
> (Segunda jornada, 652-655)

To tarnish Rosaura's honor becomes a way of proving himself. He must do it just to prove that he can:

> y asi por ver si puedo cosa es llana
> que arrojaré tu honor por la ventana.
>
> (Segunda jornada, 658-659)

His new attempt at self-assertion erupts into unbridled violence when he is interrupted by Clotaldo, whom he attempts to kill, then by Astolfo and Basilio. Oblivious to reason, Segismundo lashes out first at one then the other in terrible vengeance for the past humiliations he has been made to suffer:

> Porque aún no estoy vengado
> del modo injusto con que me has criado.
>
> (Segunda jornada, 732-733)

The more Segismundo is challenged, the more he reels against his challengers. For every attempt to subdue him is another threat to the newly released will he is trying so desperately to keep alive.[21]

---

[21] "Violence, or acts close to it, gives one a sense of counting, of mattering, of power... This in turn gives the individual a sense of significance. No human being can exist for long without some sense of his own significance." Rollo May, *Power and Innocence*, pp. 36-37. "It is important to see that... violence... is the end result of repressed anger and rage, combined with constant fear based on the patient's powerlessness. Behind the pseudo-power of the madness we can often find a person struggling for some sense of significance, some way of making a difference and establishing some self-esteem." *Power*, p. 26.

Even in the sixteenth century Luis Vives recognized pride as the misguided manifestation of a perfectly natural sentiment. He also recognized violence and vengeance as natural outcomes of uncontrolled self-assertiveness manifested as pride. *Tratado*, pp. 1315-1317.

Many modern critics have recognized Segismundo's self-assertiveness as pride. For example, Leopoldo Eulogio Palacios calls Segismundo "un monstre d'orgeuil." But these critics have failed to see Segismundo's pride as a positive reaction against his encarceration. See Palacios, *"La Vie est un songe," Laval Théologique et philosophique*, 7 (1951), pp. 123-149.

Basilio repays vengeance with vengeance. Once more he threatens his son with death —with that living death which is life without freedom. Once more he threatens to return him to the eternal nothingness of the womb (Segunda jornada, 734-737). In fulfilling his promise Basilio performs Segismundo a service, rather than a disservice, however, for it is only when he is confronted with the termination of his own "dream" that Segismundo begins to understand the functioning and limitations of the will.

Once back in the tower, Segismundo is overcome with confusion. Half asleep, half awake, he continues to babble about vengance. But once his eyes are open, the certainty he displayed at Court disappears:

> ¿Soy yo, por ventura? ¿Soy
> el que, preso y aherrojado
> llego a verme en tal estado?
> (Segunda jornada, 1095-1097)

Segismundo no longer affirms that he knows who he is, but, on the contrary, questions his own identity. To question one's own images —including one's self-image— is a step toward maturity.

He recognizes his tower as the womb-coffin to enclose him during all eternity:

> ¿No sois mi sepulcro vos,
> torre? Si.
> (Segunda jornada, 1098-1099)

Segismundo's awakening in the symbolic tower-sepulcher is his awakening to the reality of death. In the face of his own mortality, he begins to understand the temporal nature of power and in what sense life is only a dream. His sudden, unexpected return to prison teaches him that life, like a dream, may end at any time without warning. Those things we have seen and heard and those things we have valued such as power, wealth, fame, vanish from our existence; they become meaningless, for they cannot help man to forstall his inevitable end.

All life —including reality— is a dream. Even awake, that is, even aware of the temporal nature of life, man lives a dream, for he must always remain uncertain regarding which things are projections of his will and which are not —which things are appearances or images and which are reality— and also regarding the nature and time of his own end:

> ni aun ahora he dispertado;
> que según, Clotaldo, entiendo,
> todavía estoy durmiendo,
> y no estoy muy engañado;
>
> (Segunda jornada, 1112-1115)

Although it is true, as E. M. Wilson argues, that Segismundo "is still the dupe of Basilio and Clotaldo; he has still to understand that he was awake all the time that he thinks he was dreaming," and that, "Only then shall we be able to talk of him as truly converted,"[22] Segismundo has already come to the conclusion which will make possible that conversion. Calderón adopts a skeptical attitude here inasmuch as he throws into question our very ability to distinguish between what is real and what is not.[23]

---

[22] "On *La vida es sueño*," p. 75.

[23] Wilson criticizes Farinelli's assertion that *La vida es sueño* contains a skeptical message which contradicts the religious one. Farinelli argues that if a life is indeed a dream, we can hardly be held responsible for those acts we perform while dreaming. However, even if we do not accept Farinelli's thesis, we cannot overlook the skeptical message reiterated throughout the play: the dream-like quality of life and the unreliability of sense information are basic to skeptical thought. See "On *La vida es sueño*," p. 67 and Arturo Farinelli, *La vita è un sogno*. Parte seconda, Torino, 1916, pp. 283-284. For a discussion of Calderón's and Descartes' use of the skeptical thesis "life is a dream," cf. Humberto Piñera Llera, "¿Descartes en Calderón?," *La Torre*, Puerto Rico, 6 (1958), pp. 145-165.

The lesson Segismundo learns is precisely the uncertain and temporal nature of human experience:

> ...si ha sido soñado
> lo que vi palpable y cierto,
> lo que veo será incierto;
> y no es mucho que rendido,
> pues veo estando dormido,
> que sueñe estando dispierto.

> (Segunda jornada, 1116-1121)

Experience teaches Segismundo not that his existence is dreamed but thàt appearances are as deceiving as if they were dreamed:

> ...el vivir sólo es soñar;
> y la experiencia me enseña
> que el hombre que vive sueña
> lo que es hasta dispertar.

> (Segunda jornada, 1167-1170)

The difference between characters such as Aureliano and Segismundo is that the former reject experience when it contradicts what they will, while the latter learns and profits from it. Segismundo no longer projects the image of himself as all-powerful prince. He accepts, instead, that man's state is merely temporary; man dreams "lo que es", and what he is, is always subject to change or termination. Power, in the sense that Segismundo has understood it up to now, is, like all other worldly goods, illusory:

> ¿Qué es la vida? Un frenesí.
> ¿Qué es la vida? Una ilusión,
> una sombra, una ficción
> y el mayor bien es pequeño
> que toda la vida es sueño,
> y los sueños, sueños son.

> (Segunda jornada, 1195-1200)

Even the dream itself —in this case, Segismundo's experiences at Court— are subject to change and termination, not because of Basilio's scheme but because death and change in fortune are always possibilities. That Segismundo is still the dupe of Clotaldo and Basilio is not really the point. Segismundo is correct in his conclusion that those things of which we are so certain are in reality only "frenzies" or "illusions."

Before the absurdity of a meaningless world of appearances Clotaldo offers a solution: action:

> aun en sueños
> no se pierde el hacer bien.
>
> (Segunda jornada, 1159-1160)

But at this point Segismundo is too overcome by his newly formed vision of the world to heed his tutor's words. It is not until he himself is called upon to act that Clotaldo's lesson takes on meaning.

"Soñemos, alma, soñemos": Man Defines Himself by his Acts

At the beginning of the third act, Segismundo is once again offered liberty. The soldiers call him to the front:

> la libertad
> te espera; oye sus acentos.
>
> (Tercera jornada, 117-118)

Once again liberty is coupled with power. But Segismundo has learned the temporal nature of power and is reluctant to accept:

> Pues no ha de ser, no ha de ser
> mirarme otra vez sujeto
> a mi fortuna;
>
> (Tercera jornada, 131-133)

He is now aware of the changing nature of fortune and of the inevitability of death. Power seems an absurdity. Rather than accept it. Segismundo retires into a shell. He rejects the world and chooses inaction:

> que no quiero majestades
> fingidas, pompas no quiero
> fantásticas, ilusiones
> que al soplo menos ligero
> del aura han de deshacerse.

(Tercera jornada, 139-143)

Segismundo's awakening has lead him to a philosophy of resignation and despair. He adopts a stoic attitude of non-participation:

> para mí no hay fingimientos;
> que desengañado ya,
> sé bien que la vida es sueño.

(Tercera jornada, 154-156)

This sense of the futility of life and of the inefficacy of human endeavor are present in modern thought from Schopenhauer to Sartre. But resignation is not Calderón's solution. For Segismundo to opt to stay in the tower at the very moment when his countrymen clamor for his leadership would be an act of gross irresponsibility.[24] Inaction is death. To live is to dream. Segismundo must accept liberty and dream on:

> pues que la vida es tan corta,
> soñemos, alma, soñemos
> otra vez.

(Tercera jornada, 171-173)

[24] Suárez maintains that inaction constitutes a form of negative action and that evil resulting from inaction is as condemnable as any other kind. *Disputaciones*. II, p. 313.
This concept of inaction as equivalent to a negative act is essentially the same as Sartre's. Sartre maintains that by choosing not to act the individual takes a stand which defines him, for while an individual can choose not to act, he cannot choose not to be free. See *L'Etre et le néant*, p. 515. In Sartre's play *Le Diable et le bon Dieu*, Goetz, like Segismundo, faced with mounting disillusionment, retires into solitude and resists taking command

But not with the cockiness he displayed previously. The regenerated Segismundo is willing to dream, but now with a new awareness of the nature of life.[25] Now he knows better than to proceed with arrogant assuredness. Life is to be lived, to be enjoyed, to be experienced to the optimum. But it is not possessed, only borrowed. The awakening will be less difficult for those who are prepared for it:

> pero ha de ser
> con atención y consejo
> de que hemos de despertar
> deste gusto al mejor tiempo.
>
> (Tercera jornada, 173-176)

And how does one prepare for it? By one's acts.[26] Life, the dream, is not futile. It is the means by which the individual defines himself as worthy or unworthy of salvation. Life is a mere transitory period between birth and death; it is filled with illusions and deceits. But it is what is given us to give meaning to ourselves as individuals. Only now does Clotaldo's lesson become clear to Segismundo, and he repeats it almost word for word:

> Que estoy soñando y que quiero
> obrar bien, pues no se pierde
> el hacer bien, aun en sueños.
>
> (Tercera jornada, 212-214)

---

of an insurgent army. Later, made aware that to shirk action is in itself an act of bad faith, the enlightened Goetz takes his place at the head of the rebel soldiers.

[25] Pedro Salinas shows how this aspect of awareness makes Calderón differ from medieval poets such as Manrique in *Reality and the Spanish Poet,* tr. Edith Fishtine Helman (Baltimore: The Johns Hopkins Press, 1966), pp. 33-63.

[26] Action is fundamental to Calderón's ethic. In *El gran teatro del mundo,* God does not intervene in human affairs in order to leave each individual free to earn his salvation through his actions:

> por no quitarles la acción
> de merecer con sus obras (934-935)

Good deeds are positive projections of the self, a means of self-fulfillment. Regardless of their consequences or the happiness they may or may not bring to the intended benificiary, they are justifiable ends in themselves. If what we experience is indeed reality, good deeds give form and meaning to that reality. If, on the other hand, worldly life is simply a passing illusion, good deeds are justifiable because it is by our acts we will be judged upon awakening to real —that is, eternal— life:

> obrar bien es lo que importa;
> si fuera verdad, por serlo;
> si no, por ganar amigos
> para cuando despertemos.
>
> (Tercera jornada, 236-240)

But man cannot act if he is not free. Segismundo must accept the freedom he is offered and go forth into battle. By retiring to the tower and allowing Basilio to conquer the rebellious soldiers, Segismundo would render his own self-realization impossible. He was born prince and must accept his place among men. He must accept power —but, at the same time, he must learn to use it correctly. He must see that power is not his to play with, that it is a means, not an end.

What Segismundo has understood in theory he must now put into practice. This proves to be somewhat difficult. Once more in a position of power, he becomes arrogant and aggressive. The illusion of grandeur tempts him (Tercera jor-

---

The prompter, the Ley de la gracia, reminds the characters:

> obra bien, que Dios es Dios. (667)

The notion that man defines himself through his actions is fundamental to the philosophy of Sartre and other existentialist writers. Sartre writes: "... l'acte est l'expression de la liberté." L'Etre et le néant, p. 513. According to Rollo May, the predicament of the free man is precisely that he is forced to act even in the face of uncertainty: "even though man can never know for certain and even though there are no absolute answers and never will be, man has to act anyway." Love and Will, p. 270.

nada, 469-476). But the spectre of the awakening has made its mark on the young prince. It is now that he begins to exercise true power, that is, power over the self. He rejects the illusion; he controls his will; he checks his ambition:

> aqueste aplauso incierto,
> si ha de pesarme, cuando esté despierto,
> de haberlo conseguido
> para haberlo perdido,
> pues mientras menos fuere
> menos se sentirá si se perdiere.
>
> (Tercera Jornada, 479-484)

Segismundo is tempted by bad faith. He knows the applause which surrounds him to be "incierto," and yet he regrets it. To lull oneself into certainty is less painful than to accept uncertainty or absurdity. But to act in the face of uncertainty is not only agonizing but also courageous.

It is Rosaura, as A. E. Sloman and William M. Whitby have shown in important articles on the structure of *La vida es sueño,* who provides Segismundo with the opportunity to prove he has learned to govern his will. [27]

Rosaura reveals to Segismundo that his day at Court was not dreamed but actually experienced. The prince is once again thrown into confusion. What is, in effect, the difference between dream and reality?

> Luego fue verdad, no sueño;
> y si fue verdad (que es otra
> confusión y no menor)
> ¿cómo mi vida le nombra
> sueño?
>
> (Tercera jornada, 743-747)

[27] Albert E. Sloman, "The Structure of Calderón's *La vida es sueño*" and William M. Whitby, "Rosaura's Role in the Structure of *La vida es sueño,*" in *Critical Essays on the Theatre of Calderón,* ed. Bruce W. Wardropper (New York: New York University Press, 1965).

211

It is only now that Segismundo realizes to what extent he has
been deceived. Reality is indeed indistinguishable from
illusion. It is impossible to know to what degree our experiences are images or projections of our own will. The new
information does not contradict but rather reinforces his
original conclusion: the "copy" or "image" is indistinguishable from the original, and we are forced to live in
uncertainty regarding which is which:

> ¿Tan semejante es la copia
> al original, que hay duda
> en saber si es ella propia?
>> (Tercera jornada, 756-758)

Segismundo is thrown off balance by Rosaura's presence.
Once more he vacillates and almost yields to the temptation
of the moment. He is sexually attracted to Rosaura and is in a
position to take advantage of her:

> Rosaura está en mi poder,
> su hermosura el alma adora;
> gocemos, pues, la ocasión:
>> (Tercera jornada, 767-769)

But once again he checks his impulses. He knows he will be
judged by his acts. If he yields to passion now, God will hold
him responsible later:

> Si es sueño, si es vanagloria,
> ¿quién por vanagloria humana
> pierde una divina gloria?
>> (Tercera jornada, 778-780)

He knows that those moments which are temporarily so
meaningful are meaningless at the time of judgment:

> ¿Qué pasado bien no es un sueño?
>> (Tercera jornada, 782)

212

Power can be better used. Rather than lose eternity for a moment of pleasure, Segismundo chooses to undertake the restoration of Rosaura's honor.

By doing so, he will redeem her socially and himself spiritually.[28] Now Segismundo truly possesses power; before, he was possessed by it. He is able to reject apparent, temporary goods. He is truly free, for he is the slave neither of Basilio nor of his own will. He no longer feels the need to flaunt temporal power, but now sees it as a tool for performing good deeds:

> Rosaura está sin honor;
> más a un príncipe le toca
> el dar honor que quitarle.
>
> (Tercera jornada, 795-797)

It is not enough to be aware of the vanity of temporal power or to express one's good intentions. Only acts define the man:

> no te hablo, porque quiero
> que te hablen por mí mis obras,
>
> (Tercera jornada, 819-820)

Segismundo sets aside his own inclinations toward Rosaura and restores her honor by marrying her to Astolfo, while he himself takes Estrella for his bride.

Segismundo's most significant act of self-domination is his pardon of Basilio.[29] Basilio has been responsible for

---

[28] For Sartre, all acts are performed with a motive which constitutes an *engagement*: "Parler d'un acte sans motif, c'est parler d'un acte auquel manquerait la structure intentionnelle de tout acte et les partisans de la liberté, en la cherchant au niveau de l'acte en train de se faire, ne sauraient aboutir qu'à la rendre absurde." *L'Etre et la néant*, p. 512. See also "Choix et engagement" in *L'existentialisme*, p. 46. For the Christian, every individual is *engagé* in saving his own soul.

[29] For Sartre, sentiment is valid and significant only to the extent that it is proven by acts: "le sentiment se construit par les acts qu'on fait."

Segismundo's enslavement in both a literal and a symbolic sense. On the one hand, he has imprisoned him physically. On the other, it is precisely he who has most contributed to his son's enslavement by his own will. Segismundo's military victory over his father reflects symbolically his triumph over himself. To take vengeance would be to act willfully, to attempt to impose the image of the conquering prince, to flaunt power. Segismundo, now undeceived regarding the illusory nature of the world, chooses rather to relinquish the image. Rather than impose power, he offers it. He places his own life at the disposal of his father (Tercera jornada, 1050-1056). Segismundo's conversion is now complete. He has proven himself victorious over his own will. He is ready to accept the freedom offered him and the responsibility it implies.[30] Now he can go forth to dream his dream in good faith:

> toda la dicha humana,
> en fin, pasa como un sueño,
> y quiero hoy aprovecharla
> el tiempo de que me durare:
>
> (Tercera jornada, 1122-1125)

Basilio's Awakening

Like Segismundo, Basilio experiences a philosophical awakening at the end of the play.[31] Throughout most of *La*

L'Existentialisme, p. 45. Segismundo's change of heart with respect to his father is proven by the act of forgiveness.

[30] In *The Dramatic Craftsmanship of Calderón* Albert E. Sloman shows how Calderón revamped an earlier play, *Yerros de naturaleza y aciertos de la fortuna,* written by him in collaboration with Antonio Coello, in order to emphasize the questions of freedom of choice and action. (Oxford: The Dolphin Book Co., Ltd., 1969), p. 253.

[31] As E. M. Wilson has pointed out. Basilio is in a sense as much a dreamer as Segismundo. "On *La vida es sueño.*" p. 83. It is characteristic of persons of bad faith that they are dreamers, for they unconciously close their eyes to their own freedom and responsibility: "On se met de mauvaise

vida es sueño, Basilio sees himself as the victim of circumstances beyond his control.[32] He fails to recognize his
responsibility for his son's faulty upbringing.[33] When, in the
third act, Segismundo takes command of the insurgent army,
Basilio accepts with resignation his son's expected tyranny,
which he believes to be inevitable by decree of the stars. Like
Calderón's men and women of honor, he sees himself as impotent in the face of destiny.

As Alexander A. Parker has pointed out, Basilio is not an evil
but a tragic character. Like the honor figures, he is both heir
to and perpetuator of a system he has neither the insight nor
the strength to discard. Basilio's decision to encarcerate
Segismundo is not an act of defiance of fate, but an act of acceptance of what he believes to be destiny. Such a stand is
one of weakness, not of strength. Basilio is not the victim of
fate but of his own blind pretentiousness, for, as Parker
makes clear, "Spanish dramatists present no victims of
destiny or mischance, but only of wrongdoing —their own,
or someone else's."[34]

When Segismundo at last triumphs over Basilio, the latter
adopts an attitude of total resignation. He kneels before his

foi comme on s'endort et on est de mauvaise foi comme on rêve." *L'Etre et
le néant,* p. 109.

[32] As Sloman points out in his introduction to the critical edition of the *La
vida es sueño,* the question of responsibility is central to Calderón's plays,
p. xxii E. M. Wilson also discusses the question of moral responsibility, in
particular with reference to Basilio's raising of Segismundo. "On *La vida es
sueño,*" pp. 81-82.

[33] "Bad faith" consists precisely in the refusal to accept one's freedom and
the responsibility that freedom implies; it consists in "faith" in one's inability to combat the circumstances: "Le véritable problème de la mauvaise foi
vient évidemment de ce que la mauvaise foi est *foi.*" *L'Etre et le néant,*
p. 108. The process by which one takes a stand in "bad faith" is unpremedi-
tated and unconscious: "...il ne s'agit pas d'une décision réfléchie et volontaire, mais d'une détermination spontanée de notre être." *L'Etre,* p. 109,
Basilio does not "decide" to accept astrology any more than don Lope "decides" to accept the honor code.

[34] "The Spanish Drama of the Golden Age," p. 691.

son, believing himself to be destined to be reduced to total submission. However, the fate in which Basilio so tenaciously believes is belied. He had misjudged appearance for reality. He had assumed that because he saw Segismundo behaving violently, the young man was irremediably violent. But Basilio saw only one aspect of Segismundo. He never suspected that Segismundo possessed the qualities of rationality, control and compassion the young man displays at the end of the play. [35]

It is precisely at this moment of total resignation that Basilio at last faces up to fate. It is now, convinced that there is no

[35] Basilio remains blind to Segismundo's redeeming qualities precisely because he experiments in bad faith. Once an individual has taken a stand in bad faith, he develops a whole method of thinking that permits him to seize upon evidence which backs up his preconceived notions and to discard evidence which does not. See Sartre's discussion of bad faith and the use of evidence in *L'Etre et le néant*, pp. 108-109 Basilio, experimenting in bad faith, accepts the evidence supplied by Segismundo's actions but rejects the evidence supplied by his arguments. In the comedy *El astrólogo fingido*, not even when the mock astrologer Don Diego assures Leonardo that he knows nothing will the latter believe him (Vol. II, pp. 157-158). The strength of astrology is, as in the case with any determinism, in the mind of the individual who believes in it, not in the signs themselves. In the same comedy Maria rebels against the signs:

> Pero aunque planetas, signos
> y estrellas en sus celestes
> globos influyan rigores,
> y contra ti se concierten,
> no ha de dejar de ser tuya
> la que por suyo te tiene,
> y la que te da su mano. (III, p. 162)

By confronting and challenging fate, she proves the stars wrong:

> ¿Ves, Don Diego,
> como, aunque fingidamente,
> descubriendo mis secretos,
> quisiste estorbar mil veces
> mi casamiento, en efecto
> no pudiste? Luego miente
> tu ciencia. (III, p. 164)

escape, that he confronts Segismundo —with a prescience of imminent death— and allows to happen what will.[36] And it is precisely now that Segismundo performs the act of clemency that disproves the stars.

Segismundo's conversion proves that man's knowledge, based largely on appearances, is imperfect and limited. Segismundo reminds his father that no one can know the future or penetrate the secrets reserved for God:

> Lo que está determinado
> del cielo, y en azul tabla
> Dios con el dedo escribió,
> de quien son cifras y estampas
> tantos papeles azules
> que adornan letras doradas,
> nunca engaña, nunca miente;
> porque quien miente y engaña
> es quien para usar mal dellas
> las penetra y las alcanza.
>
> (Tercera jornada, 971-980)

Given the uncertainty of human knowledge, to deprive another of his freedom because of one's own premonitions or predictions is inexcusable arrogance.

Segismundo tells his father that given the opportunity to develop normally, he would have become an acceptable ruler (Tercera jornada, 985-994). The role of the father is not to stunt the potential of his offspring by imposing his own will, but to guide his child in his development.

Authoritarian rigidity can result only in the kind of violent

[36] E. M. Wilson discusses Basilio's "awakening" with respect to mortality, but associates it principally with the lesson the king learns from Clarín's death. As Wilson points out, "Both (Clarín and Basilio) were too confident, but Basilio profited from Clarín's example." "On *La vida es sueño*," p. 82. But Basilio also takes an important step toward *desengaño* when he is forced to face the reality of his own death.

self-assertion displayed by Segismundo in the first and second acts. [37] The antidotes to the rigorous, vengeful, arrogant stand taken by Basilio are an open mind and a generous heart:

La fortuna no se vence
con justicia y con venganza,
porque antes se incita más;
y así, quien vencer aguarda
a su fortuna, ha de ser
con cordura y con templanza.

(Tercera jornada, 1023-1028)

Basilio has been humbled and undeceived. He, like Segismundo, experiences *desengaño* and regeneration, for he acknowledges his errors and recognizes in Segismundo the moral rectitude he thought to be lacking.

Clotaldo: An Alternative

Clotaldo illustrates an alternative to Basilio's rigidity and arrogance. Both men find themselves in the anguishing situation of having to choose between the apparent dictates of fate and the well-being of an offspring. Clotaldo has been given the order to put to death any person who should happen upon Segismundo's tower, and by a queer twist of fortune, the first intruder is Rosaura, whom Clotaldo takes to be his son.

The sign by which Clotaldo recognizes Rosaura is the sword he had left to Violante, her mother. But there is a difference between Clotaldo's interpretation of signs and Basilio's. Recognizing in the sword what seems to be a sign of his obligation to the individual who bears it, Clotaldo proceeds with utmost caution. He does not jump to conclusions but remains acutely aware of the deceptive nature of appearances:

[37] See Parker, "The Father-Son Conflict in the Drama of Calderón."

218

Aún no sé determinarme
si tales sucesos son
ilusiones o verdades.

(Primera jornada, 396-398)

It is precisely because of his understanding of the illusory quality of appearances that he later comprehends Rosaura's ambiguous words when she intimates that she is a woman, not a man.

When Clotaldo does, after much vacillation, accept the sword as evidence, he accepts it as a symbol of his responsibility to the bearer, not as an indication of irreversible fate. The sign does not become a tool for the imposition of his will or the rigid systematization of reality, but simply another factor —an obstructive one to be sure— to be considered in the implementation of the King's mandate. Rather than yielding to an apparent fate that seems to condemn him to execute his own son, he weighs his responsibilities and examines alternate modes of action. While acknowledging his obligation to carry out the King's orders, he recognizes his duty to protect Rosaura. He decides to place the dilemma before Basilio and beg for his clemency. By so doing, he faces the situation squarely and opens the door to a possible solution.

Basilio, confronted by a similar situation, displays confidence neither in himself nor in Segismundo to overcome what he believes to be his son's inevitable tyranny. His decision to lock the prince in a tower is merely an effort to limit its effects. His attitude is essentially defeatist. Clotaldo, on the other hand, displays cautious confidence —confidence in his own and Rosaura's ability to warrant clemency, and confidence in Basilio's willingness to grant it. Clotaldo's forthright behavior proves justified when he presents the situation to the King. The circumstances have changed; Segismundo's existence is no longer a secret. Basilio grants Clotaldo's request readily and the tragedy decreed by "fate" has been avoided.

In the matter of Rosaura's honor, Clotaldo also shows himself to be cautious but unresigned. Clotaldo places honor relatively low on his hierarchy of values. Unlike Calderón's honor characters, he is not obsessed with honor or quick to take vengeance. When Rosaura tells him she has been wronged by Astolfo, he advises her —whom he still believes to be a young man— to overlook the alleged affront, for as Astolfo's vassal she cannot legitimately seek redress against him. When Rosaura intimates she is a woman, Clotaldo is reminded once more that appearances are deceiving. Although he comprenhends the meaning of Rosaura's words, he is at a loss to know how to proceed in the face of this new development:

> ¿Qué confuso laberinto
> es éste, donde no puede
> hallar la razón del hilo?
>
> (Primera jornada, 975-977)

Clotaldo's predicament seems to defy reason. His confusion proves that even the most . enlightened of individuals is sometimes overwhelmed by the labyrinth of appearances that is life.

At the beginning of the third act, the question of Rosaura's honor is still in abeyance. The young woman is determined to restore her honor and Clotaldo recognizes his responsibility to help her do so. Yet, unlike the honor characters who ignore all other considerations in their implementation of the honor code, Clotaldo's first concern is for justice. He does not boast that the knows who he is and what he must do, but identifies himself only as

> persona que hace
> y persona que padece.
>
> (Tercera jornada, 371-372)

Clotaldo owes Astolfo his life, for in the skirmish with Segismundo at Court it was he who came to Clotaldo's aid. Now Clotaldo is torn between his duty to Rosaura and his gratitude toward Astolfo. He is in still another dilemma. His simple yet elegant self-definition reflects the perennial anguish of the free man: he is an individual who acts, who does; now, faced with conflicting responsibilities, he must choose one mode of action or another without the certainty that either is superior to its alternative. This is precisely existential *angoisse* —the consternation and suffering of the individual in an ambiguous situation before his irrevocable obligation to choose.[38] It this sense, every man who acts, suffers. Only those who function within the limits of peremptory systems are spared the anguish of complete awareness of their own responsibility.

Clotaldo does not disdain honor, but he considers it inferior to certain other values, such as duty, gratitude and generosity. He offers Rosaura all his worldly wealth and proposes she enter a convent. The solution is a compromise, but is all he can offer and still comply with his conflicting responsibilities.

Rosaura is unwilling to accept her father's proposed compromise. In vain Clotaldo tries to reason with her:

> Clotaldo: Es locura.
> Rosaura: Ya lo veo.
> Clotaldo: Pues véncela.
> Rosaura: No podré.
> Clotaldo: Pues perderás...
> Rosaura: Ya lo sé.
> Clotaldo: ...vida y honor.
> Rosaura: Bien lo creo.
> Clotaldo: ¿Qué intentas?
> Rosaura: Mi muerte.
> Clotaldo: Mira que eso es despecho.
> Rosaura: Es honor.
> Clotaldo: Es desatino.
> Rosaura: Es valor.
> Clotaldo: Es frenesí.
> Rosaura: Es rabia, es ira.
>   (Tercera jornada, 454-460)

[38] See Sartre, *L'Existentialisme.* pp. 28ff and *L'Etre et le néant*, pp. 77ff.

What Rosaura sees as a necessity, Clotaldo sees as a compulsion beyond the bounds of decorum, safety or reason —reason, understood not as logical systematization but as natural order, common sense and moderation. He sees Rosaura's proposed behavior as wildly foolish and rash. Yet, rather than imposing his own will on his willful daughter, he offers advice: *"Pues, véncela."* Here Clotaldo expresses his confidence in Rosaura to overcome her passion for vengeance and to govern her acts by reason. When she maintains she is unable to do so, he warns her of the risks involved. Clotaldo displays an intimate understanding of the honor system; he knows what the outcome of vengeance may be and comprehends the danger of delivering oneself over to the dictates of apparent fate. Furthermore, he knows that honor cannot really be restored by vengeance, that Rosaura will have to bear the burden of her dishonor forever if she publicizes it by an act of violence. Unlike Basilio, Clotaldo does not view his offspring's rashness as inevitable or incorrigible. Rather than simply delivering Rosaura over to her own passion, as Basilio does with Segismundo by locking him in a tower, he considers first the consequences of such irresponsible parental indifference to the child. He knows that if he allows Rosaura to succumb to her passion he will be partially responsible for her death or further dishonor.

Rosaura declares herself ready to face death. Like all of Calderón's characters who yield to the inevitability of the circumstances, Rosaura is defeatist, negative. Libio, Aureliano, don Lope and Basilio all end their personal dramas by resigning themselves to self-destruction. Rosaura follows the same pattern. She sees her own death as the inevitable consequence of her dishonor.[39] But precisely what Rosaura identifies as honor, Clotaldo recognizes as folly or

[39] Honor is frequently seen as fate and associated with astrology in Calderón's plays. Recall Doña Angela's lament in *La dama duende:*
¡Suerte injusta, dura estrella!

absurdity (*"desatino"*). What she calls valor, he calls frenzy and rashness. *"Frenesi"* is precisely the term Segismundo uses elsewhere to refer to the fleeting, deceptive nature of life. Clotaldo recognizes honor as part of the delusion of temporal existence. He calls Rosaura's obsession a *"ciega pasión"*, for she is blind, unenlightened by reason. Furthermore, she is rash enough to undertake vengeance alone, should Clotaldo fail to offer his help. In vain he persists in seeking a less radical solution. What characterizes Clotaldo is his ability to confront the circumstances, to examine them and to seek alternate solutions in the light of reason and conscience. While he is positive in his approach and cautiously confident that a remedy can be found, Rosaura is negative and determined to follow the course she sees as inevitable.[40]

In the end Clotaldo agrees to second Rosaura in her quest for vengeance, but not without expressing his total awareness that such shortsighted tenacity is bound to have disastrous consequences:

> Pues si has de perderte, espera,
> hija, y perdámonos todos.
>
> (Tercera jornada, 467-468)

What moves Clotaldo is not the desire for vengeance, but parental love. Although he seeks a rational solution to Rosaura's dilemma, he at last agrees to sacrifice reason to love. While Basilio illustrates rigidity, Clotaldo illustrates its opposite; flexibility.

The cryptic nature of the dialogue between Clotaldo and Rosaura enhances the atmosphere of confusion which en-

---

[40] Several critics defend Rosaura's integrity and laud her idealism. Wilson praises her trueness to moral considerations. "On *La vida es sueño*," p. 85. Wardropper, alluding to the legal codes of the period, notes that "the life of honor was a principle rooted outside herself in eternal truth." "'Apenas llega'", p. 242. Sloman sees in Rosaura "a model of determination and integrity." "Introduction," p. xix. But, while Rosaura is obviously a positive character with a regenerative function in terms of Segismundo's conversion, she nevertheless encarnates the same irrational obsession with honor as characters such as Don Lope de Almeida.

velops the scene. The rapidity of the exchange, the brevity of the rejoinders, the simplicity of the words charged with emotional involvement create immense tension. Between Rosaura and Clotaldo there seems to be no comprehension, and yet the father's love is so great it bridges the gap. As Clotaldo follows Rosaura off the stage he is moved by something greater than the knowledge that he is right; he is moved by compassion.

Basilio and Clotaldo face similar situations. Both are parents of passionate, willful children who seem to be headed for disaster. But while Basilio chooses the facile solution of relegating his son to a tower and leaving him to his feelings, Clotaldo confronts Rosaura's willfulness with reason. And when he fails to convince her, he does not abandon her to her own devices but rather sacrifices his convictions in order to stand by her. Through acts of love and compassion he proves himself to be a father truly solicitous of the well-being of his child.

There is still another point of comparison between Clotaldo and Basilio: their respective attitudes toward Segismundo. For if Basilio is Segismundo's natural father, Clotaldo is his spiritual father. It is Clotaldo who raises him, giving him the only guidance he receives. It is he who shows himself to be sincerely concerned with Segismundo's development. By imposing his own will on his son, Basilio alienates him. He removes Segismundo from himself both physically and emotionally, making communication between the two impossible.[41] It is characteristic of those of Calderón's charac-

---

[41] In *En la vida todo es verdad y todo es mentira*, Astolfo, the tutor-father figure whose role is similar to Clotaldo's in *La vida es sueño*, warns Focas, the natural father of one of his charges:

> No te creas de experiencias
> de hijo a quien otro crió;
> que apartadas crianzas tienen
> muy sin cariño el calor
> de los padres
>
> (p. 1122)

ters who resign themselves to what they believe to be fate that they isolate themselves precisely at the time when communication is necessary to avoid catastrophe. Rollo May has written that, "The critical issue presented by contemporary drama... is the breakdown of communication."[42] This is a critical issue in Calderón's plays, as well.

Unlike Basilio, Clotaldo tries from the very beginning to stimulate Segismundo's consciousness of his own freedom and to instill in him the idea that freedom is realized to the maximum through self-control.[43] He tells him that the prison has been imposed on him as a restraint, for the passions must be held in check (Primera jornada, 319-327).

Once released from the tower, Segismundo at last has the opportunity to exercise his free will. Clotaldo warns him to control his violent tendencies and thereby prove the predictions about his future wrong (Tercera jornada, 299-303). Unlike Basilio, Clotaldo believes that the individual can overcome the apparent dictates of fate, and this is the lesson he tries to impart to Segismundo.

But the young prince, overwhelmed by his new-found freedom, turns against Clotaldo. He recognizes in him not the father figure who has raised him from childhood, but the enforcer of Basilio's cruel mandate. Clotaldo warns him to be careful, for he may be dreaming. He alludes not only to Basilio's scheme to return Segismundo to the tower should he prove himself unworthy of the throne, but to the temporary, illusory nature of power. But Segismudo is in no mood to listen to philosophizing.

Even in the face of Segismundo's tyrannical behavior, Clotal-

[42] *Love and Will*, p. 305.

[43] For the Catholic existentialist Jacques Maritain, the conquest of one's spiritual liberty is the first goal of education. See *Pour une philosophie de l'éducation* (Paris: Arthème Fayard, 1959), p. 28.

do is unwilling to abandon him to what seems to be his destiny. Rather, he persists in his ambition to teach the boy self-restraint:

> (A Segismundo reducir deseo,
> porque en fin le he criado...)

(Segunda jornada, 633-634)

When Segismundo turns his passion against Rosaura, Clotaldo must act swiftly, for his own daughter's physical well-being and honor are at stake. But even in these tenuous circumstances,. Clotaldo appeals to Segismundo's reason, reminding him of the fragility of all human situations (Segunda jornada, 690-692). When Segismundo does persist in his wrath, Clotaldo takes the expedient action of relieving him of his sword. Then, rather than threatening him, he throws himself at his feet and appeals to his sense of mercy. Only when this proves unsuccessful does Clotaldo resort to violence.

Once Segismundo has been returned to the tower, it is Clotaldo who helps him interpret his experiences at Court. What Segismundo saw was a dream in the sense that all life is a dream: it is temporal, unpredictable, illusory. But it is not without value:

> mas en sueños fuera bien
> honrar entonces a quien
> te crió en tantos empeños,
> Segismundo, que aun en sueños
> no se pierde el hacer bien.

(Segunda jornada, 1156-1160)

Clotaldo's message is an optimistic one.[44] Dreams are to be

---

[44] Calderón's view of life is essentially optimistic, for he sees man's ultimate reward or punishment as within his own hands. For Sartre, as well, this view that man has power over his own destiny is a cause for optimism: "il n'y a pas de doctrine plus optimiste, puisque le destin de l'homme est en lui-même." *L'Existentialisme*, p. 62.
Alexander Parker presents a point of view different from the one presented

enjoyed and taken advantage of; they are not to be disdained because they are only dreams. But in order that they may be pleasant dreams and not nightmares, they must be filled with good deeds which will result in personal fulfillment. The dream of life is granted to the individual so that he may earn his salvation. What Clotaldo advises is awareness, not pessimism.

It is from Clotaldo's patient, compassionate guidance and reasoning that Segismundo learns of the dreamlike quality of life. When he again finds himself in a position of power, Segismundo not only recognizes Clotaldo as his true spiritual father (Tercera jornada, 205-211), but proves the sincerity of his regeneration by allowing him to take leave to join Basilio, to whom Clotaldo still feels allegience. When Basilio is defeated, he sees the devolopment as the fulfillment of his predictions, but even at this moment of apparent catastrophe, Clotaldo challenges Basilio's deterministic theories:

> Aunque el hado, señor, sabe
> todos los caminos y halla
> a quien busca entre lo espeso
> de las peñas, no es cristiana
> determinación decir
> que no hay reparo en su saña.
> Sí hay, que el prudente varón
> victoria del hado alcanza.
>
> (Tercera jornada, 921-928).

Wisdom lies to a large extent in the individual's ability to distinguish between what is in his power and what is not. Certain circumstances —biological, political, social, geographical— are not in our control. These irreversible circumstances may be understood to constitute fate. But fate should not be understood in terms of predestination.[45]

here in his Commentary on *El gran teatro del mundo*, in *Readings in Spanish Literature*, pp. 128-132.

[45] Suárez maintains that within the rational bounds of the universe, no effect may be attributed to fate, but only to a "free cause," either divine or

Freedom resides precisely in how the individual faces the circumstances with which he is confronted, in whether he accepts them or rejects them, in whether he faces them or seeks to avoid them. The individual stands up to fate through the choices he makes. Prudence, understood as a cardinal virtue encompassing wisdom, discretion, sagacity and moderation, is the means by which the circumstances can best be challenged.

Clotaldo faces three different circumstances in which fate seems to dictate disaster. In the first, it seems inevitable that he should put his own daughter to death; in the second, it seems inevitable that he should betray the man who has saved his life in order to restore his daughter's honor; in the third, it seems inevitable that the prince he has raised from childhood should become a tyrant. Clotaldo meets all three situations with prudence. In each case he refuses to resign himself to what seems to be inevitable. And each time the decrees of "fate" are avoided through a change in circumstances. It is precisely Clotaldo's awareness of the fragility of human circumstance that prevents his being vulnerable to the apparent dictates of fate.

Clarín: The Lesson Unlearned

Clarín is the only truly tragic character in *La vida es sueño*. He is the only one of those characters who mistake appearance for reality who undergoes no spiritual enlightenment.

Clarín is an opportunist. At the very beginning of the play, when he and Rosaura come upon Segismundo in the tower, Clarín urges Rosaura to say it is Clotaldo who is arriving, because he thinks that will insure their being well received.

human. *Disputaciones*, III, p. 141. He then distinguishes among *hado, azar*, and *fortuna: hado* implies a necessary cause-effect relationship: *azar* focuses on the effect rather than the cause and includes cases in which the cause is unknown, out of the control of the sufferer of the effect, or one of many, thus leaving the sufferer of the effect uncertain as to the cause; *fortuna* implies accident or unknown cause. *Disputaciones*, III, p. 442-448.

Then, faced with Segismundo's fury, Clarín grabs at the first "out" he can find. If the prisoner is angry at his being overheard, Clarín will say he cannot hear.

Clarín's down-to-earth opportunism provides comic relief, but his attitude illustrates a theme basic to the play: the individual who grasps at appearances is forever victim of the circumstances. Characters such as Clarín must constantly jump from one quick solution to another in order to avoid being trapped. Unable to face any situation honestly, they are always dupes of ever changing appearances.

Clarín's opportunism is partially the result of his unwillingness to accept his role in society. Just as the prince must learn to accept his role and define himself within it, so must the valet. In the second act, Clarín tries to advance his position at Court by blackmailing Clotaldo. Clarín has guessed the relationship between the older man and Rosaura and becomes Clotaldo's valet by threatening to publicize it.

Clarín resorts not only to blackmail, but also to adulation to advance his station. Seeing Segismundo in a position of power, he sets out to win his favor. While others stand up to the arrogant prince, Clarín fawns on him even when he behaves scandalously. But the unforeseen occurs. Circumstances change. Clarín's opportunism turns against him when Segismundo is returned to the tower. Clarín, too, is thrown into prison because he knows too much.

Even before Segismundo, Clarín sees that the tower symbolizes death. He realizes that glory is transient:

> No acabes de dispertar,
> Segismundo, para verte
> perder, trocada la suerte,
> siendo tu gloria fingida,
> una sombra de la vida
> y una llama de la muerte.
>
> (Segunda jornada, 1036-1041).

But Clarín applies his observations to Segismundo, without considering that he, too, must one day face death. He is taken unawares when Clotaldo has him thrown into the cell with the prince.

Segismundo learns from his imprisonment, but Clarín does not. When soldiers come looking for their prince, Clarín responds with his customary opportunism. He pretends to be the prince they are looking for. When he is found out and the scheme turns against him, he alters his story to fit the circumstances:

> ¿Yo Segismundo? Eso niego.
> Vosotros fuisteis los que
> me segismundesasteis.
>
> (Tercera jornada, 84-86)

Later on in the third act, Rosaura's presence provides Clarín with yet another occasion for trying blackmail. He hopes to escape from the prison by menacing to reveal her identity (Tercera jornada, 838-840). His cheeky proposition is interrupted by the arrival of soldiers. Clarín, as usual, thinks first of his own interests and decides to use the opportunity to escape. No sense of duty, no feeling of responsibility influences Clarín's actions. While his experience in the tower has made Segismundo aware of the illusive nature of life, Clarín believes he can go on trusting appearances and avoiding confrontation with his own mortality. He escapes from the tower certain he will avoid the perils of battle. But there is no escaping death. Clarín is hit by a stray bullet. He had closed his eyes to the lesson of the tower; now he is confronted with the absurdity of an unexpected, meaningless death.

Clarín awakens at last to the emptiness of his pretentions. But now it is too late for him to mend his ways. It is too late for him to prepare for a meaningful death by living a meaningful life. While Segismundo learned the lesson in time to give new direction and significance to his life, Clarín did not.

230

Form and Content of *La vida es sueño*

The three acts of *La vida es sueño* might be described as exposition, confrontation and unification. In the first, the two characters central to the two parallel plots, Rosaura and Segismundo, define their predicaments. The act is constructed almost perfectly symmetrically: each of the two major characters appears and reveals his inner feelings; the two meet; each of the two clarifies his situation with Clotaldo. The act ends with the scenes at Court, which further clarify the situations of each and provide a sort of preview of the coming act. The first *jornada* could be represented graphically as follows:

Rosaura reveals her feelings	Segismundo reveals his feelings	Segismundo and Rosaura meet	Segismundo clarifies with Clotaldo	Rosaura clarifies with Clotaldo	Scenes at Court (further clarification)

The exposition is made not only through the content of the text, but also through the scenery and costumes. Rosaura is dressed as a gentleman. She is playing a masculine role, for she is actively engaged in the restoration of her honor. What is more, she is dressed as a courtier and is accompanied by a valet. She brings into the turbulent world of the emotions —represented by the landscape— the refinement of the Court. Her language, like her dress, is refined. On the exterior, she is restrained and polished. On the inside, she is passionate and violent. Segismundo is in a sense the reverse of Rosaura. He is enchained and dressed in skins. On the exterior, he is brutish and primitive. But his soliloquy reveals that on the inside he is capable of lofty sentiments and complex reasoning. Both, then, reflect the duality of human nature. Both illustrate one of the central themes of the play: the deceptive nature of appearances. Segismundo is in reality more than he appears to be: he is not a brute but a potential man. Rosaura is in reality less than she appears to be: she is

231

not a man but a woman.[46] The duality of Segismundo's nature is further represented visually by his home: the primitive-looking tower scarcely distinguishable from the landscape, but with a light inside.

It is on this terrain of intense emotions that Segismundo and Rosaura meet. Both are the center of separate dramas. Both are victims. Segismundo and Rosaura, partners in suffering, are attracted to one another. Rosaura's violence is tempered by compassion for the imprisoned prince. Segismundo's is tempered by love. But Segismundo and Rosaura are not yet ready for one another. Neither is a complete, integrated human being. Still, both are purified by the encounter. Segismundo, especially, is for a moment lifted out of his agony and elevated toward something beyond himself.

Following the encounter between Rosaura and Segismundo, the prince's situation is partially clarified by Clotaldo, who hints somewhat vaguely that he has been imprisoned because of an astrological prediction. Clotaldo then confronts Rosaura, who partially clarifies her own situation by explaining she has come to Poland to avenge an affront and by producing the sword that reveals she is Clotaldo's offspring.

These scenes are followed by the episodes at Court in which Segismundo's situation is completely clarified by Basilio, who explains why his son has been imprisoned, and Rosaura's situation is completely clarified by Rosaura herself, who somewhat obliquely explains to Clotaldo that she is a woman and has been offended by Astolfo.

The second act of the play is characterized by confrontation. Here, again, there is a kind of symmetry. Segismundo experiences a succession of conflicts until at last he comes face

---

[46] On the position of women in seventeenth-century Spanish Society and as depicted in Golden Age drama, see McKendrick, *Woman and Society in the Spanish Drama of the Golden Age.*

to face with Basilio, whom he openly accuses, giving rein to his violent passion.

This scene is followed by a meeting with Rosaura, which is in a sense exactly the reverse of their encounter in the first act.

There, they were surrounded by confusion and violence, by primitive surroundings. They awoke in each other something purifying, uplifting. Here, they are surrounded by courtly pomp and affectation, by an atmosphere of refined restraint. But now they awaken in each other emotions that drag them downward, into the depths of their passions. Segismundo yields to lust; Rosaura, to anger. While in the first act the prince showed temporary violence, then restraint, here he shows temporary retraint, then violence.

Segismundo's outburst is followed by another confrontation, this one between Rosaura and Astolfo. As in the case of Segismundo and Basilio, Rosaura meets her victimizer face to face and accuses him openly.

The act ends with the scenes in prison, the place of Segismundo's awakening, which provide a sort of preview of the next act. The second act could be represented graphically as follows:

Segismundo accuses his victimizer	Segismundo meets Rosaura	Rosaura accuses her victimizer	Scenes in the tower

The second act is nearly the reverse of the first. The first act takes place in the tower, in surroundings reflecting violent passions. It is highlighted, almost at the beginning, by Segismundo's long soliloquy on freedom, which reveals both the prince's exaltation and his reasonableness. The act is further highlighted by the meeting with Rosaura, which momen-

233

tarily lifts the prince out of his tortured environment. It ends with an abrupt switch to the Court, pointing the way to the next act. The second act takes place at Court, in refined surroundings. It is highlighted by a number of violent confrontations that contrast with the environment. Just as there was humanity hidden in the ruggedness of the countryside, there is brutishness hidden in the refinement of the Court. One of the highlights of the act is Segismundo's meeting with Rosaura, which represents a downward movement into the realm of the animal, out of the realm of the civilized —precisely the opposite of what happened in the first act. The first act ended with an abrupt change of environment; so does the second. The second act ends where the first began, in the tower, with a long soliloquy by Segismundo. But whereas in the first act the prince was exalted and immature, now he is subdued and maturing. The first two acts offer not only symmetry within themselves, but certain parallels with one another with regard to the action.

The third act is characterized by unification. It is in this act that problems are resolved: Segismundo tempers his passion and controls his will; Basilio is humbled; Rosaura retrieves her honor. This act, like the first two, contains certain internal symmetry. It begins with Segismundo's declaration of purpose: first with his renunciation of the world, then with his acceptance of his role. This section culminates with his first proof of his good intentions: he allows Clotaldo to join Basilio in battle. These scenes are paralleled by others in which Clarín declares his intention to pass himself off as Segismundo. Next comes Rosaura's declaration of intentions. She tells Clotaldo she will defy reason in her quest for vengeance. The turning point of the acts is the meeting between Rosaura and Segismundo. Here the two main plots converge. Segismundo will be instrumental in helping Rosaura retrieve her honor. Rosaura will be instrumental in Segismundo's conversion. Until now Segismundo fluctuates between resignation and aggressiveness. Once he has conquered his passion for Rosaura, he remains firm in his commitment to

234

gain salvation through good deeds and the periods of vacillation are over. Segismundo's final *desengaño* is paralleled, as was his declaration of purpose, by Clarín's actions. It is now that Clarín meets with the final *desengaño* of death. Segismundo is successful in restructuring his life; Clarín, because of his own selfish opportunism, is not. In the final scenes, first Segismundo's problem is resolved through his conqueust and forgiveness of his father; then Rosaura's is solved, through Segismundo's offering her in marriage to Astolfo. The entire act could be shown graphically as follows:

Segismundo's declaration of purpose	Rosaura's declaration of purpose	Segismundo's meeting with Rosaura pointing to the restructuring of his life	Resolution of Segismundo's problem	Resolution of Rosaura's problem
Clarín's parallel action		Clarín's death		

As in the first two acts, the settings reflect the content. The section including Segismundo's declaration of purpose and Clarín's parallel action takes place in the tower. It is significant that Segismundo returns to his initial confinement for a number of reasons. In order to be reborn, Segismundo must return to the womb. His being thrust into the Court with no previous experience or guidance represented a kind of premature, imperfect birth. Self-control, moderation, and maturity cannot be imposed on an individual from the outside. They must develop from within. Segismundo must return to the tower because he must return to himself in order to conquer his will.

The scenes involving Rosaura's declaration of purpose take place at Court. Rosaura's predicament is social. Her problem is not to conquer her passions but to retrieve her honor. It is fitting that the situation be redefined precisely in that setting that represents the epitome of social convention: the Court.

235

The last scenes take place on the battlefield. It is precisely now that Segismundo engages in battle in a moral sense. Until now he has wavered. Now he is determined to define himself through his good deeds. Rosaura, too, is now actively engaged in battle. Until this moment she had merely declared her intentions. On the battlefield she actively solicits Segismundo's aid and asks him to undertake the restoration of her honor by force.

La vida es sueño is structured around three almost perfectly symmetrical acts, each of which is highlighted by a meeting between Rosaura and Segismundo. The play as a whole also reflects a certain symmetry. The first act takes place principally in a rustic setting, with the last scenes at Court pointing toward the next act; the second, principally at Court, with the last scenes in the country pointing toward the third act. The last act contains first scenes in the country, then scenes at court, with the culmination taking place in the country, on the battlefield, representing Segismundo's final moral victory over himself. The graphic representation is shown below:

Exposition		Confrontation		Unification			
Country	C o u→ r t	Court	C o u→ n t r y	C o u n t r y	C o u r t		Country

Calderón's best known and perhaps greatest philosophical work is also one of his most carefully structured, with every element —action, setting, costume, language, form— contributing to the message conveyed by the content of the text.

236

Conclusion

Some of the themes most fundamental to existentialist thought are treated by Calderón in *La vida es sueño*. The most basic of these is the relationship between existence and freedom. As E. M. Wilson has explained, existence itself is never thrown into question in Calderón's play. The metaphor of the dream refers to *what* man is, not to the fact that he is. But existence without freedom is meaningless. Roquentin, in Sartre's *La Nausée*, realizes that his existence is no more significant than that of a root or a bench if he does not himself give it meaning. Segismundo, locked in his tower, *exists*, but in an existential sense we cannot say he *lives*, for he cannot give form and meaning to his life until he is free to perform those acts by which he will define himself —in society as worthy or unworthy of respect, before God as worthy or unworthy of salvation.

Life, understood in these terms, is preparation for judgment. Goetz, in Sartre's *Le Diable et le bon Dieu*, remarks, "...j'ai besoin qu'on me juge... Je ne vois plus mon âme parce que j'ai le nez dessus: il faut que quelqu'un me prête ses yeux.[47] Man's inability to judge himself is the result of the incertainty in which he is forced to act. Goetz 'cannot see his soul for his nose" in the sense that he cannot be sure of his motives and intentions. He needs someone to judge his acts objectively. For Calderón, judgment does not correspond to a need experienced by man, but to the very nature of human existence. It is the unavoidable destiny of all men to die and appear before their Creator for judgment. But Calderón's characters, too, must act in an atmosphere of uncertainty, due to the deceptive nature of the appearances with which they are constantly confronted. They must act having only their conscience as their guide. Maturity consists precisely in learning to accept uncertainty, and acting in spite of it. It is only when Segismundo learns to look at life as an "illusion" or,

[47] *Le Diable et le bon Dieu,* p. 220.

237

"frenzy," or, in modern terms, as an "absurdity," that he comprehends that it is up to him to give his own life meaning. Uncertainty is not an easy thing to accept. The temptation to lull oneself into intellectual certainty and consequently bad faith is one against which Segismundo must battle throughout most of the play. And once uncertainty is accepted, the spectre of futility looms before man and tempts him to withdraw from life. Segismundo, like Goetz, at first rejects the call of the rebel soldiers who summon him to the front. Segismundo retires to his tower; Goetz talks of becoming a monk. Before the penetrating eyes of Heinrich, Goetz says, "...je préfère le désespoir à l'incertitude."[48] It is easier to accept will-lessness and damnation than to accept one's responsibility in an atmosphere of uncertainty. It is easier to hide from an absurd world than to function within it.

But to withdraw is to succumb to bad faith. It is to deny one's will. The inescapability of judgment makes it imperative that every individual attempt to give meaning to his life through his acts. Heinrich tells Goetz; "...la terre est apparence: il y a le Ciel et l'Enfer, c'est tout."[49] The world is absurdity, appearance, but judgment is real. Salvation and damnation —understood either in a social or a religious sense— are real and they are eternal. That is why Heinrich tells Goetz, "La mort, c'est un attrape-nigaud pour les familles; pour le défunt, tout continue."[50] To withdraw is to deliver oneself to absurdity, to meaninglessness. To live, rather than merely to exist, is man's means of affirming himself against them. Segismundo, like Goetz, must take command of his army.

The role of the parent is precisely to make this self-affirmation possible by creating an awareness of the nature of the world and of the individual will. When the parent shirks his responsibility, a conflict may arise between the parent,

[48] *Le Diable,* p. 221.
[49] *Le Diable,* p. 226.
[50] *Le Diable,* p. 226.

who attempts to impose his own will on his offspring, and the offspring, who seeks to assert himself and give meaning to his own life. This is what happens in *La vida es sueño*. This is also what happens in Jean Anouilh's *Antigones*. Here the conflict is between Crion, the king, and his niece, Antigones, who defies her uncle's order that her dead insurgent brother should not be buried with honor. Crion, like Basilio, feels compelled by outside forces to sentence Antigones to severe punishment. Basilio's excuse is the stars; Crion's is his political position. Antigones, like Segismundo, confronts the adult in question with his bad faith, and shows him that what he regards as determining forces do not determine at all. Antigones points out to Crion that he is free to disregard or change the laws he himself made. Segismundo alleges that it is Basilio, and not the stars, who is responsible for the unfortunate situation in which the young man finds himself.

Pitted against their victimizers, both Antigones and Segismundo become aware of the absurd. Antigones learns that the corpse Crion has prevented from being buried may or may not be that of her brother; what appears to be may not be at all. Segismundo learns that his experiences at Court may have only been dreamed; here, too, what appears to be may or may not be at all. For Antigones, the question revolves around the action of her uncle. For Segismundo, it revolves around not only the scheme of Basilio, but also around the unreliability of the senses and the illusory nature of life in general. Still, in spite of —or, more correctly, precisely because of— the absurdity which surrounds them, both Antigones and Segismundo must rebel and give meaning to their lives. Antigones chooses a heroic death, which she believes will give meaning to her own existence and to her brother's dishonor. Segismundo chooses to relinquish his inclinations toward Rosaura and to victory over Basilio in order to accomplish the good deeds he believes will define him as worthy of salvation in the eyes of God.

Both Calderón and Anouilh use similar techniques in the

development of their themes: they choose works or topics that deal specifically with determinism and through the action and dialogue show that what seems to be determinism is actually the result of certain attitudes adopted by the characters. Anouilh, working with the classical Greek tragedy *Antigones* transforms it into a declaration of freedom of the will. Calderón, working with popular beliefs about astrology, does the same. In both cases, the predictions stated at the beginning of the dramas *do* come true, but not because of supernatural intervention. Crion is not determined by the Gods, but by his own will. It is his bad faith and not his political position that made his condemnation of Antigones inevitable. Basilio's hands are bound, not by the stars, but by his belief in astrology. Both push their victims into situations in which they must rebel violently in order to assert themselves as individuals. The causes and effects are comprehensible within an entirely rational framework, but the individuals Basilio and Crion are too blinded by their own faith to see them.

La vida es sueño is different from the plays previously analyzed in this study in that it presents an example of a character who develops and changes throughout the action of the play. It is *La vida es sueño* that best illustrates Calderón's concept of man's ability to reach an awareness of himself and to give direction to his own life. In this sense, it is Calderón's most existential play.

CHAPTER V

REASON AND THE QUEST FOR THE UNKNOWN GOD: *EL MAGICO PRODIGIOSO*

Cipriano's Conversion, Step I: Reason vs. the Will to Rationalize

Calderón's *El mágico prodigioso* is based on the story of Saints Cyprian and Justina of Antioch.[1] In it, the magician Cyprian attempts to seduce the Christian woman Justina by resorting to necromancy. Having failed, he realizes the futility of his craft, converts to Christianity and dies a martyr.

In *El mágico prodigioso*, Cipriano's conversion is accomplished in three steps: in the first, Cipriano postulates the existence of God through means of reason; in the second, he discovers the futility of temporal pleasures through experience; in the third, he discovers God through divine revelation made possible through love and faith.

Like the other plays analyzed thus far, *El mágico prodigioso*

---

[1] There has been some question as to the authenticity of Calderón's authorship of *El mágico prodigioso*. In "Calderón y *El mágico prodigioso*," *HE*, 19 (1951), pp. 11-36 and 93-103, H. C. Heaton claims the Yepes version in a *refundición* of an earlier play which may or may not have been written by Calderón. Albert E. Sloman refutes Heaton's allegation in *"El mágico prodigioso*: Calderón Defended Against the Charge of Theft" *HR*, 20 (1952), 212-222.

241

centers around a character beset by confusion. As the play opens, Cipriano is meditating on Pliny's definition of God —"Dios es una bondad suma,/ una esencia, una sustancia,/ todo vista, todo manos"— which he finds mysterious and obscure. Unlike characters such as Aureliano, don Lope and Segismundo, Cipriano at this point recognizes the unfulfilling nature of temporal values and rejects them. This is made clear in two episodes. In the first, Cipriano sends his servants Moscón and Clarín off to the festivities at Antioch without him, choosing rather to search for the message in the confusing passages of Pliny. In the second, Cipriano breaks up a duel of honor between his friends Lelio and Floro, arguing that such a duel will only defame the lady whom they both love. He uses reason to dissuade them from taking vegeance on one another and displays perceptiveness regarding the workings of honor when he explains that dueling will not only cause scandal, but will fail to resolve the argument, since the death of one of the adversaries will cause further accusations, further vegeance and further scandals, harming both Justina, the lady in question, and the suitors. He therefore urges Lelio and Floro to ask Justina to choose between them and offers himself as an intermediary.

Rather than worldly goods such as sensual pleasures or honor, Cipriano seeks truth.[2] As he sits alone in the woods by the edge of the sea, meditating on his texts, he is accosted by a stranger, the Devil, disguised as a gentleman traveller. The role of the Devil in *El mágico prodigioso* has been discussed extensively by Alexander Parker, who, basing himself on the Thomistic observations on the nature of ignorance, concludes: "He (the Devil) represents that defect of

___

[2] Everett W. Hesse argues convincingly that truth is the connecting link between the dual plots of *El mágico prodigioso*, the first involving Cipriano's conversion and the second his romantic attraction toward Justina: Cipriano finds the true God through his true love for Justina. See "The Function of the Romantic Action in *El mágico prodigioso*," *Bulletin of the Comediantes*, 17, No. 1 (1965), pp. 5-7.

242

reason which is the ignorance that, through voluntary inattention to a truth that is accessible and which it is necessary to know, leads the will to make a wrong choice".[3] Parker sees as the key to the comprehension of the play the Devil's observation:

> Esa es la ignorancia
> a la vista de las ciencias,
> no saber aprovecharlas,

(Primera jornada, 119-121)

The point, is, of course, that the truth is accessible to the seeker who searches with an open mind, but not to the individual who picks and chooses evidence in accordance with preconceived ideas. In order to achieve truth, one must be willing to see both sides of the question. The Devil, then, represents what we have called elsewhere the will to rationalize —the tendency to see only what one wants to see or to select and mold the available evidence to fit one's goals.

The Devil is a complex dramatic figure. On the one hand, he is a real character, corresponding to a concrete theological entity.[4] On the other, he is a projection of each of the other characters of the play. The success of *El mágico prodigioso* depends, at least partially, on Calderón's ability to make the Devil credible on both planes.

At the beginning of the first act, Cipriano is on his way to discovering the answers to his questions concerning God. He uses reason correctly: to ask questions. He has an open mind and makes no attempt to adjust evidence for his own purposes. He is not guilty of any "voluntary inattention to a truth that is accessible." But the Devil's presence represents a po-

---

[3] "The Devil in the Drama of Calderón", in *Critical Essays on the Theater of Calderón,* ed. by Bruce W. Wardropper, p. 19.

[4] Saint Augustine warns specifically against entering into partnership with the Devil in order to attain knowledge. *On Christian Doctrine,* II, 39 (Chicago: Encyclopedia Britannica, 1952) p. 654.

tential danger in Cipriano's reasoning —the same danger to which Aurealiano, Cosme, don Lope, Segismundo and Basilio succumb.

With an open mind, Cipriano contends with the Devil —that is, with his own will to rationalize—. He enters into a formal debate with himself in which he demolishes his own preconceived notions regarding the authenticity of the Roman gods he has always accepted. Reason leads him to the postulation of a First Cause which fits Pliny's description; yet, he cannot conceive of the nature of this unknown God. The Devil, unable to rebuke Cipriano's arguments, leaves. Reason has triumphed over the will to rationalize.

It is significant that in this episode the Devil wears a disguise and that Cipriano does not recognize him for who he is. [5] The Devil's disguise is the artistic device by which Calderón represents a point of theology: man cannot see the Devil until, by an act of his own will, he has sinned. The Devil is merely a potential with which sin —the result of man's yielding to his own misguided will— makes direct confrontation possible. In the same way, an individual does not adopt a position of "good faith" or of "bad faith" con-

---

[5] In *No hay más fortuna que Dios,* Bien and Mal appear in disguises. Most of the characters, preoccupied with their own selfish concerns, remain blind or oblivious to Bien. Nevertheless, Bien remains in the world:

> pero aun con todo, a la mira
> estaré, mostrando en esto
> que ellos son los que me apartan
> y no soy yo el que me ausento.

> (1352-1355)

The point is that good is attainable, but it is up to the individual to recognize it. It is man's nature to be attracted to the good, although he may be sidetracked by his own willful illusions. The Devil, counting on the fact that men are easily led astray, argues that the advantage in the battle between good and evil is his:

244

sciously, but as a result of his own honest or dishonest approach to the evidence confronting him.[6]

Lelio and Floro: The Will to Rationalize vs. Reason

Lelio and Floro, unlike Cipriano, seek satisfaction in worldly goods and adhere to the honor code. While Cipriano uses

> Sí, mas la ventaja es mía;
> pues a los humanos ojos
> más cerca está el Mal que el Bien. (654-656)

But Justicia sets the record straight when she argues:

> A quien mirare ambicioso
> Bien y Mal, porque en la esencia
> más lo está el Bien. (657-659)

Only the ambitious, presumptuous person who considers his own material welfare above all mistakes good and evil. Alexander Parker writes in reference to these lines: "Good is intrisically more desireable; and this fact is evident to the morally clearsighted, who have no selfish bias." *No hay más fortuna que Dios*, ed. A. A. Parker, (Manchester: University of Manchester Press) 1962, p. 64.

Justicia's words have their basis in the belief that all created things are good and tend to good, evil being a privation, imperfection or disorder brought about by free will.

The doctrine of the nonsubstantiality or negative character of evil has its sources in the teachings of both Saint Augustine and Saint Thomas and was explained by Suárez in his *Disputaciones:* "...el mal de culpa propiamente es un mal del hombre en cuanto que es racional y usa del libre arbitrio; y por ello no siempre se dice de sola la privación, sino también del acto positivo, pero con todo no por razón de sólo lo positivo sino en cuanto que carece de la debida rectitud. Por consiguiente, este mal por razón del acto que incluye puede oponerse contrariamente al acto bueno o de virtud, y lo mismo proporcionalmente hay que decir acerca de los hábitos. Y del mismo modo, el mismo acto se dice contrario a la razón porque carece de la debida rectitud; por lo cual no sólo es malo porque excluye del sujeto al acto contrario o al hábito bueno (lo cual parece que se supone en los argumentos), sino porque él mismo es disconforme con la naturaleza racional, y es disconforme no por la entidad positiva precisa, sino en cuanto que ésta es soporte de una carencia de la rectitud debida..." Suárez, *Disputaciones,* Vol. II, pp. 291-292.

[6] See Chapter 1, Note 16.

245

reason to point out the futility of an honor duel, Lelio and Floro distort reason in order to prove that no matter which of them Justina may prefer, there will be cause for vengeance:

> luego excusada
> acción es que ello lo diga,
> pues con cualquier circunstancia
> hemos en apelación
> de volver a las espadas
> (Primera jornada, 457-461)

That is, Lelio and Floro rationalize dueling. Once honor is accepted as a premise, vengance is always justifiable and truth is no longer an issue. There is no longer room for the kind of dialog Cipriano entertains with himself —or the Devil— regarding the Roman gods. Doubt must be discarded and all evidence arranged to warrant violence.

This difference in attitude explains why Lelio's and Floro's confrontation with the Devil is so different from Cipriano's. Prevented from dueling by their mutual friend, both suitors steal to Justina's house during the night. There, they wait underneath her balcony, the presence of each unknown to the other. The Devil, making the most of the occasion, leaps from the balcony and both Lelio and Floro, suspecting a betrayal on Justina's part, rush forward with bared swords. The duel is prevented once again by Cipriano's intervention. But the Devil has accomplished his purpose; he has sown the seeds of suspicion.

The Devil was unsuccessful in his confrontation with Cipriano because the latter combatted him with an open mind and a healthy reason. He is successful in his confrontation with Lelio and Floro for precisely the opposite reason: both are predisposed to interpret the evidence he presents to them in accordance with a preconceived idea. Lelio and Floro have closed minds; they have a system. Capitalizing on their

246

superstition, the Devil provides them with just enough fuel to ignite the senses and set the cogs' of fantasy spinning. When Lelio and Floro see the amorphous shadow they immediately latch on to the bit of information provided by the senses —in this case, sight— and interpret it as evidence that a man has been to Justina's room.

The Devil plays on appearances. For men of honor, the appearance of guilt is enough to justify vengeance. In this way, the Devil allows men of honor to rationalize sin. Rationalization is the act of explaining one's act —consciously or unconsciously— on grounds ostensible rational, but in reality only apparent. I results when reason is twisted or misrepresented in subservience to the will —in this case, the will to vengeance. It is reason contaminated by arrogance and pride, the sins of the Devil, and it occurs when the pretentious individual allows himself to pretend to know what he does not know at all.

The contrast between Cipriano's attitude and his friends' is represented visually by the contexts in which they find themselves in confrontation with the Devil. Cipriano is outdoors, in "la amena soledad" or an "apacible estancia," surrounded by "flores, rosas y plantas." He is at ease with himself, although confused about Pliny's definition of God. He meets the Devil in broad daylight. We know this because he has just told his servants to leave for the celebration in Antioch and not to return until the sun sets. Cipriano is surrounded by light because he is guided by the light of reason, even in the face of confusion. The openness of the atmosphere relfects Cipriano's openness of mind; it is not here that the Devil can work his magic.

Floro's and Lelio's first meeting with the Devil is, in contrast, at night, in an atmosphere of darkness and shadows. Lelio opens the scene with reference to the "oscura noche" which extends her "manto negro", over the "umbrales" where he is

247

hiding. Both men hear identified noises; both speak of violence and have their swords ready: It is in this atmosphere of murkiness and closed-mindedness that the Devil is effective.

Lelio's and Floro's second meeting with the Devil is similar to their first. Lelio enters Justina's house and, basing himself on the evidence of the shadow of what he believes to be a man jumping from her balcony, accuses her of unvirtuous conduct. The Devil, once again playing on Lelio's suspicious nature, appears and disappears. As before, the young man assumes Justina is betraying him and becomes jealous. Justina, defending herself against his false accusations, correctly identifies the shadow as a product of his fantasy:

> En el viento
> te finge tu fantasia
> ilusiones.
> (Segunda jornada, 1555-1557)

And when Lelio enters the room into which he thought he saw the shadow disappear, he finds nothing and is forced to admit that Justina is right:

> (Ap.) Ahora acabo de creer
> que sombra los celos hacen,
> (Segunda jornada, 1579-1580)

What follows is a series of misunderstandings resulting from Lelio's mistake. Lisandro, Justina's guardian, enters and Lelio is forced to hide. Next Floro enters, but he, too, is forced to hide when the maid announces the arrival of the Governor. Floro and Lelio confront each other and each assumes the other is Justina's lover. The episode ends when the Governor, who is Lelio's father, discovers the two young men and has them thrown into prison.

What Calderón illustrates through Lelio's and Floro's con-

248

frontations with the Devil is how the closed mind, resulting from an unhealthy will, distorts evidence and makes false assumptions until it involves the individual in a net of misunderstandings of potentially tragic consequences.

As was the case in Lelio's and Floro's first confrontation with the Devil, the episode takes place in a closed atmosphere of shadows and hiding.

Cipriano's Conversion, Step II: Experience and Futility

In the first half of the first act of *El mágico prodigioso,* Cipriano showed himself to be unmoved by sensual, temporal pleasures. Cipriano's first meeting with Justina on behalf of his friends Lelio and Floro causes a change in his attitude and initiates the second movement of the play. Cipriano's meeting with Justina ignites his senses and turns his head from his books to worldly pursuits. His change of heart is represented visually by his change in costume. During most of the first act he is dressed as a student. At the end of the act, he doffs his student's garments and asks for fancy clothes, a sword and feathers with which to adorn himself. Appearance is now important to him. He wishes to appeal to Justina's senses. In this second section of *El mágico prodigioso* Cipriano is no longer characterized as rational, but as sensual. It is sensual satisfaction, not spiritual elevation, he seeks from his relationship with Justina. And it is now the senses, not reason, to which he appeals for knowledge.

It is precisely because of this new sensuality that Cipriano cannot capture the message in Justina's words when, during their first meeting, she gives him the clue to her identity:

> porque es mi rigor de suerte,
> de suerte mis males fieros,
> que es imposible quereros,
> Cipriano, hasta la muerte.
>
> (Segunda jornada, 1100-1103)

249

Born to a Christian martyr and raised as a Christian by Lisandro in a city in which followers of her faith suffer severe harassment, Justina cannot give her love to any man until freed from persecution by death. But Cipriano seeks no message beyond what he hears, and interprets her words only in terms of his own goal. Gone is the delving mind capable of penetrating beyond the immediately obvious. He answers her in courtly language, revealing his new worldliness. He plays on the love-death metaphor which characterizes Renaissance love poetry and emphasizes his own sensuality.[7]

Once he has left Justina, Cipriano finds himself again in a state of utter confusion. But he no longer uses reason as a tool to seek his way out of the maze. He looks, rather, for quick, ready-made solutions. He finds one in necromancy. His state of mind is revealed in the passage which immediately precedes his second confrontation with the Devil:

> Confusa memoria mía,
> no tan poderosa estés,
> que me persuadas que es
> otra alma la que me guía.
>   Idólatra me cegué,
> ambicioso me perdí,
> porque una hermosura vi,
> porque una deidad miré:
>   y entre confusos desvelos
> de un equívoco rigor,
> conozco a quien tengo amor,
> y no de quien tengo celos.
>
> (Segunda jornada, 1176-1187)

The beginning of Cipriano's monologue reveals immediately that his contact with reality is no longer direct, but through

---

[7] See Chapter 4, p. 185-186.

the memory, in itself a representation or projection.[8] His memory is qualified as confused. This confused image of reality is now what guides him; it is so powerful he seems to be lead on by a soul other than his own.

In the next stanza the sensual nature of his outlook becomes still more evident. There are numerous references to sight; *cegué, hermosura, vi, miré* all involve sight. The reference to idolatry may be understood on two levels. In a literal sense, it is precisely because of his paganism and idolatry that Cipriano cannot marry the Christian Justina. On a symbolic level, it is precisely because of his materialism that he cannot attain her spiritually. An idolater is a person who worships the physical representation of a god —an image designed to appeal to the senses. What characterizes Cipriano during this second segment of the play is his inability to go beyond the senses.

The second line of the stanza picks up the theme of pride, the Devil's sin. This line, too, may be understood on both a literal and a symbolic level. On the first level, Cipriano "was lost" because of his ambition; that is, because he aimed too high, for the goddess Justina instead of for a mortal woman, his failure was inevitable. In terms of the symbolism of the play, it is the pride he displays in thinking he can mold the universe to his will by his manipulation of the occult that is responsible for his coming so close to perdition.

In the third stanza he returns to the themes of confusion and blindness. Here, confusion is associated with anxiety and

[8] The "representative" function of memory is described by Vives as follows: "Es la memoria aquella facultad del alma por la cual aquello que uno conoció mediante algún sentido externo o interno consérvalo en la mente. Así, pues, toda su actuación está vuelta hacia dentro, y la memoria es como la tabla que un pintor iluminó. Así como la tabla, mirada con los ojos, produce una noción, la memoria la realiza por los ojos del alma, que entiende o conoce." *Tratado*, p. 1185.

rigorousness. Cipriano is becoming the same kind of tortured, incomprehensible, willful character we have analyzed in reference to other plays. He is lead on by a jealousy without cause, bred on suspicion and nourished by unclear images embellished by the imagination.[9] He functions exactly as Lelio and Floro do in the scenes already discussed.

The senses stimulated, passion, thought and imagination ignite each other one by one in domino style:

> Y tanto aquesta pasión
> arrastra mi pensamiento
> tanto (¡ay de mí!) este tormento
> lleva mi imaginación,
>   que diera (despecho es loco,
> indigno de un noble ingenio)
> al más diabólico genio
> (harto al infierno provoco),
>   Ya rendido, y ya sujeto
> a penar y padecer,
> por gozar a esta mujer,
> diera el alma.
>   (Segunda jornada, 1188-1199)

Cipriano's monologue describes a complex psychological process by which the will sets the imagination in motion.[10] It is now, with the imagination functioning fully, that the Devil —the will to rationalize— appears and offers to teach Cipriano the occult sciences. For what is magic but a means by which to control natural events according to our own will? The Devil's presence represents man's unabashed pride in assuming he can willfully manipulate reality. Cipriano not only permits the Devil to make an entrée, but summons him forth by allowing will to manipulate reason.

[9] "Los celos nacen de los suspicaces y hace a la vez a los suspicaces y los hace sumamente propensos a la credulidad de todo lo peor." Vives, *Tratado*, p. 1298.
[10] See Vives, *Tratado*, Parte III.

252

The Devil appears in a new disguise, as victim of a shipwreck, cast upon the banks by an angry sea—a traditional image of man in the sea of life, tossed about by uncontrollable forces and plagued by confusion. The Devil obligates Cipriano's will by asking for his help, offering in return to teach him the art of black magic. That is, he gives Cipriano the opportunity to rationalize his acceptance of the offer. Cipriano knows, and says in the second stanza of the passage quoted above, that to enter into negotiations with the Devil is wrong. It is now that he engages in a "voluntary inattention to a truth". He closes his eyes to what he knows to be wrong and justifies his action to himself. He does not see the danger lurking in the Devil's offer because he chooses not to. This is the significance of the Devil's disguise and of his proposal.

To think of Cipriano as the unwitting victim of the Devil would be contrary to Catholic theology, especially as interpreted by Suárez,[11] perhaps the most influential Spanish theologian during Calderón's lifetime. Cipriano accepts the Devil's offer not out of friendship, but out of selfishness. He has a motive: to seduce Justina through necromancy. There is no doubt but that he accepts the Devil of his own free will:

> Demonio: ¿Ya me adquieres
> por tuyo?
> Cipriano: Con los brazos
> firme nuestra amistad eternos lazos.
> (Segunda jornada, 1424-1426)

Cipriano's voluntary blindness contrasts with the perceptiveness of his servants Moscón and Clarín, who "smell the sulpher" and "sniff the smoke" and comment half-

[11] "Con respecto a los ángeles, debe decirse que un ángel, por su natural virtud, no puede producir inmediatamente en el entendimiento una inmutación que lo haga pasar al juicio o acto segundo, ya que esto es exclusivo de Dios, su autor. Según ello, mucho menos podrá un ángel malo obligar al entendimiento a un asentimiento falso; lo más que podrá hacer será, valiéndose de sugestiones y persuasiones, inducir a un asentimiento falso por modo de enseñanza, aunque siempre le quedará al hombre la posibilidad de disentir o, por lo menos, de no asentir, si quiere." Suárez, *Disputaciones*, Vol. II, p. 196.

seriously throughout the second and third acts regarding the identity of their master's mysterious friend.[12]

The Devil's end of the bargain consists of producing Justina for Cipriano's enjoyment. Cipriano's reason balks at the proposal because he knows that the will is free and cannot be forced and that the Devil therefore cannot bring Justina to him without her consent:

> sobre el libre albedrío
> ni hay conjuros ni hay encantos.
> (Segunda jornada, 1086-1087)

He knows, too, that the doubting mind can perceive the clever illusions projected by a distorted will:

> Los engaños
> son para alegres amigos
> no para desconfiados.
> (Segunda jornada, 1905-1907)

But in this struggle between the reason and the will to rationalize, the latter proves triumphant. Cipriano allows his imagination free rein; he gives himself over to his senses. This is illustrated dramatically by the trick the Devil plays on Cipriano. He asks him what he sees in the distance and Cipriano answers that he sees a mountain. The Devil then makes him see the mountain move. Throughout the episode the point is the Devil's manipulation of the senses, not the actual movement of the mountain:

> ¡No *vi* más confuso asombro!
> ¡No *vi* prodigio más raro!
> (Segunda jornada, 1926-1927)

---

[12] Regarding the role of Moscón and Clarín, see Martin Franzbach, "Die 'Lustige Person' (gracioso) auf der spanischen Buhen und ihre Funktion, dargelegt and Calderón's *El mágico prodigioso*," *Die neueren Sprachen*, 14 (1965), 61-72, and Alexander Parker, "The Rôle of the Graciosos in *El mágico prodigioso*," in Hans Flasche, *Litterae hispanae et lusitanae*, Munich, 1968, pp. 317-330.

Then, still playing on the senses, the Devil makes Cipriano see the image of Justina sleeping.

The Devil's magic represents the unhealthy will projecting images in accordance with its own inclinations. When Cipriano attempts to verify whether or not the image of Justina corresponds to any objective reality, the scene immediately disappears. He is left with the choice of doubting and rejecting what he has seen or accepting it; that is, it is up to him whether he signs the contract with the Devil or not. The element of choice persists throughout the play. Once Cipriano chooses to sign the contract, however, he becomes the victim of his own willfulness and converts himself, albeit unwittingly —for he still is unaware of the Devil's true identity— into another man of "bad faith". The signing of the document represents that moment at which the individual rejects reason and puts it at the service of the will; it is that moment in which he allows himself to be blinded or deceived. This voluntary blindness is once again represented dramatically by darkness: the Devil leads Cipriano to a cave, and it is there that the lessons in black magic take place.

But even after an individual has allowed himself to be deceived, he is capable of repentence and regeneration.[13] He is choiceless only as long as he allows himself to be so. At the beginning of the third act, Cipriano wanders of his own free will out of the cave and into the sunlight, much to the Devil's displeasure. Cipriano's passage from the darkness of the cave to the light of day represents dramatically his passage from the darkness of sin and spiritual ignorance to the light of

[13] The ability of man to redirect his life by a conscious choice was topical in seventeenth-century Spanish drama and central to the plots of many plays, for example, Calderón's *La vida es sueño* (see Chapter 4) and Tirso de Molina's *El burlador de Sevilla*. On the individual's ability to correct his own false judgments Suárez clarifies: "el entendimiento, siempre que profiere un juicio falso, puede sufrir mutación y proferir uno verdadero." *Disputaciones*, Vol. II, p. 195.

purity and reason. The Devil is angry with Cipriano because his leaving the cave foretells his coming conversion. The Devil knows he is losing his grip on his pupil.

Since the Devil's magic rests only in his ability to play on a receptive will by mobilizing the senses and the imagination, he cannot actually change reality but represents, rather, man's tendency to distort it.[14] The most dramatic illustration of this is the episode in which, having completed his apprenticeship with the Devil, Cipriano asks him to comply with his side of the agreement and to produce Justina. The best the Devil can do is manipulate representations and images. Once again working in an atmosphere of darkness and shadows, the Devil produces the illusion of Justina for Cipriano. But when the young man examines what the Devil has given him in the light —representing, of course, the light of his own reason— he discovers the Devil has failed to produce the promised prize. Instead of Justina, Cipriano is left holding a drab, shrouded skeleton.

Face to face with his own illusion, Cipriano is forced to acknowledge it is exactly that: an illusion. Experience teaches him the deceptive nature of the projections of the will.

---

[14] In *Los encantos de la culpa,* Calderón illustrates allegorically the tendency of the senses to get out of hand and plunge man into vice when they go uncontrolled by Understanding. In this *auto* Entendimiento admonishes Ulises for succumbing to the enticements offerred by the senses:

> ¿Así
> Ulises, te has olvidado
> de ti mismo? ¿Así entregado
> a unos placeres fingidos,
> que sin mí y con tus Sentidos
> aquí vives engañado?

(1136-1142)

Ulises, like Cipriano, loses control of himself by allowing his will to be swayed by representations nourished by the senses. Cf. Vives. *Tratado,* pp. 1278-1289 and Suárez, *Disputaciones,* Vol. II, pp. 185ff.

But it is more than simply the illusory quality of his own particular daydream that Cipriano is forced to confront, for his experience brings him headlong into confrontation with the very concept of nothingness. He is forced to ask himself what there is outside of his own projection and his own particular vision of the world. He senses in the emptiness of his illusion the terrible emptiness of death; he perceives "un trasunto/de la muerte" (III, 2566-2567). This is the significance of the skeleton he is left holding in place of Justina. And he surmises that all worldly pleasure and values are of the same nature as his own dream. This is the significance of the skeleton's words:

> Así, Cipriano, son
> todas las glorias del mundo.
>
> (Tercera jornada, 2547-48)

Once he understands the transient nature of worldly goods, Cipriano is once again able to reject the Devil. He returns to the rational attitude he held at the beginning of the play and debates with his adversary. Now he is able to discard his inclination to remold reality according to his will. Yet he cannot accept the apparent futility of life which seems to be the obvious conclusion to be drawn from his experience. He reasons there must be something beyond the nothingness confronting him. But he does not alone postulate the existence of the Christian God. What brings Cipriano to knowledge of the Christian God is his love for Justina.

Once Cipriano has accepted the Christian God, he reasons that since He gave Justina strength to resist the temptation of the Devil, He could also free him, Cipriano, of the contract he has signed in blood. Hearing his student call out to the God of the Christians, the Devil hurls him away. Experience and reason have taught Cipriano humility. Love has given him faith. Gone is the will to rationalize. This is the significance of the Devil's exit.

257

Justina and the Devil: Strength through Faith

Just as the other characters in the play must contend with their own will to rationalize, so must Justina. The Devil knows he cannot force her will, but he can work on her senses and ignite her imagination, hoping her will will be swayed by its own projection:

> aunque el gran poder mío
> no puede hacer vasallo un albedrío,
> puede representalle
> tan extraños deleites, que se halle
> empeñado a buscallos,
> y inclinarlos podré, si no forzallos.
>
> (Tercera jornada, 2118-2123)

The Devil storms Justina with erotic fantasies. The words *fantasía* and *fantasma* occur repeatedly in his vocabulary. The word *imaginar* and its derivatives occur repeatedly in hers:

> Demonio: De mil torpes *fantasmas* que en el viento
> su casto pensamiento
> hoy se informe, su honesta *fantasía*
> se llene;
> (Tercera jornada, 2172-2175)

> Justina: Calla, ruiseñor; no aquí
> *imaginar* me hagas ya,
> (Tercera jornada, 2214-2215)
> Pesada *imaginación.*
> (Tercera jornada, 2219)

The Devil's purpose is, of course, to represent sensual pleasure as so attractive to Justina that she loses control of her will and wants Cirpiano as much as he wants her. It is the only way he will be able to meet the terms of his contract with Cipriano. Justina does feel strangely attracted to Cipriano, but she knows her own strength. She correctly identifies the Devil as a projection of her own confused fantasy:

> ¿Eres monstruo que ha formado
> mi confuso desvarío?
> (Tercera jornada, 2285-2286)

Once she has recognized the enemy, she can use her free will to reject him:

> Pues no lograrás tu intento;
> que esta pena, esta pasión
> que afligió mi pensamiento,
> llevó la imaginación
> pero no el consentimiento.
> (Tercera jornada, 2292-2295)

Justina is not bound, just as Cipriano was not bound, to sign a contract with the Devil —that is, to allow her will to be swayed by its own projections. The Devil's efforts to convince her otherwise are ineffective because she knows a licentious thought in itself does not constitute a sin. She knows man is defined by his acts, not merely by his thoughts. As long as she maintains control over her acts, she is able to combat the Devil. She is not responsible for the images her will projects, but she alone is responsible for what she does about them:

> que aunque es llano'
> que el pensar es empezar,
> no está en mi mano el pensar
> y está el obrar en mi mano.
> (Tercera jornada, 2303-2306)

Justina understands what Cipriano failed to grasp, that man need not succumb to his will. This is the significance of the scene in which the Devil tries to move Justina physically and is unable to. It is precisely the point of free will that it cannot be forced:

> No fuera libre albedrío
> si se dejara forzar.
> (Tercera jornada, 2320-2321)

259

The Devil threatens to leave her defamed for life by playing on the suspicions of others if she fails to do his bidding, but she recognizes that the appearance of honor is not honor:

> Desa ofensa al cielo apelo,
> porque desvanezca el cielo
> la apariencia de mi fama,
> bien como al aire la llama,
> bien como la flor al hielo.
>
> (Tercera jornada, 2347-2351)

It is here, in a play constructed in a specifically Christian context, and not in the honor plays, that Calderón presents a solution to the honor problem. It is not by seeking vengeance but by focusing on a higher sense of honor that Justina answers the Devil. For characters such as don Lope and don Luis, there is no solution other than violence, but Justina finds a solution to the unwarranted accusations against her virtue in faith. She can appeal to heaven for protection.

What gives Justina her immense strength in her combat with the Devil is her faith. As a Christian, she can appeal to the God who is until the end of the play unknown to Cipriano. Caught in a siege of passion, she leaves her home for the cleansing atmosphere of the small secret church maintained by the Christian community of Antioch.

The erotic images which moved Cipriano do not succeed in moving Justina. The Devil cannot produce a real woman for his apprentice to make love to. Cipriano is left with his illusions and dreams. Justina's faith prevents her from being put in the same position.

Cipriano's Conversion, Step III: Revelation through Love

Reason and experience initiate Cipriano's conversion, but they alone cannot accomplish the task.[15] Salvation is achieved through love, the perfect love of God for man which makes possible the miracle of Revelation. It is through his love for Justina, divorced now from the exclusively sensual desire which characterized his early attraction toward her, that Cipriano discovers divine love.

[15] In *El día mayor de los días* Calderón illustrates allegorically the inability of human thought to penetrate the divine mysteries:

> Ingenio:
>
> Ya sé que eres loco y no
> loco de atar, pues no hay cuerda
> imaginación que tú
> no rompas.
>
> Pensamiento:
>
> Pues ya que es fuerza
> que por loco tolerado
> me sufras, dame licencia
> de decirte que no pienses
> penetrar eso que piensas.
>
> (p. 1637)

Ingenio notes that sometimes even a *loco* can be right. Human thoght is frivolous and daring; one can never be certain where it will lead. But Pensamiento responds that he is inadequate when it comes to divine secrets:

> Ingenio:
>
> Dices bien; y pues hoy muestras
> estar en razón, que un loco
> con algo tal vez acierta,
> ¿qué haré en las dudas que sabes?
>
> Pensamiento:
>
> Yo no puedo decir dellas
> más de que solo hay un Sabio
> que puede satisfacerlas.
>
> (p. 1637)

That is, only God, through Revelation, can answer man's questions regarding the divine. Ingenio, accompanied by Pensamiento, cannot penetrate the truth he seeks to know. He learns it only through revelation. Tiempo explains the principle of the Resurrection and Noche asks:

> ¿Quién eso asegura? (p. 1659)

Cipriano, disillusioned with the temporal, accuses the Devil of failing to fulfill his obligations according to their contract. Cipriano has learned the transient, empty nature of those things to which he formerly gave importance. He recognizes that the Devil provides only representations and illusions:

> sólo fantasmas hallo
> adonde hermosuras busco.
>
> (Tercera jornada, 2611-2612)

The only answer to doubt is the word of God. Thus, it is the Zagal who answers:

> Yo,
> pues que volviendo a nacer,
> con el Grano que murió
> en la tierra y dio después
> ciento por uno, en aqueste
> Blanco Pan deposité
> alma y cuerpo, en que realmente
> el hombre llegue a tener
> refacción de Cuerpo y Alma.
>
> (p. 1659)

Hearing these words of divine revelation, Ingenio no longer doubts. When Tiempo asks:

> ¿Quédate algo que saber,
> Ingenio?

he answers:

> No, sino mucho
> que admirar.
> (p. 1659)

Human genius must remain forever in awe *(admiración)* of the Word.

In *El tesoro escondido,* Idolatría doubts the Sacrament, since he sees bread and wine, and not flesh and blood before the altar. Inspiración, in order to make him and the other characters see the truth rather than what is reflected by the senses, puts out the light. The gesture is symbolic: in order to reach divine light one must not only mortify the senses but also put out the light of reason:

> Idol: Si en vez de alumbrar apagas
> la Luz, ¿cómo hemos de verla?

The Devil promises to try again, but the undeceived Cipriano now rebukes him. He realizes he cannot bend reality to suit his will, and therefore tells the Devil he wishes to be released from his contract. Cipriano once again enters into formal debate with the Devil and once again postulates the existence of a supreme being. Yet, he remains ignorant of the identity of this mysterious God. This is information inaccessible through reason.

It is now that Justina's Christianity becomes even more meaningful to him. The Devil must admit he has been ineffective with her because her faith in the Christian God

> Insp: Como aquesta maravilla
> se ha de mirar tan a ciegas,
> que el Oído ha de escucharla
> y cautivo ha de creerla
> de la Fe el Entendimiento;
> y para que mejor veas,
> que sin luz hay luz de luz,
> finge una nube en tu idea,
> que se signifique ser
> Belén, cielo de la tierra,
> mirando en él coronada
> la Humana Naturaleza,
> que es el Arca del Tesoro.
>
> (p. 1688)

Once faith or "inspiration" has come forth, the individual is ready for revelation. Now the Zagal enters to reveal the word of God:

> Todos: ¿Quién afirma esa propuesta?
> Zagal: Yo, que soy la Luz del Mundo,
> Luz que es tan verdadera,
> que quien sus reflejos vio
> no pisará las tineblas;
> porque también soy camino
> seguro, y verdad tan cierta,
> que como este Pan y Vino
> es mi Carne y Sangre mesma.
>
> (p. 1688)

Page numbers refer to *Obras completas,* Vol. III.

provides her with the strength to resist him. It is only now that the Devil identifies himself. Cipriano, with the new awareness Justina's faith has given him, recognizes his adversary and also the possibility of his own salvation. Reason has not revealed God, but once Cipriano knows God through revelation he can reason backwards and hypothesize that if God exists and possesses infinite power, He has it in his power to pardon him his sins. Cipriano calls out to the Christian God and the Devil hurls him away with the words:

> Este te ha dado la vida.
>
> (Tercera jornada, 2757)

Cipriano's knowledge of the Christian God has been made possible through his love for Justina; the love which unites man and woman reflects the more perfect love which unites God and man. It is the Christian God who has given Cipriano life —eternal life— and enabled him to recognize and be cleansed of those sins represented by the Devil. And Cipriano has not come to Him through his sciences —"la docta Minerva" (Tercera jornada, 2889)—, but through love —"la enamorada Venus" (Tercera jornada, 2890).

Faith has given Cipriano a new awareness of himself and of his own freedom. It has given him the strength and insight to recognize and reject evil. For Calderón, freedom may be realized to its fullest by the man of faith in his continuous struggle for his own salvation.

Cipriano's conversion is completed and sanctified with his union with Justina in martyrdom. The Governor has long searched for an excuse to rid Antioch of Justina and thereby assure that his son Lelio will refrain from dueling. He finds an excuse in Justina's Christianity, which he discovers when the Christian church is raided and she is found there praying. When Cipriano, too, declares himself a Christian, he, like

264

Justina, is taken prisoner. Thrown together unexpectedly by
circumstance, both Ciprino and Justina mistrust their senses:

Cipriano:	(Ap.) Mas no es ella, que en el aire la *finge* mi *pensamiento.*
Justina:	(Ap.) Mas no es él: por divertirme, *fantasmas* me *finge* el viento.
Cipriano:	Sombra de mi *fantasía...*
Justina:	*Ilusión* de mi deseo...
Cipriano:	Asombro de mis sentidos...
Justina:	Horror de mis *pensamientos...*

The italicized words indicate that Cipriano now takes
precisely the same attitude as Justina regarding the projections of the will and the senses. At last he is completely free
of his will to rationalize. Justina explains to Cipriano God's
infinite goodness and His boundless mercy. Until that
moment Cipriano doubts, for he knows the extent of his sins.
But guided by Justina's faith and strength he pronounces the
saving words:

> Así Justina, lo creo
> (Tercera Jornada, 3025)

Faith gives Cipriano the courage to face death:

> Fe, valor y ánimo tengo;
> (Tercera jornada, 3040)

Death is no longer eternal nothingness for him, but eternal
life in union with God and the woman he loves. It is now that
Justina's promise to love him only in death becomes
meaningful to Cipriano. Through her, he has found salvation
and perfect love, unblemished by carnal desire.

The death of the martyrs is accompanied by one final appearance of the Devil, who explains that Justina's honor is
impeccable. This last pronouncement by the Devil signifies
that in the light of faith, all illusions must be dispelled and

rejected. For the Devil's craft is nothing but fantasy and leads only to futility. Before the real prodigious magician, God, he must acknowledge his powerlessness.

Conclusion

El mágico prodigioso shares with much existentialist thought the view that reason and experience lead the individual to a recognition of the fundamental futility of the temporal world. The individual, in the face of such futility, must either accept the meaninglessness of his own life or seek some justification for it. By distorting reason, he may rationalize his own existence. Honor, wealth, beauty, may become objectives of life. Yet, such a solution proves ultimately inadequate, for it masks a lie. Calderón personifies the tendency to rationalize in the Devil, whose different relations with the other characters in the play illustrate their own particular concession to or rejection of this temptation.

The existentialists are by no means unanimous in their solution to the problem of futility. Yet, for the most part, they seek temporal fulfillment through the varied manifestations of the human will. For Heidegger, complete control of the will enables the individual to free himself from his own illusions or projections and comprehend intuitively a certain poetic truth which transcends reason and creates a common bond between man and his surroundings. For Sartre, an existentialist of completely different background and ideology, the will is the impetus of the act by which the individual defines himself in terms of a cause. Every act, then, represents a kind of *engagement* on the part of the person who performs it, whether or not he recognizes it as such.

Calderón, unlike most existentialists, views the question of futility within a specifically Christian context. His characters are, in a sense, *engagés* in terms of their own personal

266

salvation and they do define themselves as worthy or unworthy of a rewarding afterlife by means of their acts. But
while this notion of salvation as a sort of religious *engagement* does provide a valid point of comparison between
Calderón and Sartre, it also points up certain irreconcilable
differences between seventeenth and twentieth-century man
in general and Calderón and the existentialists in particular.

For Calderón, Cipriano's pessimism and sense of futility are
the inevitable consequences of the rational mind working
within a pagan framework. Once Cipriano finds faith, his
pessimism dissipates. The existence of God gives meaning to
the universe. It provides the possibility of salvation after life
and therefore meaning for those acts performed during life.

Throughout this study I have stressed Calderón's distrust of
systems. But Calderón applies this distrust only to what he
conceives as man-made systems, never to the theological
system he considers divine in origin. Human systems are subject to scrutiny by human reason, but the divine system is
not, since human reason is by definition imperfect and
therefore inadequate for the task. For the seventeenth-century
fideist, the imperfection of human reason became in itself an
argument to reinforce his belief, for, considering himself imperfect and therefore unqualified to question the doctrine of
the Church, he argued that dogma must be accepted blindly
on faith.[16] Cipriano is guided by reason, but he is saved by
faith. Once the Christian God is revealed to him, he no
longer has recourse to reason. His debates cease. His doubts
are dispelled. Further questioning and probing are unnecessary.

For the existentialist —even for the Christian existentialist—
the problem is quite different. For twentieth-century man,

[16] This was the skeptics' principal argument in favor of blind faith. See
Popkin, p. 46.

religion is no longer inviolable by human reason. Religion is perceived as another human system, subject to inquiry. Calderón excludes religion from his criticism of the will to rationalize, but existentialism does not. The existentialist writers have by and large seen religion as simply another means of imposing meaning on a meaningless universe and comfortably justifying human existence while assuaging man's fears about death. By the mid-nineteenth century Kierkegaard had already pointed out the emptiness of religion as practiced in Europe and qualified as a "poet relationship" what he saw as an abstract ideal with no practical reality in the lives of those who professed it.[17] Nietzsche signaled the bankruptcy of religion as a vital force in Western thought when he declared God dead in 1882.[18]

Miguel de Unamuno, perhaps better than any other writer, has described the irreconcilable antagonism between reason and religion which exists for modern man. Reason, imperfect and superficial though it may be, nervertheless constitutes a human reality. For Unamuno, reason corrodes belief, leaving man in a futile, godless universe, where there can be no finality in life nor immortality in death. And yet, the will to find some purpose in life and to extend oneself beyond the nothingness of death constitutes another very deeply rooted human reality. This conflict between reason and this vital life-force Unamuno qualifies as a "trágico combate."[19] God corresponds to that which is egotistical in us, to our inner self. The "authentic," unreasonable or a-reasonable self, which Unamuno calls "el hombre de carne y hueso"[20] is in all of us the antithesis of the other human reality, the rational

---

[17] *Attack upon Christiandom,* tr. by Walter Lowrie, (Princeton: Princeton University Press 1944), p. 202
[18] *Ecce Homo.* p. 344
[19] *Del sentimiento trágico de la vida,* p. 73.
[20] Unamuno opposes the "flesh and blood" man to the "intellectual" or "rational" man in many of his writings. See *Del sentimiento* and *Tres novelas ejemplares y un prólogo.*

self. The continuous struggle between the two is what Unamuno calls "el irreconciliable conflicto entre la razón y el sentimiento vital."[21]

Unlike seventeenth-century man, twentieth-century man can no longer use the inadequacy of human reason as an argument to reinforce blind faith. He can no longer leave faith unquestioned. Unlike Calderón's Ciprïano, Unamuno's don Manuel Bueno[22] cannot accept God on the basis of Revelation and cast away the seeds of pessimism and doubt reason has sown. For twentieth-century man, reason is a constant hindrance to faith.

The Christian existentialist must justify his faith in the face of the menace of reason. He must consciously choose to believe *in spite of* reason. Unamuno saw in don Quijote and in Nicodemo el Fariseo admirable characters whose will to believe overrode their reason.[23] Kierkegaard saw the same in Abraham in his struggle with the angel.[24] He admired in Abraham his continuing faith in spite of the absurdity, the cruelty, and the inexplicability of the sacrifice God asked him to perform. Gabriel Marcel, who, like Unamuno, rejects the notion of an ordered universe designed by God and governed by causality, spends long pages of his *Journal Métaphysique* attempting to justify his Catholicism.[25]

For the seventeenth-century fideist, such justifications were unnecessary and even unthinkable. There could be no conflict between faith and reason because faith could not be submitted to the criterion of reason. In order to believe the existentialist must bridge the schism between faith and reason by an act of

[21] *Del sentimiento*, p. 98.

[22] Protagonist of Unamuno's short novel, *San Manuel Bueno, Mártir*.

[23] *Vida de Don Quijote y Sancho* and *"Nicodemo el Fariseo"* in *La agonía del cristianismo*, (New York: Las Américas, 1967).

[24] *Fear and Trembling*, pp. 19-20.

[25] Paris: Gallimard, 1935.

the will. The seventeenth-century fideist *did* believe; he did not *choose* to believe. For the existentialist, faith is a matter of conscious choice. The act of believing, like any other act, functions as a means by which the individual asserts and defines himself.

These very different views of faith and reason are indicative of the fundamentally different world views held by Calderón on the one hand and the existentialists on the other. In the two hundred and fifty years which elapse between Calderón's most productive period and the beginnings of existentialism the notion of a world rationally ordered by an unfathomable divine intelligence belonging to a perfect God has given way to the view of an irrational, absurd world without finality. In our zeal in pointing out the similarities between Calderón's system and the existentialists', we must not overlook this fundamental, irreconcilable difference.

CHAPTER VI

THE INTEGRATED SELF: *LA ESTATUA DE PROMETEO*

The Myths of Prometheus

La estatua de Prometeo combines several Greek and Roman myths about Prometheus. In one, Prometheus creates mankind out of clay and water. In another, in vengeance for Zeus's mistreatment of man, Prometheus steals fire from the gods and gives it to man, teaching him many useful arts and sciences. In still another, Zeus orders Hephaestus to create Pandora, the first woman on earth, as a punishment for man and his protector, Prometheus. The gods endow Pandora with beauty and charm, as well as curiosity and deceit, and Zeus sends her as wife to Epimetheus, Prometheus' simple brother. Zeus gives Pandora a box which contains a host of evils to plague mankinds, and orders her never to open it. But in spite of Prometheus' warnings, Epimetheus allows her to open the box, which she does, letting loose those ills which have afflicted the human race ever since. Only hope remains in the box. Zeus, angry with Prometheus, has him chained to a mountain peak in the Caucasus, but later restores his freedom in appreciation for a favor.

Critics have been divided over the question of Calderón's intentions in writing *La estatua de Prometeo*. Some scholars, such as Angel Valbuena Prat[1] and Charles Aubrun,[2] maintain that the work is fundamentally a Christian allegory. Others, such as W. G. Chapman[3] and Raymond Trousson,[4] insist that such an interpretation is unjustifiable. Although the text of the play does not itself specifically refer to the story of the creation, the fall and the redemption, there are a number of factors which make it possible to entertain the thought that Calderón may have had Christian symbolism in mind when he wrote the play.

For one thing, the myth of Prometheus had been interpreted allegorically in Christian terms and Calderón had access to such interpretations. For example, the Jesuit Father Baltasar de Victoria included it in his *Teatro de los Dioses de la gentilidad,* which appeared in 1620. Juan Pérez de Moya wrote in his *Philosophia secreta,* which was published in 1585, 1599, 1611, 1628 and again in 1673: "El fuego que trujo (Prometeo) del cielo con que dió ser a su estatua que había formado, es el divino fuego o ánima que Dios inspiró en el hombre. Y así por Prometeo se entiende el poderoso Dios que crió el mundo y el hombre de nada."[5]

Mythology played an important part in Jesuit teaching as a source of moral instruction.[6] We know that Calderón was a pupil at the Colegio Imperial de la Compañía de Jesús in

[1] Angel Valbuena Prat, *Historia de la literatura española,* Vol. II (Barcelona: Noguer, 1957), p. 599.
[2] Charles V. Aubrun, Introduction to *La estatua de Prometeo* (Paris: Centre de Documentation Universitaire, 1961).
[3] Chapman, W. G., "Las comedias mitológicas de Calderón", *RL,* V (1954), pp. 35-67.
[4] Raymond Trousson, "Une synthèse tardive: *La estatua de Prometeo".
Le Thème de Prométhée dans la littérature européenne* (Geneva: Droz, 1964), p. 175.
[5] Juan Pérez de Moya, *Philosophia secreta,* Vol. II (Madrid: Nueva Biblioteca de Autores Españoles -Los Clásicos Olvidados, 1928), pp. 194-195.
[6] See Trousson, "Une synthèse," p. 167.

Madrid for five formative years. Furthermore, he wrote his nineteen mythological dramas during the thirty years preceding his death, precisely the period during which he was a Church father. *La estatua de Prometeo* was written toward the end of his career —it was created in 1669 and performed at the Buen Retiro in 1673 or 1674—[7] when he was engaged primarily in writing *autos sacramentales*. It is not so improbable, then, that like the *autos, La estatua de Prometeo* caches a religious theme.

Yet, these facts do not in any way prove that it was Calderón's intention that the work be understood as allegorical drama. They are mentioned here only to suggest that such an interpretation is possible within Calderón's historical context. Prometeo and Epimeteo might be understood to constitute together a kind of primal man, or Adam, who creates a woman, Pandora, out of clay and water just as Adam gave form to Eve through his rib, the substance of which was dust.[8] This primal woman brings sin into the world, just as Eve did. Because of a wrong committed in her behalf, Prometeo is condemned to eternal suffering but is later pardoned by Apollo, paralleling Adam's fall, the condemnation of mankind and its redemption through Christ.

Whether or not we adhere to this Christian interpretation of Calderón's play, we can understand Prometeo and Epimeteo as traditional symbols of reason and passion, forming together the *homo duplex* of Italian mythological studies. The works of the Italian mythographs —Comes, Cartari, Gyraldi— and Boccaccio's *De geneologiis* were well known throughout Europe and were surely at Calderón's disposal.[9] Calderón's *La estatua de Prometeo* is, Raymond Trousson points out, the culmination of a long tradition of interpretations of the myth in which Prometheus is seen as a

[7] Aubrun, "Introduction", p. 1
[8] *Genesis,* 3:19
[9] See Trousson, "Une synthèse", p. 168

273

symbol a reason. However, as Trousson notes, Calderón's
work is not merely a compilation of existing interpretations.
Rather, Calderón brings to the classic story his special view
of the role of reason, enthusiastic, yet tempered with the
awareness of the potential dangers of reason when it goes unchecked by conscience. Trousson sees in Calderón's
Prometeo, "le héros avide de savoir, mais tempéré par la
réflexion et la sagesse."[10] As such, he is a more sophisticated,
more mature Prometheus than Boccaccio's. Trousson finds in
Calderón's interpretation of the myth a view much closer to
Aeschylus' than in any earlier European interpretation. He
suggests that Calderón may even have known the original
Greek *Prometheus Bound* and have used it as a source.

Prometeo and Epimeteo

Calderón's *La estatua de Prometeo* revolves around twin
brothers, Prometeo and Epimeteo, of very different inclinations. Prometeo is a philosopher and a teacher; Epimeteo
is given to the cultivation of military pursuits. Together they
live in the Caucasus, surrounded by shepherds and shepherdesses. Prometeo has retired to the mountaintop, where he
lives symbolically "above" the masses; he is closer to the
heavens physically because he has cultivated the sciences and
raised himself above the primitive, brute state of man. The
mountainside is overrun by thick, uncultivated underbrush
and, as the first act opens, it is night. The "cerviz inculta" of
the valley and the darkness symbolize the rough, rude nature
of the people and the darkness of their ignorance.

Prometeo summons the people forth and bids them bring
their instruments —crude, primitive instruments like the
crude, primitive people who play them— for there will be a
celebration. They appear with their *zampoñas rudas*
(Primera jornada, 14) and *rudos albogues* (Primera jornada,

[10] Trousson, p. 176

274

15), which produce *harmonías confusas* (Primera jornada, 16). Throughout the play the people express themselves in music —not pure refined harmonies, but simple songs of a primitive, emotional character. They sing in exultation, in anger, in fear. Here, their song is in endecasyllables which, while continuing the assonance, contrast with Prometeo's *romance*. Epimeteo, who has come with them, remarks on their lack of order *(demandadas cuadrillas;* Primera jornada, 33); the scene is one of confusion, festiveness, and simple, unpretentious exuberance.

Prometeo reminds the people that he had always been inclined to study. Puzzled by the fact that he and his brother, although born under the same star, were so different in inclination, he had become especially interested in astrology.[11] Seeking to explain how one cause —that is, one horoscope— could give such dissimilar effects, he traveled near and far in search of answers. His relation is rich in imagery; learning is repeatedly associated with light (*"la clara lumbre pura/ de la enseñanza";* Primera jornada; 109-110) and ignorance with darkness (*"Pisaba, bien como ciego,/ Que anda tropezando a oscuras";* Primera jornada, 112-113).

He then returned to Caucasus to bring the people the fruits of his learning. He had wanted to establish a government based on the light of reason, but the people, guided by a simple, basic Old Testament ethic that punishes the thief and the murderer, reject the new proposal. They distrust Prometeo and fear ambition might cause him to manipulate reason to subjugate them.

This episode is open to a number of interpretations. Charles Aubrun, in his introduction to the critical edition of *La estatua de Prometeo,* maintains that the people reject

---

[11] The fact that twins, conceived and born under the same horoscope, are often very different in nature is one of Saint Augustine's arguments against the validity of astrology. See *The City of God,* V, 1-6.

Prometeo because "Prométhée n'était guidé que par l'abominable raison d'Etat," that the state rather than the individual had become an end for him, and that the people fear and therefore turn against "cette machiavélique Raison."[12] But it is not clear from the text that Prometeo is as ambitious and rigid as Aubrun —and the people of Caucasus— say he is. It is clear, however, that Calderón presents the abuse of reason— whether Prometeo is guilty of it or not— as a very real possibility.

This same episode may be interpreted quite differently. Considered in a Christian context, it could be said that the people, ignorant and primitive, prefer to adhere to their inflexible Old Testament ethic and reject Prometeo's proposal for a more enlightened, reasonable type of government.

Prometeo, saddened by the people's rejection of him, retires to the mountain top. There he erects a statue to Minerva, goddess of the sciences and wisdom, whom he reveres more than any of the other gods of Olympus. It is to the unveiling of this statue that Prometeo has called the people of Caucasus.

The Creation

The creation of Pandora takes place in two very obvious and distinct stages. In the first, Pandora is given form by Prometeo, who molds her out of clay in the image of Minerva. In the second, se is given life by the sun ray Prometeo steals from Apollo. In the first act she remains an inanimate object, a work of art.

As such, Prometeo's statue is the product of his fantasy, the concretization of an abstract idea. She is, like all works of art, a representation of something pure and intangible whose source lies deep in the mind of its creator. She is an image.

[12] Aubrun, p. 13.

276

The principal difference between her and the images which haunt Aureliano or delude Segismundo is that she has been given physical form by the individual who projects her. This is art: an illusion made tangible; a fantasy given form.

The statue is a concrete representation of Reason, the abstract perfection man strives toward. This symbolism is doubly complex, since in the play Calderón has himself personified Reason in the character of Minerva.

Prometeo describes inspiration as a bright fire that ignites his fantasy even in the darkness of night, that is, even in the presence of incertitude:

> Di en aprehender su hermosura,
> Tan viva en mi fantasía,
> Que no había parte alguna
> En que no me pareciese
> Mirarla con tan aguda
> Vehemencia, que aun en la sombra
> De la noche siempre oscura,
> (Pues hasta ahora no vió luz
> En ella humana criatura)
> Jurara que un vivo fuego
> Para mirarla me alumbra.
>
> (Primera jornada, 231-241)

The statue reproduces not something Prometeo has actually seen in the daylight, but something he has apprehended with the mind's eye —something so vivid and bright it can be clearly perceived or intuited in spite of the physical darkness which surrounds its creator.[13]

This representation of an intangible reality is imperfect.

[13] Heidegger expresses a similar notion of artistic creation in "Holderlin or the Essence of Poetry". For him, it was the artist's capacity to obviate his own prohections which enabled him to perceive poetic essence, then to capture it and give it form.

Flowers and ornaments hide the coarse clay form Prometeo has molded, giving it the appearance of charm and grace. This image Prometeo offers to the people instead of the laws he had originally intended. And yet, both the statue and the laws have one thing in common: both are imperfect simulacra of divine reason.

Upon seeing the statue Epimeteo falls in love with it and proposes a temple be built in honor of Minerva where it will be kept. His intention is to take it away from the people and keep it where only he can enjoy it. In a sense, the statue is as much Epimeteo's as Prometeo's, for Epimeteo gives it meaning in a way his brother cannot. In a later scene, Epimeteo and Merlín, the *gracioso* of the play, discuss the statue. Merlín argues that it is nothing more than a mass of clay, while Epimeteo praises it idealistically as though it were a live woman. The episode tells us something both about love and about art. In love, it is the lover who assigns value to the loved one, who idealizes her and creates an illusion around her, amplifying in his mind those characteristics he finds appealing and overlooking those he does not. In art, a similar phenomenon occurs. The receptive audience gives the art form life in a way its creator cannot. The audience in a sense recreates the art form for itself, giving it a meaning its creator may not originally have intended it to have. For Prometeo, the statue is a representation of Minerva —that is, of a concept buried deep in his mind; for Epimeteo, it is a meaningful reality unto itself. In art, one man's creation may be another's inspiration. Calderón knew and understood this, for he himself had been inspired for many of his plays in the work of others.[14]

In Prometeo's statue, art and nature are joined (*"La naturaleza/ Y el arte se juntan"*; Primera jornada, 381-82), a

[14] See Sloman, *The Dramatic Craftsmanship of Calderón*

union which seems to represent an ideal for Calderón, for he achieves the same union in this very play, in which the natural setting of the Buen Retiro compliments the artifical set and stage devices.

Accompanied by their crude instruments the shepherds sing the praises of Prometeo's statue. Their confused music is a manifestation of man's devotion on a primitive level, but the dissonance of their song is also symbolic, for the statue which is to be reborn as a woman will sow the seeds of discord in the Caucasus.

Prometeo and Epimeteo Understood as Symbols

Calderón displays extraordinary dexterity in creating characters which are viable both as persons and as symbols. Prometeo and Epimeteo are perfectly believable inventions understood as two individuals who choose careers in accordance with their particular inclinations. However, the brothers may also be understood as allegories of two aspects of the human character, reason and will. As such, they complement each other, living together in harmony in the body of the Caucasus, Prometeo, representing reason, at the head, Epimeteo, representing will, in the tangled underbrush of the vicera.

Both have as their objective the good of the total self. Reason tries to guide it by bringing it government, that is, control. Will gives it arms for war, that is, vigor, vitality, the capacity for movement. Both are potentially evil; reason may become tyrannical when deprived of the gut intuitiveness of the will; will is blind and destructive without the control and guidance of reason. Both need to be held in check by conscience. Functioning together normally, they form a harmonious, integrated self.

Reason proposes that which it conceives as reasonable; will may either accept or reject these proposals. Epimeteo, rightly or wrongly, rejects out of fear Prometeo's implementation of a new government.

Both will and reason are in natural harmony with God; human will tends to conform with the divine will and human reason, with divine reason.[15] Accordingly, both Prometeo and Epimeteo worship the gods, each choosing for special reverence that goddess who best represents his own character.

Reason, the intellectual faculty, is capable of giving form to the abstract and so it is Prometeo who constructs the statue of Minerva. Will is the faculty which is enticed by the senses, which in turn ignite the passions, and so it is Epimeteo who falls in love with it. Reason is capable of distinguishing between the real and the representation and guides the will to the real, which is sometimes invisible. Will may prefer the representation, which is visible, and therefore pleasing to the senses. When this occurs, there arises discord between will and reason. The primary source of discord between the twin faculties in man is woman.

Minerva and Pallas

The people's celebration is interrupted by Timantes, the old man. The figure of the old man is topical in European literature; he represents knowledge, attained not through reason, but through experience.[16]

[15] These concepts of the natural harmony of human will and reason and divine will and reason are accepted theology and are expounded by Augustine, *City of God* XXii, 30 and Thomas Aquinas, *Suma Theologica,* I, Q. 82. Art. 2; Q. 95. Art. 1; II, 1st part, Q. 1, Arts. 7-8; Q. 4x, Art. teenth century theologians; see Vives, *Tratado,* p. 1192-1198 and Súarez, *Disputaciones,* V, XXIX, XXX.

[16] For a discussion of the old man as a traditional symbol of experience, see Curtius, *European Literature,* p. 98-100.

Timantes warns the people that the Caucasus has been attacked by a monster. The group disbands, and the shepherds once more burst into song. This time the music reflects both their fear and determination before the imminent danger. These two basic reactions are reflected once again in the quick, comical dialogue between Merlín and Libya, his female counterpart. He shows himself to be cowardly and fearful, while she is curious and determined.

The terrifying monster is Minerva, who appears dressed in animal skins. Her disguise symbolizes the dual potential of reason. To the people, reason appears as a beast —something to be feared and rejected. That is why they reject Prometeo's proposal for a reasonable government. But reason is a monster only when it is misapplied. The people see reason only superficially; that is, from the outside. Prometeo, on the other hand, recognizes that reason is fundamentally a good to be cultivated. That is why before him Minerva doffs her animal skins. She may be seen as either destructive or sweet:

> Pues los horrores que das
> Quitas con suavidades,
> (Primera jornada, 479-480)

While she is intrinsically good, man may use her for either good or evil. To each man she is as he sees her, and so she appears to Prometeo just as he imagined her; to him she is

> ...la que copié
> En fantásticas ideas.
> (Primera jornada, 437-474)

And she is dressed identically to his crude imitation of her:

> En aquel propio traje
> Que tu idea me copia.
> (Primera jornada, 496-497)

Calderón uses artistic devices to distinguish the divine characters from the human ones. Minerva, unlike Prometeo

281

and Epimeteo, sings in *recitativo*, reflecting the celestial harmony of the heavens. She uses *quintillas*, an elegant form reserved for deities in this play, which contrast with Prometeo's more usual *redondillas*.

Prometeo's meeting with Minerva throws him into a state of confusion and doubt. Is she real or simply another representation? He can only be sure that he did in fact cast a statue of her:

> Ilusión o fantasía,
> Que aparentemente ví,
> Que realmente retraté,
>
> (Primera jornada, 486-487)

That is, man cannot be certain what is real and what is representation, only of the fact that he does indeed project representations. Prometeo's distinguishing characteristic is that he is aware of this.

Minerva convinces Prometeo of her superior nature; she is real and more perfect than what man, in his imperfection, can create.

She comes to Prometeo at night, in a place penetrated neither by light, nor by bird nor by beast —in Christian terms, neither by spirit, nor dove nor life,[17] a trinity of symbols representing God. Even in the presence of reason, Prometeo is in spiritual darkness.

The goddess offers to grant Prometeo any of his wishes. He asks to be taken to the heavens so that he may observe first hand the astronomical bodies which have intrigued him for so long, for knowledge is not attained through books and debates, but through experience, experimentation and observation.[18] She agrees to take him, if he dares to go:

[17] Aubrun discusses the symbolism of the scene in "Introduction", p. 15.
[18] Calderón's view of education seems to correspond with that of early skeptics such as Sánchez. See *Que nada se sabe*.

282

> ...si tú te atrevieras
> A penetrar osado...
> (Primera jornada, 554-558)

Calderón characterizes the scholar as a man of daring. In an age when science was leading men to discoveries never before imagined, there seemed no limit to where reason might lead. To delve into the secrets of the universe might bring satisfaction, but it also represented a risk, tempting man to postulate in realms beyond his capacity to comprehend. The daring and spectacular nature of the undertaking is conveyed by the daring and spectacular nature of Prometeo's and Minerva's exit on a tree branch.

In the meantime, Epimeteo has continued to search for the monster only to find himself suddenly face to face with Pallas, goddess of war, who reprimands him for falling in love with the statue of Minerva. Pallas, like Minerva, is the personification of an abstract concept. Just as Minerva represents pure or perfect Reason, Pallas represents pure or perfect Force. Twin sisters of opposite inclinations, Minerva and Pallas parallel exactly Prometeo and Epimeteo. They are the divine ideals of which the brothers represent the human application.

Epimeteo has fallen in love with an image, *"una inanimada/ fingida belleza."* Prometeo gave the statue form, but did not lose sight of the fact that it is a mere representation. Epimeteo, moved by passion, ignores its real nature. Pallas speaks derrogatively of Prometeo, *"aquese ignorante sabio,"* for she knows that reason's creation can be a dangerous temptation for the will because when the will is unduly swayed by a representation it loses control of itself and is ultimately debilitated. By falling in love with a statue, Epimeteo risks losing his forcefulness and therefore of being disloyal to the ideal of Force. By yielding to the attraction of the statue of the goddess of wisdom, he is being untrue to his

283

own nature, which is characterized by force, not by reason. Human will is at odds with divine will.

Pallas, angered, orders Epimeteo to destroy the statue and leaves. Epimeteo is unable to follow her as Prometeo did Minerva. The way is closed by underbrush *("me cierran/ el paso troncos y ramas")* representing visceral, brute passions, and Prometeo is not there to guide him. That is, will is unable to function properly because reason is absent and the senses are ignited. Epimeteo is plunged into confusion:

> ¿Quién habrá visto tan ciega
> confusión como buscar
> a un hermano y a una fiera,
> y en vez de fiera y hermano
> hallar deidad tan violenta,
> que se explique favorable
> para declararse adversa.
>
> (Primera jornada, 721-727)

Will is, by definition, blind.[19] Without the guidance of reason it is capricious. This is why Epimeteo now finds himself in a state of "blind confusion," emphasized by the use of juxtaposition and opposites in his speech *(hermano, fiera; fiera, hermano; favorable, adversa)*. He is torn first one way, then the other.

Finally Epimeteo finds a compromise solution, a means of leaving intact the statue without offending Pallas. But the solution is based on a deceit; it is an unreasonable solution, for there can be no compromises with the gods. Still, Epimeteo is determined to satisfy his desire.

The Theft of Apollo's Ray

Prometeo, flown to the heavens by Minerva, perceives Apollo at a distance. Reason elevates man to the realm of the gods.

---

[19] Thomas Aquinas, *Summa,* II, part. 1, Q. 9.

In Christian terms, Apollo may be understood to represent God, or the principle of eternal life. He sings, not like Minerva and Pallas, but in melody and accompanied by a chorus.

Prometeo, like Cipriano in *El mágico prodigioso,* has been brought close to God by science. But he has not yet touched God. Like Cipriano, he longs for that knowledge science cannot give him. A spark of the divine is what he most covets. Apollo, the sun, is not only light, he is fire; he is not only the source of science, he is the source of life. Life-giving spirit can come only from him. There is no other source of fire but Apollo. It is only by attaining a spark of his light that one comprehends that

> ...quien da luz a las gentes
> es quien da a las gentes ciencia.
>
> (Primera jornada, 763-764)

Since Reason, represented by Minerva, cannot provide man with the life giving spark, Prometeo must steal it himself. In the presence of Apollo, Prometeo feels his senses to be in suspension.[20] He is in a state to receive God. He reaches out and steals a ray from Apollo, which he dedicates to his own creation, the statue of Minerva.

Distribution and Significance of the Characters

By the end of the first act all the major characters except Discordia have been introduced, and it is possible to discern a pattern in their distribution. They fall into three groups: the

[20] This is a state described by many mystics, for example, Santa Teresa, San Juan de la Cruz, Miguel de Molinos. This is not to infer that Calderón is in any sense a mystic, but rather that Prometeo is prepared to ignore the temptation of the senses in order to receive spiritual redemption.

gods, the Titans and the people. The gods, Apollo, Minerva and Pallas may be seen to form a symbolic trinity. They are distinguished by their speech. All three sing in *recitativo,* although Apollo, the male and most powerful of the group, also sings in melody. Together they may be understood to represent God, with Apollo symbolizing the eternal; Minerva, divine reason and Pallas, divine will, the two faculties of God.

On the second level are Prometeo and Epimeteo. According to Greek mythology, Prometheus and Epimetheus were twin sons of the Titans or primeval gods Iapetus and Clymene. In Calderón's play they are not specifically sons of gods, but are rather human extentions or imitations of gods. Together they represent Man, "created in the image of God,"[21] with imperfect reason and will paralleling God's perfect faculties. Although human reason and will normally tend to conform with their divine ideals, the will is free and therefore may deviate from divine will, just as Epimeteo deviates from Pallas. Human reason always is in harmony with divine reason, except in those cases in which is made subservient to the will and abused, which does not occur in *La estatua de Prometeo.*

Prometeo creates Pandora who is like those who gave her form, for she speaks rather than sings when at last she is given life.

On the bottom layer are the people, who express themselves either in song or in speech, but who in either case express a simpler, more basic attachment to life than either of the other two groups. They are good, for they respect the teachings of the Old Testament, but they are primitive and unenlightened.

---

[21] *Génesis,* 1:26; the passage is clarified as follows: *In our image and likeness:* endowment with intellect and free will in imitation of God's perfections of understanding and willing.

They are like the beasts who populate the earth before the coming of man in *Genesis*.

These three groups may be seen to parallel the three strata of characters in the Biblical account of the creation: God on the highest level; Adam and Eve on the second; the beasts on the third.

The Creation of Pandora

As *Jornada* II opens, Epimeteo and Merlín grope in the dark of night for the niche in which the coveted statue of Minerva is hidden. Will unguided by reason (light) directs itself toward that which it deems good. While Epimeteo extols the statue's beauty as though it were a woman, Merlín, representative of the people, babbles about the basic necessities of life: food, clothes, wages. He is unable to understand why Epimeteo refuses to obey Pallas' command. For him the statue is no more than clay. What is more, the commandments of the gods are not to be questioned. His is a simple, down-to-earth approach to life. Like Manrique in *A secreto agravio, secreta venganza,* whose unquestioning adherence to the Ten Commandments makes it impossible for him to accept the honor code, Merlín accepts the gods' rulings unembellished. In Calderón's theater it is often the *gracioso* who illustrates a healthy, uncomplicated Old-Testament ethic, while it is the individual who is in some sense superior, either socially or intellectually or both, who must struggle with the temptations put to the will.

Epimeteo, like Cipriano in *El mágico prodigioso,* characterizes himself as an idolater (Segunda jornada, 1023), for, like Cipriano, he is attracted by visual representations. Epimeteo, embellishing the statue by means of his imagination, sees it as something unique, while Merlín argues it has the same blank face as other pretty girls, (Segunda jornada, 1030). Merlín, who does not fantasize as Epimeteo does, is, like his

287

namesake, a wise man. His only considerations are practical: a statue will undoubtedly be less demanding and expensive to maintain than a real woman. But his fears are also practical, for he knows that if Pallas discovers Epimeteo's scheme, she will take offense and punish him. Epimeteo disdainfully dismisses Merlín's warning:

> ...Deidad que tiene envidia,
> ¿Por qué no tendrá ignorancia?
> (Segunda jornada, 1067-1068)

Epimeteo, in his willfulness, chooses to disregard the truth.

As they stumble in the dark, Merlín calls out for Minerva's aid and miraculously a light appears. It seems one has only to appeal to reason to obtain guidance. But one must appeal to reason in good faith. Epimeteo immediately assumes that Minerva has come to light his way to the niche. He assumes reason to be subservient to the will. But he is deceived by appearances. In reality, it is Prometeo who approaches with the ray he has stolen from Apollo. Epimeteo and Merlin hide, and Merlín must turn away from the blinding ray, for the people are not yet equipped to be enlightened, as they showed by rejecting Prometeo's laws.

Prometeo opens the niche and places the stolen ray in the statue's hand. Immediately it comes to life, for now it possesses spirit, symbolized by fire. A chorus identifies the divine source in song:

> ...quien da ciencia da
> Voz al barro y luz al alma.
> (Segunda jornada, 1170-1172)

According to the Christian interpretation, God, identified in the play only as "quien", is represented in the mythological context by Apollo.

288

The statue is alive and therefore must be given a name. She will be called Pandora, which means *"providencia del tiempo"* (Segunda jornada, 1491). As primal woman, she is the procreative force which will assure future generations. She is the hope of humanity for continued survival in spite of the evils which plague it. She is, in Calderón's play as well as in Greek mythology, source both of man's ills and man's hope.

Pandora's meeting with Epimeteo illustrates the confrontation of man's willful, passionate aspect, with woman. Epimeteo is both moved and confused by the fire that

> Abrasa como que hiela,
> Y hiela como que abrasa.
>
> (Segunda jornada, 1213-1214)

Epimeteo's *concepto* reflects the ambivalence of his sentiments. He is astounded by the inexplicable phenomenon of Pandora's new-found life. She both "burns" by arousing his passion and "freezes" by her cold disdain.

Epimeteo and Prometeo, unaware of each other's presence, both call the people to witness the miracle. Both use identical words. In theological and philosophical terms, will and reason, components of man's dual character and rivals for its control, echo one another in their praise of God and their admiration for His creation.

Pandora is as naive, awed and helpless as a baby. She is aware of herself as a mysterious new force on the face of the earth, but is ignorant of her nature, origin and identity:

> Músicas al aire inquietan,
> La tierra, el fuego y el agua.
> ¿Quién soy yo, Dioses, que he puesto
> El orbe en confusión tanta?
>
> (Segunda jornada, 1232-1235)

The totality of the universe, represented by the elements earth, fire and water, has been upset by the birth of the new creature, woman. Pandora, like the gestating Segismundo, is not sure who she is, yet is aware of her immense potential and capacity for self-assertion, for already she has thrown the orbe into confusión.[22]

Pandora mistrusts all she sees and hears. If she is confused about her own identity, she is even more so about Prometeo's. (Segunda jornada, 1263). She intuits that she owes her life to the mysterious life-source identified as "quien" by the divine chorus, but she is unsure of all else. She has not yet been subjected to the rationalizing forces that distort one's clarity of vision.

Prometeo, at first confused by appearances, takes Pandora for the goddess in whose image she was created. But he soon distinguishes her by her voice. Pandora, a woman and not a goddess, merely speaks, as he and his brother do. Rejoicing amid the confusion, Prometeo and Epimeteo are reunited. In Christian terms, they have seen in the creation of Pandora the miracle of life and the presence of the Creator, symbolized by the three stages of flame:

> En tres edades del fuego,
> Pasando de luz a brasa,
> Y desde brasa a ceniza.
> (Segunda jornada, 1370-1372)

Flame, smouldering matter and ashes represent the trinity of forms of fire. Will and reason are united in their love for God, awakened by the presence of woman.[23] The rival brothers are at peace with one another.

[22] Trousson describes Pandora's awakening in existential terms: "elle est, pour employer le langage de la philosophie moderne, un existence qui découvre soudain son essence." "Une syntèse," p. 174.

[23] The same point is illustrated dramatically in a quite different manner in *El mágico prodigioso,* in which Cipriano is converted through Justina's love. See Chapter 5.

But while woman may be instrumental in helping man achieve spiritual tranquility, she is also responsible for his inner discord.[24] Already Epimeteo hears Pallas' war cries. He had been presumptuous and foolish to believe he could outsmart the gods. Pandora begs him to remain and worship the flame she holds in her hand. Her metaphor may be understood to compare fire with Old Testament God who is gentle when content and tyrannical when angered. Like Him, fire can be either beneficial or destructive.

Pallas, angered at Epimeteo's disobedience, calls on Discordia, for Force needs discord in order to produce violence. Discordia, we are reminded later on in Act III, is the bastard daughter of Pluto, god of the underworld. She leads to death those who are ensnared by her deceits. Unlike the gods and the Titans, she can both speak and sing. She belongs both to the realm of the divine and the realm of the human. In the heavens there is discord among the gods; in nature, among the elements; on earth, among individuals; within the individual, between reason and will.

Discord promises to present Pandora with an urn containing evils, which, when allowed to escape, will plague mankind forever. Neither Pallas nor Discordia can herself cast evil into the world. Man, or more specifically, woman brings suffering into mankind.

The shepherds sing and dance in honor of Pandora, whom they take to be a new deity. The bucolic, care-free abandon of the peasants in their peaceful valley is reminiscent of the harmony of the Garden of Eden. Discordia, like the serpent who tempted Eve, blends in with the group, undetected. The shep-

---

[24] Pérez de Moya sees Pandora as the archetypal woman, author of man's misfortune: "fué necesario que en alguna manera pusiese la fábula haber mujeres; y no fué otra manera mejor que decir que vinieron de la ira de los dioses, así como las fiebres y enfermedades." *Filosophia secreta,* p. 194. He does not specifically relate Pandora to Eve, however.

herds and shepherdesses offer Pandora all the gifts of the earth, just as all of nature was Eve's to enjoy. Discordia, singing and dancing with the others, gives Pandora the box. Pandora is, until now, innocent. She is humble and recognizes herself as merely and object of clay, on whom the miracle of life has been bestowed. She knows she is not the goddess the people take her for. Eve, too, was innocent in the Garden of Eden, until, by eating the fruit of the Tree of Knowledge she learned to recognize the difference between good and evil. Pandora, in appreciation for the tribute the people have paid her, preparès to open the urn and distribute its contents among them, but Timantes stops her. The old man momentarily prevents the catastrophe by reminding Pandora of her true nature. She is not a goddess, but she was created in the image of a goddess and her spirit is divine in origin. She is, then, at least a semi-goddess. In Christian terms, as the female aspect of Man, she, too, was created in the image of God. We may also understand Timante's comment as a statement on the nature of love: man, moved by passion and imagination, idealizes woman and converts her into a semigoddess, making her either an end in herself or a means by which he can attain God.

Timante's words touch off an argument between Prometeo and Epimeteo; the presence of woman has already begun to sow discord between will and reason. Now Pandora opens her urn and lets loose the evils. Like Eve, Pandora is victim of a deceit and like her, she unwittingly introduces sin into the world.

Discordia curses mankind for all eternity, condemning Prometeo to be loved without loving in return and Epimeteo to love without being loved; thus, the cold, impassionate nature of reason and the agressive, passionate nature of the will. Discordia's exit is followed by an earthquake and a storm that throw the Caucasus into darkness and confusion. The success of the scene depends on a set and on sound effects that convey an atmosphere of terror —the terror of an eternity without redemption, a never-ending nothingness:

> Anticipada la noche,
> Tocando arma al universo,
> Desarragadas desdobla
> Tupidas sombras sin tiempo.
>
> (Segunda jornada, 1783-1786)

The urn has exuded a blinding smoke. Mankind, blinded by evils of its own making, stumbles about in a confused universe. In desperation, the people turn to the gods, begging, in song, for protection. Epimeteo joins forces with Pallas in an attempt to pacify her wrath. Prometeo sides with Minerva in hopes she will calm Apollo's anger.

Pandora brings sin to the world, but she is not alone in her guilt. Just as Adam ate the forbidden fruit as well as Eve, so Epimeteo and Prometeo are guilty of sins. Prometeo, who like Adam was driven by a desire for knowledge, stole a ray of light from Apollo. Like Adam, who blames Eve for his error, both Epimeteo and Prometeo blame Pándora. Epimeteo tells her:

> ...si en ti tuve la culpa,
> En ti la disculpa tengo.
>
> (Segunda jornada, 1809-1810)

Prometeo says:

> Que al mirarte, como causa
> De las ansias que padezco,...
>
> (Segunda jornada, 1819-1820)

Epimeteo, who loves Pandora, wishes to take her with him; Prometeo, whom she loves, rejects her. Their attitudes reflect

293

the ambivalent attitude of man toward woman. On the one hand, he is attracted by her; she pleases his will because she arouses his passion. On the other, he is repelled by her because he recognizes she is responsible for his downfall by causing him to sin.

At the end of the second act, Prometeo and Epimeteo have declared themselves enemies; will and reason have been split assunder and each goes its separate way.

Apollo, the Angry God

Apollo is, at the beginning of the third act, reminiscent of the angry god of the Old Testament, hurling forth his indignation in furious *décimas*. Because he has been wronged by Prometeo, he condemns all humanity:

> Todos son
> Cómplices del robo...
>> (Tercera jornada, 1875-1876)

Just as, according to Christian theology, all are guilty of Original Sin, perpetuated generation after generation, all are guilty of Prometeo's crime and must be punished for it:

> Perezcan todos...
>> Tercera jornada, 1879)

Encouraged by Pallas, Apollo gives vent to his anger until he is interrupted by Minerva, who tries to calm his rage by arguing that the tiny ray hardly missed by him has brought great benefits to humanity. Pallas contradicts that Apollo's light must be given freely by him, not stolen. Minerva answers that Apollo's light, originating in the perfect being, gives man that spark of perfection which likens him to a god.

294

In *Genesis,* God is angered at Adam's having eaten from the tree of knowledge precisely because having done so, Adam is likened to Him, for the is then able to discern good from evil. Pallas contends that a theft is sinful no matter what positive consequences might result, just as disobedience to God is sinful no matter what the positive consequence might be. For example, Adam's and Eve's fall made possible the redemption and the biological procreation of mankind, but was, nevertheless, a sinful act. Minerva argues that because of the theft, men can now see clearly; that is, they can see the difference between good and evil and therefore be redeemed.

Apollo remains undecided. He sends both sisters back to earth to fight it out between them. He will not intervene. In Christian terms, in the eternal battle between will and reason for control of man's soul, God remains neutral; whether or not an individual chooses to allow reason to govern his actions depends solely on himself, not on divine intervention.

In the ensuing battle between Minerva and Pallas it is the former who is better equipped, for reason 'applies to the science of war just as to the other sciences. In other words, reason is capable of comprehending and subduing the will through understanding.

The War Between the Brothers

In Caucasus, the people side up either with one of the brothers or the other. Minerva joins Prometeo, who readily recognizes her by her voice. Unlike Discordia, Minerva cannot disguise her voice and lie. Reason cannot misrepresent the truth, although man can render a false or inaccurate representation of the truth by distorting logic.

Epimeteo approaches and Minerva hides. In order to avoid being recognized by her voice, she pretends to be an inanimate statue. While Epimeteo and Merlín try to explain the statue's strange silence, Pandora appears and Minerva slips out while Epimeteo's attention is diverted. That is, while man is preoccupied with images, reason is absent or at least inactive. Epimeteo is thoroughly confused. Unlike Prometeo who, guided by intellect, is able to distinguish reality from representation, Epimeteo cannot. Merlín perspicaciously sensses that one of the two is a representation, and playing on the double sense of *representar*, "to represent" and also "to act", he provides the key to the mystery:

¡Oh para representanta
Qué buena era! pues es cierto,
No errara el papel y fuera
En la tramoya sin miedo.

(Tercera jornada, 2274-2277)

Minerva is both an actress and a representation. She is acting the part of a statue; she is representing her own representation. Pandora, of course, is also a representation, for she is an image of Minerva. Thus, the scene is a complex net of representations and double representations as is life, in which what is reasonable does not always appear to be so and appearances may be mistaken for reality. Incidentally, Merlín's pun also tells us the means by which the actress playing Minerva is made to disappear: through the use of stage machinery. The complexity of the scene, Merlín's humor and Epimeteo's frustration, Merlín's pragmatism and Epimeteo's passion, convey the notion of the individual in the confusion of life.

Neither Merlín nor Epimeteo adequately explains the two Minervas. Epimeteo is confused by his imagination, which is spurred on by his jealousy of his brother, the object of Pandora's affections:

Pandora: ¿Qué culpa tengo que haga
Amor en su pensamiento
Caso la imaginación?

(Tercera jornada, 2368)

Merlín is confused by his senses:

> Merlín: No miento,
> El día que estoy viendo cosas.
> Que son cosas que estoy viendo.
>
> (Tercera jornada, 2317-2319)

Prometeo's meeting with Pandora is quite different from Merlín's and Epimeteo's. Although he momentarily takes her for Minerva, he soon recognizes her as Pandora. Prometeo is bothered by Pandora without understanding why. Each of her separate parts is pleasing, yet considered as a totality he finds her somehow lacking. He seeks something beyond the mere image, but what? While will is satisfied by the image, reason finds it unfulfilling and seeks something beyond. Pandora asks who could possibly deny his own creation, and Prometeo begins to answer, "he who has seen...," but is interrupted by the call to war. "He who has seen the gods cannot be satisfied by facsimiles," Prometeo might have said. Just as Segismundo and Cipriano learned through reason and experience to distinguish between reality and appearance and to seek the reality of the divine, so does Prometeo.

Prometeo joins his followers and prepares for battle. Epimeteo is surprised that Timantes has joined his brother's forces. The old man explains that he prefers to be on Prometeo's side because the fire brought by Prometeo brings warmth and protection by day and light by night; in Christian terms, the spark of the divine —or, more clearly, the light of faith— brings comfort to the person who knows God (who lives in daylight) and enlightenment to the person who does not (who lives in night). But, asks Epimeteo, what good are comfort and enlightenment if Apollo is to remain forever enraged:

> ¿Qué importa si todo eso
> Para en que Apollo castigue
> En todos su atrevimiento?
>
> (Tercera jornada, 2459-2461)

The angry God of the Old Testament leaves man no hope for redemption. Timante's explanations fall on empty ears as Epimeteo prepares for battle.

Discordia appears, descending from the heavens and singing. Deceitfully posing as "ambassador of the gods," she praises the people for their Old Testament ethic, which requires punishment without mercy for the thief and the murderer, "an eye for an eye and a tooth for a tooth." She calls a truce and declares that only Prometeo and Pandora are to be castigated for the suffering they have brought upon the people. The punishment will be in accordance with the laws of the Caucasus. Prometeo, the thief of Apollo's ray, will be locked in a prison where a ravenous bird will pick out and devour his heart. The following day his heart will be renewed and devoured again, and so the cycle will continue for all eternity.

Pandora, the murderess *(pues es/También homicida quien mata de amor;* Tercera jornada, 2522-2523) will be burned and all Caucasus set aflame:

> Hoguera será, que lleve en pavesas
> De leves cenizas el aire veloz.
> (Tercera jornada, 2530-2531)

Understood in Christian terms, this is the hell —endless torture and fire— which awaits all sinners without the miracle of redemption.

Prometeo, who only shortly before shunned Pandora's affections, now declares himself ready to defend her at any sacrifice. Aubrun found this sudden change of heart illogical, a deviation from the natural development of the tragedy.[25] It is quite logical, however, if we consider the play within a religious framework. Man, made in the image of God as are

---

[25] Aubrun. p. 25.

Prometeo and Pandora, can be saved from Original Sin only by sacrifice. Prometeo, the Adam figure, now evolves into a Christ figure, willing to die for the being created in the image of God.[26] If Pandora, the representation and symbol of the temporal, is to be rejected because she is only an image, she is also to be valued because she can be redeemed.

The people, including Timantes, turn against Prometeo and demand he be taken prisoner, just as the mob turned against Christ and by doing so participated in the fulfillment of the divine plan for Man's salvation.

Prometeo and Pandora lament their misfortune:

> Prometeo: ¡Ay de quien el bien que hizo,
> En mal convertido vió!
> > (Tercera jornada, 2567-2568)

> Pandora: ¡Ay de quien nació milagro
> Para fallecer horror!
> > (Tercera jornada, 2569-2570)

Prometeo, like Christ, brings light to the world and is condemned. Pandora, born of a miracle through the light of Apollo's ray just as Adam and Eve were born of the miracle of creation, is fated to die at the hand of discord: mankind is fated to suffer eternally without redemption for the sins of its first mother. Pandora's words may also be construed as a lament for the death of Christ, born of a miracle —thait is, as a result of immaculate conception— to die in horror, that is, crucified.

The two victims are blindfolded and covered, lest the people

---

[26] Everett W. Hesse sees the struggle between Prometeo and Epimeteo as simply a conflict between good and evil. This interpretation seems to be unsound given the reconciliation at the end of the play. See *Calderón de la Barca.* (New York: Twayne Publishers, 1967), p. 128.

take mercy on them if they see their suffering. According to the laws of Caucasus, once the faces of the condemned have been shielded from the sun there can be no exoneration; once one is shielded from the divine light, there can be no hope of salvation. Prometeo and Pandora are to be taken to the mountain, where Pandora's torch is to be put out. The light Prometeo gave her is not eternal at all. It flickers and dies, leaving mankind to suffer eternal torment.

Minerva, distressed over the apparent fate of her protegées, appeals to Apollo for mercy. Pallas opposes her and the two struggle. Minerva, applying the science of war, overwhelms her opponent; the force of reason is stronger than brute force. Discordia contends that Minerva's victory will change nothing, for the execution will be effectuated before Minerva can accuse her and Pallas to Jupiter. In her view, discord is the inevitable consequence of the dual character of human nature.

The people, expressing themselves in song, lament the fate of Prometeo and Pandora. The two victims also sing; through their suffering they are united:

> ¡Ay de quien vio...
> El bien convertido en mal...
> Y el mal en peor!
>
> (Tercera jornada, 2653, 5,7)

Epimeteo, in order that they might see each other in their suffering, uncovers the faces of Prometeo and Pandora and the people, witnessing the sad scene, feel compassion. Like Christ, Prometeo has taught mankind mercy through his suffering. Now mankind is prepared to receive grace.

Forgiveness and Redemption

Apollo appears and demands the people suspend the execution. He is surrounded by brilliant sunlight, and the

300

people, overwhelmed, ask the cause of such brightness. Apollo tells the people who he is. Understood as a God-symbol, he is first cause and can be known only by revelation. That is why he must identify himself to the people.

Apollo, in his boundless mercy, forgives Prometeo and allows him to keep the ray he has stolen. Pandora's torch will no longer flicker, but burn eternally; in Christian terms, God has bestowed eternal life upon man. Discord will dissipate and the evils brought about by Pandora will be dispelled. The horror of eternal damnation will be replaced by the joy of eternal salvation:

> El mal convertido en bien,
> Y el bien en mejor.
>
> (Tercera jornada, 2712-2713)

Prometeo and Epimeteo, reason and will, recognize they have been at fault to wage war against one another. They are brothers and must remain allies. They are both good, although when separated from one another they may become inflexible and distortive. Epimeteo is not put to death for his attempt to assert himself over Prometeo; will must not be extinguished, but simply held in check and allowed to function normally, for a healthy will is good and necessary.

Prometeo and Pandora marry. Pandora will become the true mother of mankind and assure the proliferation of the race. She will fulfill her mission, as expressed by the meaning of her name: "providence of time." Merlín and Libya also marry, out of theatrical convention and also to assure the proliferation of the lesser beings.

Conclusion

The conflict between reason and will is a central issue for many existentialists. The existentialist writers have dealt with

301

the dilemma in varying ways. For some, such as Unamuno —for whom the irreconcilable antogonism between reason and the will to believe led to a "tragic sense of life"— there could be no solution; the conflict was inevitable unless the supremacy of one or the other were arbitrarily imposed. For others, such as Jaspers, there could be no harmony between the two unless reason was defined and limited. For still others —Sartre, for example— the imposition of reason could lead to a mechanistic view of man which obviated free will; he, and other French existentialists, stress the active role of will rather than reason in confronting the problems posed by a hostile universe. For the existentialists, in general, the conflict between will and reason remains a conflict.

For Calderón, too, the struggle between the two is a fundamental human problem. It is, as such, the source of the dramatic action of many of his plays. It is central to all of the plays analyzed in this study: to the conflict between the "willful" Aureliano and the "reasonable" Cenobia; to. the friction between the superstitious Cosme and the open-minded don Manuel; to the inner turmoil experienced by don Lope, torn between his awarenesss of the unreasonableness of the honor code and the submission of his will to a society that he feels forces him to abide by it; to the conflict between Segismundo's need for self-assertion as well as his need to govern his actions; to Cipriano's tendency to rationalize and his consciousness of the dangers of doing so; and finally, to the battle between will and reason illustrated allegorically through the temporary animosity between Prometeo and Epimeteo. But Calderón, unlike the existentialists, resolves the problem.

For Calderón, both the will and reason have a natural active role. The balanced individual is neither will-less nor irrational, but rather he allows each faculty to perform normally; reason guiding the will; the will, healthy and strong, following those courses of action which reason deems appropriate. Calderón's solution is, of course, standard theology. Yet it is a viable solution even for modern man, for whom theology does not necessary constitute authority. The particular circumstances confronting us are very different from those which face Calderón's characters. It is, nonetheless, by achieving a harmonious balance between the two faculties, will and reason, that one can avoid the perils of rationalization, resulting from the subordination of reason to the will, on the one hand, and impotence, resulting from the ineffectiveness of the will, on the other.

CONCLUSION

The foregoing chapters suggest that Calderón was in a sense a precursor of the modern existentialist playwrights and novelists, in particular, of Sartre. The similarities between Calderón and these modern writers are most meaningful in terms of the kinds of characters they create. Like Sartre, Camus, Anouilh, and other writers of the same school, Calderón created characters faced with situations of great complexity to which they, as individuals free and responsible for their acts, must react. It is through the choices they make and the consequent acts they perform that these characters define themselves —as tyrants, as heroes, as men of honor, as individuals worthy of salvation or damnation.

The sense of uncertainty that permeates Calderón's plays results, we have said, from the characters' awareness of the deceptive nature of appearances. The sense of uncertainty that permeates the existentialist play and novel stems from the characters' sense of the absence of moral absolutes and of the lack of finality of human existence. In both cases, the characters experience a sense of anguish at having to make decisions in the face of doubt. The vacillations of the principal characters as they agonize in situations that are ambivalent, yet nevertheless require decisions, constitute dramatic crises. Calderón's plays typically revolve around one or more such crises. Aureliano's vacillation before the symbols of his new-found power, don Manuel's before the inexplicable happenings in his room, don Lope's in the face of the apparent threat to his honor, Segismundo's before the wonders of the

305

palace, Cipriano's before the Devil's deceptive magic, and Epimeteo's before his attraction to Pandora and his duty to Pallas are characteristic of these crises. In each of the forementioned situations, the character must choose and act. For example, Aureliano decides to reject doubt and accept the emperorship; don Manuel, to search for a reasonable explanation of the mystery; don Lope, to take vengeance, etc. This pattern of crisis, decision and consequent action accounts largely for the tremendous dramatic tension of Calderón's plays.

The lack of self-assuredness that typifies Calderón's characters gives them a decidely unheroic aspect. Their vacillations, uncertainties, and search for self-fulfillment recall the anguish of the antiheroes of modern existentialist fiction.

In the face of uncertainty Calderón's characters typically adopt one of two attitudes. Some, such as Aureliano, Cosme, don Lope, and Basilio, reject it, seeking to impose, rather, some form of intellectual certainty. It is characteristic of these persons that they trust appearances, interpreting them as evidence to dispel their doubts and to reinforce their preconceived notions. These characters typically see themselves as predestined; they hide behind what they believe to be their fate in order to justify their actions. They do not believe in their own freedom nor do they accept responsibility for their acts. Rather, they live in a world of inventions. Eventually, they become trapped in their own web of lies. By that time they have become alienated and emotionally unstable. These characters, except for those who experience a spiritual awakening during the course of the play, remain blind and insatiable of worldly goods until death. In seventeenth-century terms, they are *engañados*, men and women deceived by the information conveyed by the senses and unwilling to acknowledge any reallity beyond that which is immediately obvious. These characters are similar to the men and women of bad faith of modern fiction.

306

Others of Calderón's characters accept uncertainty, realizing that appearances are deceiving and the senses, unreliable. It is characteristic of these persons —Cenobia, Decio, don Manuel, Clotaldo— that they proceed with caution, weighing and considering each circumstance as it arises, never seeking to impose explanations. These characters are the *desengañados*. They are similar to the modern existentialist characters of good faith.

Calderón's characters also bear a resemblance to those produced by modern existentialist fiction in their awareness of and concern for their own temporality. Some, *engañados* such as Aureliano, both fear and seek death. Others, the *desengaños* —for example, Segismundo after his conversion— are able to accept death as both inevitable and meaningful. What gives death significance for both Calderón's characters and those produced by modern existential fiction is judgment. Judgment is the assessment of the total sum of one's deeds. Just as Pierre realizes at the end of Sartre's *Les Jeux son faits* that he has only one lifetime during which to define himself as a revolutionary, so does Segismundo realize he has only one lifetime during which to define himself as worthy of salvation. To deliver himself to a life of inaction would be to rob himself of the opportunity to achieve that goal.

In a Christian context, the judge is God and judgment is Final Judgment. But even those of Calderón's characters who do not function within the Christian framework are conscious of the inevitability of judgment. Aureliano seeks witnesses who will judge him powerful and ferocious. Don Lope's vengeance is perfomed precisely so that his supposed accusers —society, in general, and don Juan and King Sebastian, in particular— might judge him as he wishes to be judged: as a man of honor. The murders of don Luis and doña Leonor and the final decision to follow King Sebastián to Africa are the acts by which don Lope defines himself as honorable. For him, as for the characters in Sartre's *Huis-Clos,* "l'enfer, c'est les autres." That is, others judge one, impartially and objectively,

307

by one's acts. Whether the judge is God or other people, it is what one does that determines what one is.

Both Calderón's and Sartre's characters act in terms of a commitment. Every Christian is committed to the salvation of his own soul. At the end of *La vida es sueño,* Segismundo understands that he will be judged by God in terms of this commitment. In *A secreto agravio, secreta venganza,* don Lope's commitment is to honor. He seeks to be judged only by his peers and his king. He makes the mistake of seeking salvation in a purely social context. That is why the death of the principal character, which in Calderón's religious plays such as *El mágico prodigioso,* constitutes a happy or poetic ending, in *A secreto agravio, secreta venganza,* constitutes a tragic one. For Calderón, a Christian himself, don Lope's commitment is the wrong one.

Calderón's attitude toward such characters as don Lope is both compassionate and reprehensive. On the one hand, such characters are blind and pitiful; on the other, they are reprehensible, for they reject their own freedom and the Christian values of charity, compassion, forgiveness. Calderón, as a Christian, is himself *engagé.* His works are, in a sense, morality plays. He shows the tyrant, the opportunist, the man of honor, in their true light·—tragic and unheroic. Like Sartre, Calderón creates a *littérature engagée,* committed to the causes of freedom and self-awareness, understood in Christian terms. Characters such as don Lope are to be recognized for what they are and rejected.

Like Sartre's, Calderón's fictional world is non-elitist. Self-realization is a possibility for characters of all social stations. In *La vida es sueño,* the *gracioso* is a spiritually void opportunist. In *A secreto agravio, secreta venganza,* the *gracioso* is morally upright and acutely aware of the vacuity of don Lope's value system. In *La gran Cenobia,* one monarch is empty and fatuous while the other is magnanimous and politically adept. In *La vida es sueño,* the heroine is impetuous and idealistic; in *A secreto agravio, secreta venganza,* she is weak and deceitful; in *La dama duende,* she is clever and independent; in *La gran Cenobia,* she is generous, intelligent and competent. None of Calderón's characters is predetermined by sociological factors, by sex, or otherwise. Every character, king or valet, aristocrat or peasant, man or woman, is presented as free and capable of *desengaño.*

The extent to which Calderón's characters are self-determined becomes obvious when we compare them to characters produced by French and English theater of approximately the same periòd. Racine's protagonists are typically members of the royalty determined by the gods to suffer some dire fate against which their wills are impotent. Corneille's are likewise members of the royalty or aristocracy who follow one determined, heroic course from the beginning of the play to the end. The painful vacillations and intense self-awareness that characterize Calderón's creations are absent from French theater. English theater created more complex characters, but even they lack the sense of self-determination that typifies Calderón's characters. Shakespeare's heroes are frequently the victims of villains. In the tragedy *Othello,* the good Moor is the dupe of his evil enemy Iago, who tricks him into believing that Desdemona has been disloyal to him. In the comedy *Much Ado about Nothing,* the young suitor Claudio is tricked by don John and his servants into believing that Hero has deceived him. In Calderón's plays, this type of villain is conspicuously absent. The characters are the dupes of their own willfulness and faulty view of reality, not of others. They alone are responsible for their own fate. In *A secreto agravio, secreta venganza,* there is no character similar to Iago or don John. Don Lope alone plants the seeds of suspicion in his own mind and is ultimately responsible for his own self-destruction. At the end of Shakespeare's two plays, the villain confesses, the lady is exonerated, the protagonist's honor is left intact. The hero remains a hero. Things are

309

returned to their rightful order. In Calderón's dramas, there is no such clearing of the air. The characters remain blind to the hideous fact that they have toppled their own world, except, of course, in those cases in which, like Segismundo or Cipriano, they awaken to the reality of their own responsibility.

The reason for the many similarities between the literary creations of Calderón and those of many modern existentialists must, for the time being, remain in the realm of speculation. One possible link might be German romanticism. We know, of course, that many of the early German romantics were passionately fond of Calderón. Some of them were devout Catholics and were especially attracted to Calderón's religious plays. The German Catholic romantic critics —starting with the Schlegel brothers— were undoubtedly responsible for Calderón's renewed favor in the nineteenth century. Calderón remained a favorite with the Germans throughout the romantic period, even when the romantic movement lost its distinctly Catholic tendencies. We know that both Schopenhauer and Nietszche read Calderón. Although the German critics undoubtedly misunderstood some aspects of Calderón's dramas —notably his attitude toward honor— they did appreciate his view of the individual, self-aware and responsible, yet vacillating and uncertain in a hostile universe. The typical romantic hero, rebellious, impetuous, arrogant and defiant of fate, is to a great extent inspired by Calderonian characters such as Eusebio in *La devoción de la Cruz*. The culmination of this ideal is perhaps Nietzsche's superman.

The influence of Nietzsche on existentialist thought has been studied by a number of historians of existentialism, among them, Walter Kaufmann[1] and William Barret.[2] Suffice it to

[1] *From Shakespeare to Existentialism* (Garden City: Doubleday, 1960), pp. 207-240.
[2] *Irrational Man*, pp. 177-205.

mention here that Nietzsche's rejection of traditional ethics, his search for personally authentic values and moral honesty, his total rejection of preconceived schemes, and his view of the perfectibility of the will have been a major influence in modern existentialist thought. It seems plausible, then, that German Romanticism, which culminated in a sense in Nietzsche, who, in turn, so greatly influenced the existentialist writers, might be considered one important link between these writers and Calderón.

There is another possible explanation for the great similarity between several of the existentialist writers, in particular Sartre, and Calderón: many of these writers, including Sartre, were of Catholic background and even studied under the Jesuits. Their views are in many cases similar to those presented by standard Catholic theology. The main difference is that for the existentialists, the existence of God and one's natural commitment to Him are no longer taken as a matter of fact.

These suggestions are, of course, only speculative. Yet it is interesting to note that several existentialist writers, in particular Camus, have shown great interest in the Spanish theater. Camus translated two Spanish plays, Calderón's *La devoción de la Cruz* and Lope's *El Caballero de Olmedo*. Sartre's play *Le Diable et le bon Dieu* shows a striking similarity both to Calderón's *La vida es sueño* and to Cervantes' *El rufián dichoso*. Whether or not these similarities were intentional or merely accidental, they reflect an extraordinary coincidence in outlook. As we read Calderón's plays, we cannot help but be struck by their modernity and their universality. In an age in which the relevance of many traditional subjects of study in being questioned, we must place Calderón's theater among the most relevant.

Selected Bibliography

Editions of Calderón's Works

Complete Works

Obras completas. Tomo I: Dramas. Ed. Luis Astrana Marin. Madrid: Aguilar, 1951

Obras completas. Tomo I: Dramas. Ed. Angel Briones. Madrid: Aguilar, 1966.

Obras completas. Tomo II: Comedias. Ed. Angel Valbuena Briones. Madrid: Aguilar, 1960.

Obras completas. Tomo III: Autos sacramentales. Ed. Angel Valbuena Prat. Madrid: Aguilar, 1967.

Collections that Include Works Mentioned in this Study

Autos sacramentales. Tomo 1: La cena del rey Baltasar; El gran teatro del mundo; La vida es sueño. Ed. Angel Valbuena Prat. 3rd ed. Mądrid: Espasa-Calpe, 1951 (Clas. Castellanos)

Autos sacramentales. Tomo II: El pleito matrimonial del cuerpo y el alma; Los encantos de la culpa; Tu prójimo como a ti. Ed. Angel Valbuena Prat, 3rd ed. Madrid: Espasa-Calpe, 1952 (Clas. Castellanos).

Autos sacramentales. Barcelona: Plaza y Janés, 1961.

Autos sacramentales: El gran teatro del mundo; La vida es sueño; La cena del rey Baltasar; Los encantos de la culpa; Tu prójimo como a ti. Barcelona: Iberia, 1964.

313

Comedias de capa y espada. Tomo II: La dama duende; No hay cosa como callar. Ed. Angel Valbuena Briones. Madrid: Espasa-Calpe. (Clas. Castellanos).

Comedias religiosas. Tomo I: La devoción de la Cruz; El mágico prodigioso. Ed. Angel Valbuena Prat. Madrid: Espasa-Calpe, 1953 (Clas. Castellanos).

Dramas de honor. Tomo I: A secreto agravio, secreta venganza. Tomo II: El médico de su honra; El pintor de su deshonra. Ed. Angel Valbuena Briones. Madrid: Espasa-Calpe, 1953 (Clas. Castellanos)

Dramas de honor. Tomo I: A secreto agravio, secreta venganza. Tomo II: El médico de su honra; El pintor de su deshonra. Ed. Angel Valbuena Briones. Madrid: Espasa-Calpe, 1956 (Clas. Castellanos).

Dramen in der Übertragung von Johann Diederich Gries (welt-liche Schauspiele) und Joseph von Eichendorff (geistliche Schauspiele), mit einen Nachwort von Edmund Schramm. Munich: Winkler Verlag, 1963.

Eight Dramas of Calderón. Trans. Edward Fitzgerald. Garden City: Doubleday, 1961.

Estudio y antología. Ed. José Inocencio Tejedor Sanz. Madrid: Compañia Bibliográfica Española, 1967.

Four Plays. Trans. Edwin Honig. New York. Hill and Wang, 1961.

Obra dramática. Ed. J. Alcina Franch and E. Veres. Barcelona: Elite, 1959.

Obras selectas. Adaptación de Fernando Laina. Madrid: Hernando, 1951.

Obras. Teatro doctrinal y religioso. Ed. Angel Valbuena Prat. Barcelona: Vergara, 1965.

Piesi, Per. s ispan. Introd. by N. B. Tomashevskiy. Moscow: Iskusstvo, 1961.

Six Plays. Trans. Denis Florence MacCarthy, and revised by Henry W. Wells, New York: Las Américas, 1961.

Spanische Welttheater. 4 Meisterdramen. Ed. Wilhelm von Scholz. Munich: List, 1961.

Sus mejores poesías. Barcelona: Bruguera, 1954.

Teatro. Trans. Ferdinando Carlesi. Introd. by Mario Casella. Florence: Sansoni, 1949.

Tragedias. Tomo I: La vida es sueño; La hija del aire; El mayor monstruo del mundo. Ed. Francisco Ruiz Ramón. Madrid: Alianza Editorial, 1967.

Tragedias. Tomo II: A secreto agravio, secreta venganza; El médico de su honra; El pintor de su deshonra. Ed. Francisco Ruiz Ramón. Madrid: Alianza Editorial, 1968.

Tragedias. Tomo III: La devoción de la Cruz; El mágico prodigioso; Los cabellos de Absalón; La cisma de Inglaterra. Ed. Francisco Ruiz Ramón. Madrid: Alianza Editorial, 1969.

Trois autos sacramentales. Trans. Mathilde Pomès. Paris: Klincksieck, 1957.

Trois comédies: La Vie est un songe; Le Médecin de son honneur; L'Alcalde de Zalamea. Ed. Alexandre Arnoux. Paris: Grasset, 1955.

315

Veinticinco siglos de teatro. Ed. Enrique Ortenbach. Barcelona: Fomento Internacional de Cultura, 1959.

El alcalde de Zalamea y dos entremeses: El dragoncillo, La rabia. Ed. Julio Durán Cerda. Santiago de Chile: Edit. Universitaria, 1956.

El alcalde de Zalamea; La vida es sueño. Ed. Jorge Campos. Madrid: Taurus, 1959.

El alcalde de Zalamea; La vida es sueño. 11th ed. Madrid: Espasa-Calpe, 1959.

El alcalde de Zalamea; La vida es sueño. Madrid: Edaf, 1964.

El alcalde de Zalamea; La vida es sueño; El gran teatro del mundo. Ed. Cipriano Rivas Xerif. Mexico: Ateneo, 1965.

El alcalde de Zalamea; La vida es sueño; El gran teatro del mundo. Ed. Amando Isasi Angulo. Barcelona: Bruguera, 1968.

El alcalde de Zalamea; La vida es sueño; El mágico prodigioso, 3rd ed. Madrid: Aguilar, 1959.

La devoción de la Cruz; El gran teatro del mundo. 3rd ed. Madrid: Espasa-Calpe, 1961.

La devoción de la Cruz; El mágico prodigioso; Los cabellos de Absalón; La sibila de Oriente y gran reina de Sabá. In Nicolás González Ruiz (ed.), *Piezas maestras del teatro teológico español, Tomo II: Comedias,* 2nd ed., Madrid: Bib. de Autores Cristianos, 1953, pp. 133-160.

La Dévotion à la Croix; La Vie est un songe (with Lope de Vega's *Fontovejuna; L'Enlèvement d'Hélène*). In Paul Verdevoye, (trans. and ed.), *Les Baroques* Paris: Mazenod, 1959.

El mágico prodigioso; Casa con dos puertas mala es de guardar. 4th ed. Madrid: Espasa-Calpe, 1961.

El médico de su honra; El pintor de su deshonra. Ed. Angel Valbuena Briones. Madrid: Espasa-Calpe, 1965.

No hay burlas con el amor; El médico de su honra. 3rd ed. Madrid: Espasa-Calpe, 1962.

El pleito matrimonial del cuerpo y el alma; La cena de Baltasar; El gran teatro del mundo; Los encantos de la culpa; Tu prójimo como a ti; La vida es sueño. In *Autos sacramentales eucarísticos,* ed. Alejandro Sanvisens, Barcelona: Edit. Cervantes, 1952.

El pleito matrimonial del cuerpo y el alma; El veneno y la triaca; La cena de Baltasar; La vida es sueño; La hidalga del valle; El gran teatro del mundo; Los encantos de la culpa; Las órdenes militares; A María el corazón; Sueños hay que verdad son; El santo rey don Fernando I; A Dios por razón de estado; El gran mercado del mundo; La devoción de la misa; El pintor de su deshonra. In Nicolás González Ruiz (ed.), *Autos sacramentales,* 2nd ed., Madrid: Bib. de Autores Cristianos, 1953, pp. 297-792.

Der Standhafte Prinz; Der Arzt seiner Ehre. Trans. August Wilhelm Schlegel and Johann Diederich Gries. Munich: Goldmann, 1961.

El príncipe constante; La vida es sueño; El alcalde de Zalamea; Los encantos de la culpa. Ed. José María Pemán. Barcelona: Eito, 1951.

La vida es sueño; El alcalde de Zalamea. Ed. Augusto
Cortina. Madrid: Espasa-Calpe, 1955.

Das Leben, ein Traum; Der Richter von Zalamea. Trans.
Johann Diederich Gries, Munich: Doldmann, 1960.

La vida es sueño; El alcalde de Zalamea. Ed. Stugis E.
Leavitt. New York: Dell, 1964.

*La vida es sueño; El alcalde de Zalamea; El mágico
prodigioso.* 4th ed. Ed. Federico Sainz de Robles.
Madrid: Aguilar, 1961.

*La vida es sueño; El alcalde de Zalamea; El mágico
prodigioso.* New York: Doubleday, 1961.

*La vida es sueño; El alcalde de Zalamea; El mágico
prodigioso; El médico de su honra; El gran teatro del
mundo.* In Antonio Espina (ed.), *Las mejores escenas
del teatro español e hispanoamericano desde sus
orígenes hasta la época actual,* Madrid: Aguilar, 1959.

*La vida es sueño; El alcalde de Zalamea; El mágico prodi-
gioso; El príncipe constante.* Ed. José Bergua. Madrid:
Ibéricas, 1955.

*La vida es sueño; El alcalde de Zalamea; El médico de su
honra.* Barcelona: Maucci, 1961.

*Life is a Dream; Love after Death; The Wonder-Working
Magician.* In Eric Bentley (ed.), *The Classic Theatre,
Vol. III: Six Spanish Plays,* Garden City: Doubleday,
1959.

La Vie est un songe; La Dévotion à la croix (also *L'Etoile de
Séville* and Cervantes' *Le Retable des merveilles*). In
Calderón, Lope de Vega, et Cervantes, *Théâtre*

espagnol, trans. Alexandre Arnoux, Albert et Jules Super-vielle, et Dominique Aubier, Paris: Club des libraires de France, 1957.

La vida es sueño; El principe constante; El alcalde de Zalamea; La cena del rey Baltasar. In Vicente Gómez-Bravo (ed.), *Silva dramática. Asuntos del teatro español dispuestos para estudio literario,* 4th ed., Madrid: Razón y Fe, 1967.

Individual Works Mentioned in this Study

A secreto agravio, secreta venganza.

A secreto agravio, secreta venganza, 3rd ed. Madrid: España-Calpe, 1964

A secreto agravio, secreta venganza. Ed. Edward Nagy, Zaragoza: Ebro, 1966 (Clas. Ebro).

El Alcalde de Zalamea.

El alcalde de Zalamea. Ed. André Nougé. Toulouse-Paris: Privat-Didier, 1952.

L'Alcalde de Zalamea. Trans. Alexandre André Arnoux. Paris: 1953.

El alcalde de Zalamea. Ed. Fermín Estrella Gutiérrez. Buenos Aires: Kapelusz, 1954.

El alcalde de Zalamea. (Extracts.) Paris: 1954 (Col. Mil renglones.)

319

Der Richter von Zalamea. Trans. J.D. Gries. Leipzig: Reclam, 1954.

El alcalde de Zalamea. Madrid: Escelicer, 1959.

L'Alcalde de Zalamea. Trans. Robert Marrast. Paris: Aubier, 1959.

Alcadele din Zalamea. Trans. Emanuel Avilar. Ed. Paul Alexandru Georgescu. Bucharest: Editura de Stat Pentru Literatura si Arta, 1959.

The Mayor of Zalamea. Trans. William E. Colford. Great Neck, N.Y.: Barron's, 1959.

Zalamejský Rychtár. Trans. Joroslov Pokorny. Ed. Milso Fiala. Prague: Orbis, 1959.

L'Alcalde de Zalamea. Trans. Georges Pillement. Paris: TNP. 1961.

El alcalde de Zalamea. Ed. Gabriel Espino, 7th ed. Zaragoza: Ebro, 1962.

El alcalde de Zalamea. Ed. Peter N. Dunn. Oxford: Pergamon, 1966.

El alcalde de Zalamea (El garrote más bien dado, según el texto de 1651). Ed. Everett W. Hesse. Buenos Aires: Plus Ultra, 1967.

La dama duende.

La dama duende. Ed. Herbert Kock. Halle: Max Niemeyer Verlag, 1952.

La dama duende. Ed. Pilar Diez y Jiménez de Castellanos. 2nd ed. Zaragoza: Ebro, 1957 (Clas. Ebro).

(La dama duende) Drilledjaevelen. Danish adaptation by Jean Louis Petersen. Copenhagen: Gyldendal, 1959.

La dama duende. Ed. Eugenio Castelli. Buenos Aires: Edit. Huemul, 1965.

La dama duende. Ed. José Luis Alonso. Madrid: Editora Nacional, 1966.

La devoción de la Cruz.

La devoción de la Cruz. Ed. Sidney F. Wexler. Doct. diss., New York University, 1952.

La dévotion à la Croix. Trans. Albert Camus. Paris: Gallimard, 1953.

La devoción de la Cruz. Ed. Isidoro Montiel. 4th ed. Zaragoza: Ebro, 1961.

La devoción de la Cruz. Ed. Sidney F. Wexler. Salamanca: Anaya, 1966.

En la vida todo es verdad y todo mentira.

En la vida todo es verdad y todo mentira. Ed. Don William Cruickshank. London, 1971.

La estatua de Prometeo

La estatua de Prometeo. Ed. Charles V. Aubrun. Paris: Centre de Documentation Universitaire, 1961.

La estatua de Prometeo. Ed. Charles V. Aubrun. Paris: Centre de Recherches de l'Institut d'Etudes Hispaniques, 1965.

El gran teatro del mundo.

El gran teatro del mundo. Ed. Juan Loveluck M. In *Autos sacramentales por Lope de Vega y otros,* Santiago de Chile: Zig-Zag, 1953.

The Great Theater of the World. Trans. Mack H. Singleton. In *Masterpieces of the Spanish Golden Age.* ed. Angel Flores, New York: Rinehart, 1957.

El gran teatro del mundo. Ed. Eugenio Frutos Cortés. Salamanca: Anaya, 1958.

Das grosse Welttheater. Trans. (and arranged for staging) by Hans Urs. von Balthasar. Einsiedeln: Hohannes, 1959.

Das Einsiedler grosse Welttheater. Trans. Joseph von Eichendorff: Einsiedeln, Gesellschaft der geistlichen Spiele, 1960.

El gran teatro del mundo. An edition and translation of the Nahuatl version by William A., Hunter. In *Middle American Research Institute,* Publication 27, New Orleans: 1960, pp. 107-221. (Doct. dist., Tulane Univ., 1954).

El gran teatro del mundo. Adaptation "a lectura dialogada." Madrid: Gráficas Ibarra, 1962.

Das grosse Welttheater. Ed. Joseph von Eichendorff and Fritz Schalk. Stuttgart: Reclam, 1962.

El gran teatro del mundo. In Anthony Zahareas and Barbara Mujica (eds.) *Readings in Spanish Literature,* Commentary by Alexander A. Parker, New York: Oxford University Press, 1975.

La hija del aire.

La hija del aire. A Critical Annotated Edition of the "Primera Parte", with a Study of the Semiramis Legend and its Dramatic Treatment by Calderón in Relation to Earlier Dramatizations of the Theme. Ed. G. Edward. Unpub. doct. diss., University of London (King's College), 1960-61

El mágico prodigioso.

El mágico prodigioso. Ed. Angel Valbuena Prat. Zaragoza: Ebro, 1953 (Clas. Ebro).

Der wundertätige Magier. Ed. Eugen Gürster. Stuttgart: Reclam, 1962.

Le Magicien prodigieux. Trans. and ed. Bernard Sesé. Paris: Editions Montaigne, 1969.

El médico de su honra.

The Surgeon of His Honour. Ed. Roy Campbell. Introd. by Everett W. Hesse. Madison: Univ. of Wisconsin Press, 1960.

El médico de su honra. Ed. C. A. Jones. Oxford: Oxford Univers. Press, 1961.

No hay más fortuna que Dios.

No hay más fortuna que Dios. Ed. Alexander A. Parker. Manchester: Manchester Univ. Press, 1949.

El pintor de su deshonra.

El pintor de su deshonra. Ed. Manuel Ruiz Lagos. Madrid: Ediciones Alcalá, 1969.

La vida es sueño.

La vita è un sogno. Trans. A. Monteverdi. In C. Pavolini (ed.), *Tutto il teatro di tutti i tempi,* Rome: 1953.

La vida es sueño. Ed. Rafael Gastón. Zaragoza: Ebro, 1954 (Clas. Ebro).

La vida es sueño. Ed. Martín de Riquer. Barcelona: Juventud, 1954.

Life is a Dream. Trans. William E. Colford. Great Neck, N. Y.: Barron's, 1958.

La vida es sueño. Ed. Everett W. Hesse. New York: Scribner, 1961.

La vida es sueño. Ed. Albert E. Sloman. Manchester: Manchester Univ. Press, 1961.

Das Leben ist ein Traum. Ed. Eugen Gürster. Stuttgart: Reclam, 1962.

Life Is a Dream. Trans. Edward and Elizabeth Huberman. In Angel Flores (ed.), *Spanish Drama,* New York: Bantam Books, 1962.

La vie est un songe. Adaptation by M. C. Valène and André Charpak. Paris: L'Avant-Scène, No. 258, 1962.

La vida es sueño. Buenos Aires: Edit. La Mandrágora, 1963.

La vida es sueño. Madrid: Alfil, 1964.

La vida es sueño. Buenos Aires: Losada, 1965.

La vida es sueño. Ed. Carmelo Samona. Roma: De Santis, 1966.

La vita è sogno. Il drama e l'auto sacramental. Ed. Luisa Orioli. Milan: Adelphi, 1967.

La vida es sueño. In José Martel, Hymen Alpern and Leonard Mades (eds.), *Diez comedias del Siglo de Oro,* New York: Harper and Row, 1968.

Life's a Dream. Trans. Kathleen Raine and R. M. Nadal. London: Hamish Hamilton, 1968.

General Studies on Calderón

Alonso, Dámaso. "La correlación en la estructura del teatro calderoniano." In Dámaso Alonso and Carlos Bousoño, *Seis calas en la expresión literaria española,* Madrid: Gredos, 1951, pp. 115-86.

Artiles, Jenaro. "Bibliografía sobre el problema del honor y la honra en el drama español." In *Filología y crítica hispánica: Homenaje al Prof. Federico Sánchez Escribano,* ed. Alberto Porquera-Mayo and Carlos Rojas, Madrid-Atlanta: Ediciones Alcalá-Emory Univ., 1969, pp. 235-41.

Aubrun, Charles V. "Le Déterminisme naturel et la causalité surnaturelle chez Calderón." In *Le Théâtre Tragique,* Paris: Centre National de la Recherche Scientifique, 1962, pp. 199-209.

—————. *Histoire du théâtre espagnol.* Paris: Presses Universitaires de France, 1965, pp. 63-78 (Col. Que sais-je?).

—————. *La Comédie espagnole* (1600-1680). Paris: Presses Universitaires de France, 1966.

Ayala, Francisco. "Sobre el punto de honor castellano." *Revista de Occidente,* 2a. Epoca 1, No 5 (1953), pp. 151-74.

Bandler, Jane Yankovic. *Comic Mechanisms in the Cape and Sword Plays of Calderón de la Barca.* Unpubl. Doc. Diss. (1975).

Le Baroque au Théâtre et la Théâtralité du Baroque. Actes 1966 de la 2e session des Journées internationales d'étude du Baroque. Montauban: Centre National de Recherches du Baroque, 1967, p. 151.

Bertrand, J.J.A. "Los comienzos del hispanismo alemán." *Clavileño,* 3, No. 14 (1952), pp. 11-14.

—————. "Encuentros de F. Schiller con España." *Clavileño,* 6, No. 35 (1955), pp. 38-42.

Beysterveldt, A.A. van. *Répercussion du souci de la pureté de sang sur la conception de l'honneur dans la "Comedia nueva" espagnole.* Leiden: E. J. Brill, 1966.

Bomli, P.W. *La Femme dans l'Espagne du Siècle d'Or.* The Hague: Martinus Nijhoff, 1950.

Bravo-Villasante, Carmen. *La mujer vestida de hombre en el teatro español (Siglos XVI-XVII).* Madrid: Revista de Occidente, 1955.

Brenan, Gerald. *The Literature of the Spanish People.* Cambridge: Univ. Press, 1951, pp. 275-314.

Camus, Albert. Introduction to *La Dévotion à la Croix.* Paris: Gallimard, 1953.

Casalduero, Joaquín de. "Algunas características de la literatura española del Renacimiento y del Barroco." In *Filología y crítica hispánica: Homenaje al Prof. Federico Sánchez Escribano,* ed. Alberto Porqueras-Mayo and Carlos Rojas, Madrid-Atlanta: Ediciones Alcalá-Emory Univ., 1969, pp. 87-96.

Castro, Américo. *La realidad histórica de España.* Mexico: Porrúa, 1954, p. 421-601.

————. "El drama de la honra en España y en su literatura:" *Cuadernos del Congreso por la Libertad de la Cultura,* No. 38 (1959), pp. 3-15; No. 39 (1959), pp. 16-28.

————. *De la edad conflictiva.* I: *El drama de la honra en España y en su literatura.* Madrid: Taurus, 1961.

Chandler, Richard Eugene, and Kessel Schwartz. *A New History of Spanish Literature.* Baton Rouge: Louisiana State Univ. Press, 1961, pp. 91-94.

Chapman, W. G. "Las comedias mitológicas de Calderón." *Revista de Literatura,* 5 (1954), pp. 35-67.

Couche, John Philip, "Camus' Dramatic Adaptations and Translations," *The French Review,* 33, No. 1, (Oct., 1959), pp. 27-36.

Dunn, Peter N. "Honour and the Christian Background in Calderón." *Bulletin of Hispanic Studies,* 37 (1960), pp. 75-105 (Also in Wardropper, Bruce, *Critical Essays,* 1965, pp. 25-60).

Durán, Manuel. "Camus and the Spanish Theater." *Yale French Studies,* No. 25 (1960), pp. 123-31.

327

Durán, Manuel and González Echeverría, Roberto. *Calderón y la crítica, historia y antología*. Madrid: Gredos, 1976.

Escobar López, Ignacio. "Teatro sacramental y existencial de Calderón de la Barca." *Cuadernos hispanoamericanos*. No. 134 (1961), pp. 219-34 (Also in *Revista de la Univ. de los Andes*, 3, 1960, pp. 50-62 and *Bol. de la Acad. Colombiana*, 10, 1960, pp. 313-28.)

Farinelli, Arturo. *Poesía y crítica*. Temas hispanoamericanos. Madrid, Consejo Superior de Investigaciones Científicas, 1954, pp. 109-15.

Frutos Cortés, Eugenio. "La filosofía del barroco y el pensamiento de Calderón." *Rev. de la Univ. de Buenos Aires*, 9 (1951), pp. 173-230.

————. *La filosofía de Calderón en sus Autos sacramentales*. Zaragoza, Institución "Fernando el Católico," Consejo Superior de Investigaciones Científicas, 1952.

Gilman, Stephen. "The *Comedia* in the Light of Recent Criticism Including the New Criticism." *Bulletin of the Comediantes*, 12, No. 1 (1960), pp. 1-5.

Green, Otis H. *Spain and the Western Tradition: The Castilian Mind in Literature from "El Cid" to Calderón*. 4 vols. Madison: Univ. of Wisconsin Press, 1963-66; Vol. I, pp. 258-62; Vol. II, pp. 31-32, 114-15, 124-25, 136-37, 143-45, 210-11, Vol III, pp. 185-86; Vol. IV, pp. 58-60, 78-81, 172-74, 222-23, 244-47, 275-77.

Hesse, Everett W. *Calderón de la Barca*. New York: Twayne Publishers, 1967.

Hilborn, Harry W. *A Chronology of the Plays of Calderón.*
Toronto: University of Toronto Press, 1938.

Honig, Edwin. Introduction to Calderón de la Barca, Pedro,
Four Plays, New York: Hill and Wang, 1961.

—————. "The Concept of Honor in the Dramas of
Calderón." *New Mexico Quarterly,* 35 (1965), pp. 105-
17.

—————. "The Seizures of Honor in Calderón." *Kenyon
Review,* 23 (1961), pp. 426-47.

—————.*Calderón and the Seizures of Honor.* Cambridge,
Mass.: Harvard University Press, 1972.

Iriarte, Joaquín. "Calderón o la temática moderna." In *Pen-
sadores e historiadores: I. Casa de Austria (1500-
1700),* Madrid: Edit. Razón y Fe, 1960, pp. 401-63.

—————. "Schopenhauer, admirador de Gracián y de
Calderón." *Razón y Fe,* 162 (1960), pp. 405-18.

Jones, C. A. *The Code of Honour in the Spanish Golden
Age Drama, with Special Reference to Calderón.*
Unpub, doct. diss., Oxford Univ., 1955.

—————. "Honor in Spanish Golden-Age Drama: Its Relation to Real Life and to Morals." *Bulletin of Hispanic
Studies,* 35 (1958), pp. 199-210.

—————. "Spanish Honour as Historical Phenomenon,
Convention and Artistic Motive." *Hispanic Review,* 33
(1965), pp. 32-29.

—————. "Brecht y el drama del Siglo de Oro."
Segismundo, 3 (1967), pp. 39-55.

329

Lionetti, Harold. "La preocupación del 'más allá'." *Hispania*, 41 (1958), pp. 26-29.

Lorenz, Erika. "Calderón und die Astrologie." *Romanistische Jahrbuch*, 12 (1961), pp. 265-77.

Lund, Harry. *Pedro Calderón de la Barca: A Biography*. Edinburg (Texas): Privately Printed (Andrés Noriega Press), 1963.

Manson, William R. *Attitudes toward Authority as Expressed in Typical Spanish Plays of the Golden Age*. Unpub. doct. diss., Univ. of North Carolina, 1963.

Maravall, José Antonio. "Una interpretación histórico-social del teatro barroco." *Cuadernos hispanoamericanos*, 78 (1969), pp. 621-49; 79 (1969), pp. 74-108.

McPheeters, E.W. "Camus' Translations of Plays by Lope and Calderón," *Symposium*, 12, (1958) pp. 52-64.

Menéndez Pelayo, Marcelino. *Calderón y su teatro*. Buenos Aires: Emecé: n. d.

Parker, Alexander A. Commentary to *El gran tratro del mundo*. In *Readings in Spanish Literature*. (eds.) Anthony Zahareas and Barbara Mujica, New York: Oxford University Press, 1975.

—————. *The Approach to the Spanish Drama of the Golden Age*. London, The Hispanic and Luso-Brazilian Councils, 1957. (Col. Diamante, 6) (Reprinted in *Tulane Drama Review*, 4, 1959, pp. 42-59).

—————. *The Allegorical Drama of Calderón. An Introduction to the Autos Sacramentales*. Oxford: Dolphin, 1962, 1968.

————. "The Father-Son Conflict in the Drama of Calderón." *Forum for Mod. Lang. Studies,* 2 (1966), pp. 99-113.

————."The Spanish Drama of the Golden Age: A method of Analysis and Interpretation." In *The Great Playwrights: Twenty-four Plays with Commentaries by Critics and Scholars, I.* Chosen and introduced by Eric Bently. Garden City: Doubleday, 1970, pp. 679-707 (This article is a revision of "The Approach", cited above.)

————. "Toward a Definition of Calderonian Tragedy." *Bulletin of Hispanic Studies,* 39 (1962), pp. 222-37.

————. "On Edwin Honig's *Calderón and the Seizures of Honor.*" Bulletin of the Comediantes, 26 (1974), pp. 68-71.

Parker, Jack H. and Fox, Arthur M. *Calderón de la Barca Studies, 1951-69.* Toronto: University of Toronto Press, 1971.

Podol, Peter, *The Evolution of the Honor Theme in Modern Spanish Literature* Unpub. doct. diss., Univ. of Pennsylvania, 1968.

Prince, Alvin Lafayette, III. *The Role of the King in Selected Works of Calderón de la Barca.* Unpubl. Doc. Diss. (1975).

Roig Gironella, J. "La angustia existencial por el no ser del ser y el teatro de Calderón." *Gran Mundo* (Madrid), 7 (1953), pp. 555-80.

Sauvage, Micheline. *Calderón dramaturge.* Paris: L'Arche, 1959.

Serrano Plaja, "El absurdo en Camus y en Calderón de la Barca." *Mélanges à la Mémoire de Jean Serrailh, II* Paris: Centre de Recherches de l'Institut d'Etudes Hispaniques, 1967, pp. 389-405.

Serrano Poncela, Segundo. "Unamuno y los clásicos." *Torre, 9,* Nos. 35-36. (1961), pp. 505-35.

Seator, Lynette. "An Existential View of Man in Four Dramas of Calderón." *Hispano,* 49 (1973), pp. 17-43.

Shergold, N.D. *The Staging of Secular Drama in Spain, 1655-1700.* Unpubl. doct. diss., Cambridge Univ., 1954.

————. *A History of the Spanish Stage from Medieval Times until the End of the Seventeenth Century.* Oxford: Clarendon Press, 1967.

Shergold, N.D., and J. E. Varey. *Los autos sacramentales en Madrid en la época de Calderón, 1637-1681: Estudios y Documentos.* Madrid: Ed. de Historia, Geografía y Arte, 1961.

Sloman, Albert E. *The Dramatic Craftsmanship of Calderón: His Use of Earlier Plays.* Oxford: Dolphin, 1958.

Valbuena Briones, Angel. *Ensayo sobre la obra de Calderón.* Madrid: Ateneo, 1958.

————. "El concepto del hado en el teatro de Calderón." *Bulletin Hispanique,* 63 (1961), pp. 48-53.

————. "El simbolismo en el teatro de Calderón: La caída del caballo." *Romanische Fornschungen,* 74 (1962), pp. 60-76.

Valbuena Prat, Angel. *Calderón.* Barcelona: Juventud, 1941.

——————. *Historia del teatro español.* Barcelona: Noguer, 1956.

——————. *Historia de la literatura española.* 5th ed., revised. 3 vols. Barcelona: Noguer 1957.

——————. *El teatro español en su Siglo de Oro.* Barcelona: Edit. Planeta, 1969.

Wardropper, Bruce W. (ed.) *Critical Essays on the Theatre of Calderón.* New York: New York Univ. Press, 1965.

Wilson, Edward M. "The Four Elements in the Imagery of Calderón." *The Modern Language Review,* 3331, No. 1 (1936) pp. 34-47

——————. "On the Pando Editions of Calderón's Autos." *Hispanic Review,* 27 (1959), pp. 324-44.

——————. "The Two Editions of Calderón's Primera Parte of 1640." *The Library,* Fifth Series, 14 (1959), pp. 175-91.

Studies on or Related to Individual Works
Discussed in this Investigation

A secreto agravio, secreta venganza.

Honig, Edwin. "Dehumanizing Honor," in *Calderón and the Seizures of Honor.* Cambridge, Mass: Harvard University Press, 1972, pp. 37-52.

May, T.E. "The Folly and Wit of Secret Vengeance: Calderón's *A secreto agravio, secreta venganza.*" *Forum for Modern Language Studies,* 2, No. 2 (April, 1966) pp. 114-22.

333

Mujica, Barbara. *Calderón's don Lope de Almeida: A Kafkian Character.* New York: Plaza Mayor, 1971.

Valbuena Briones, Angel. Introduction to *A secreto agravio, secreta venganza.* Madrid: Espasa-Calpe, 1956.

Wilson, Edward M. "La discreción de don Lope de Almeida." *Clavileño,* 2, No. 9 (1951), pp. 1-10).

—————. "Notes on the Text of *A secreto agravio, secreta venganza.*" *Bulletin of Hispanic Studies,* 35 (1958), pp. 72-82.

La dama duende

Acrete, Julio C. "Calderón de la Barca." *Primer Acto,* No. 78 (1966), p. 64 (Review of performance by José Luis Alonso, 1966).

Aragonés, Juan Emilio. "*La dama duende* y el otro Calderón." *La Estafeta Literaria,* 342 (April 23, 1966), pp. 12-13 (Review of performance by José Luis Alonso, 1966).

Armas, Frederick A. de. "Céspedes y Meneses and Calderón's *La dama duende.*" *Romance Notes,* 11 (1970), 598-603.

Dalbor, John B. "*La dama duende,* de Calderón, y *The Parson's Wedding,* de Killigrew." *Hispano,* 2 (1958), pp. 41-50.

Fucilla, Joseph G. "*La dama duende* and *La viuda valenciana.*" *Bulletin of the Comediantes,* 22 (1970), 29-32.

Gättke, Walter. "Zu Calderóns Komödie *Dame Kobold.*" *Die Volksbühne* (Hamburg), 14 (1963), pp. 47-48.

Honig, Edwin. "Flickers of Incest on the Face of Honor: Calderón's Phantom Lady." *Tulane Drama Review*, 6 (1962), pp. 69-105.

Horst, Robert ter. "The Ruling Temper of Calderón's *La dama duende.*" *Bulletin of the Comediantes*, 27 (1975), pp. 68-72.

Kuehne, Alyce de. "Los planos de la realidad aparente y la realidad auténtica en *La dama duende* de Calderón." *Pacific Coast Philology*, 2 (1967), pp. 40-46.

Mujica, Barbara. "Tragic Elements in Calderón's *La dama duende.*" *Kentucky Romance Quarterly*, 16, iv (1969), pp. 303-28.

Quinto, José María de. "*La dama duende* o el verso encontrado." *Insula*, 21, No. 234. (May, 1966), p. 14 (Review of Performance by José Luis Alonso).

Santaló, José Luis. "*La dama duende,* en el Español." *Arbor*, 64, No. 245, (1966), pp. 89-90 (Review of performance by José Luis Alonso).

Schindler, Otto G. "Calderón's *Dame Kobod* aus dem Stegreif." *Maske und Kothern* (Graz-Wien), 15 (1969), pp. 325-41.

Schwarz, Egon. *Hofmannsthal und Calderón.* The Hague: Mounon; Cambridge, Mass: Harvard Univ. Press, 1962.

Valbuena Briones, Angel. Introduction to *La dama duende.* Madrid: Espasa-Calpe, 1962.

————. "La técnica dramática y el efecto cómico en *La dama duende,* de Calderón." *Arbor*, 349, (1975), pp. 15-26.

La estatua de Prometeo.

Aubrun, Charles V. Introduction to *La estatua de Prometeo.* Paris: Centre de Documentation Universitaire, 1961.

—————. "Realismo y poesía en el teatro: Abstracciones morales y referencias a lo real en la tragedia lírica de Calderón." *Revista de la Univ. Nacional de la Plata,* 18 (1964), pp. 297-305.

Chapman, W. G. "Las comedias mitológicas de Calderón." *Romanische Forschungen,* 5 (1954), pp. 35-67.

Trousson, Raymond. "Une synthèse tardive: *La estatua de Prometeo.*" In *Le Thème de Prométhée dans la littérature européene.* Geneva: Droz, 1965, pp. 167-78.
    Rev. Pierre Moreau, *Revue de littérature comparée,* 42 (1968), pp. 291-96.

La gran Cenobia.

Février, James Germain. *Essai sur l'histoire politique et économique de Palmyre,* Paris: Vrin, 1931.

Valbuena Briones, Angel. "Nota preliminar," in *Obras completas,* I. Madrid: Aguilar. 1966, p. 70.

—————. "El tema de la fortuna en *La gran Cenobia.*" *Quaderni Ibero-Americani,* 45-46 (1975), pp. 217-23.

El mágico prodigioso.

Aubrun, Charles V. "*El mágico prodigioso:* Sa signification et sa structure." *Studia Ibérica: Festschrift für Hans Flasche.* Eds. Karl-Hermann Korner and Klaus Rühl. Bern: Francke, 1973, pp. 35-46.

Franzback, Martin. "Die 'Lustige Person' *(gracioso)* auf der spanichen "Bühne und ihre Funktion, dargelegt an Calderóns *El mágico prodigioso*." *Die neueren Sprachen,* 14 (1965) pp. 61-72.

Fucilla, Joseph G. "Un'Imitazione dell'*Aminta* nel *Mágico prodigioso* di Calderón." Studi Tassiani. 6 (1956), pp. 29-33.

González Echevarría, Roberto. "En torno al tema de *El mágico prodigioso."* *Rev. de Estudios Hispánicos,* 3 (1969), pp. 207-20.

Heaton, H. C. "Calderón y *El mágico prodigioso."* *Hispanic Review,* 19 (1951) pp. 11-36 and 93-103.

Hesse, Everett W. "The Function of the Romantic Action in *El mágico prodigioso."* *Bulletin of the Comediantes,* 17, No. 1 (1965), pp. 5-7.

Martin, Eleanor J. "Calderón's *La gran Cenobia:* Source Play for *La vida es sueño?"* *Bulletin of the Comediantes,* 26 (1974), pp. 22-30.

May T.E. "The Symbolism of *El mágico prodigioso."* *Romanic Review,* 54 (1963), pp. 95-112.

Parker, Alexander A. "The Devil in the Drama of Calderón." In Wardropper, Bruce, *Critical Essays...*

——————. "The Role of the *Graciosos* in *El mágico prodigioso,"* In Hans Flasche, *Litterae hispanae et lusitanae,* Munich: 1968, pp. 317-30.

Sloman, Albert E. *"El mágico prodigioso:* Calderón Defended Against the Charge of Theft." *Hispanic Review,* 20 (1952) pp. 212-222.

337

La vida es sueño.

Ayala, Francisco. " 'Porque no sepas que sé'." *Quaderni Ibero-Americani,* 4, No. 28 (1962), pp. 193-202.

――――. *Realidad y ensueño.* Madrid: Gredos, 1963.

Bandera, Cesareo. "El 'confuso abismo' de *La vida es sueño. Modern Language Notes,* 87 (1972), pp. 214-31.

――――. "La muerte de Clarín y apuntes sobre la tragedia calderoniana." *Barroco,* 4 (1972), pp. 57-75.

Buchanan, Milton A. "The Presidential Address: Calderón's *Life is a Dream." Publications of the Modern Language Assoc. of America,* 47 (1932), pp. 1315-21.

Casalduero, Joaquín de. "Sentido y forma de *La vida es sueño." Cuadernos del Congreso por la Libertad de la Cultura,* 51 (1961), pp. 3-13.

Cilveti, Angel L. *El significado de La vida es sueño.* Valencia: Albatros, 1971.

――――. "La función de la metáfora en *La vida es sueño." Nueva Rev. de Filología Hispánica,* 22 (1973), pp. 17-38.

Cope, Jackson I. "The Platonic Metamorphoses of Calderón's *La vida es sueño." Modern Language Notes,* 86 (1971), pp. 225-41.

Dunn, Peter N. "The Horoscope Motif in *La vida es sueño." Atlante* I (1953).

Farinelli, Arturo. *La vita è un sogno, Parte seconda.* Torino: 1916, pp. 283-84.

Feal, Gisèle and Carlos. "*La vida es sueño:* De la psicología al mito." *Reflexión* 2, I, 1 (1972), pp. 35-55.

Halkhoree, Premraj. "A Note on the Ending of Calderón's *La vida es sueño.*" *Bulletin of the Comediantes,* 24 (1972), pp. 8-11.

Hall, H.B. "Segismundo and the Rebel Soldier." *Bulletin of Hispanic Studies,* 45 (1968), pp. 189-200.

Hesse, Everett W. "Psychic Phenomena in *La vida es sueño.*" *Estudios literarios de hispanistas norteamericanos dedicados a Helmut Hatzfeld con motivo de su 80 aniversario.* (Eds.) Josep M. Sola-Solé, Alessandro Crisfulli, and Bruno Damiani. Barcelona: Hispam, 1975, pp. 275-86.

Honig, Edwin. "The Magnanimous Prince and the Price of Consciousness: *Life is a Dream.*" In *Calderón and the Seizures of Honor...*

Johnson, Carroll B. "Segismundo en palacio: Nota sobre *La vida es sueño,* Jornada II." *Duquesne Hispanic Review,* 8, ii (1969), 7-17.

Martínez Almendrez, Gregorio. *"La vida es sueño* de Calderón y los problemas del existencialismo actual." *Studium Generale* (Porto, Germany 1, (1953), pp. 97-125.

May, T. E., "Brutes and Stars in *La vida es sueño." Hispanic Studies in Honour of Joseph Manson.* Eds. Dorothy M. Atkinson and Anthony H. Clarke. Oxford: Dolphin, 1972.

Merrick, Carol A. "Clotaldo's Role in *La vida es sueño." Bulletin of Hispanic Studies,* 50 (1973), pp. 256-69.

Palacios, Leopoldo Eulogio. *"La Vie est un songe."* Laval *Théologique et philosophique,* 7 (1951), pp. 123-49.

Parker, Alexander A. "Calderón's Rebel Soldier and Poetic Justice." *Bulletin of Hispanic Studies,* 46 (1969), pp. 120-27.

Paterson, Alan K. G. "The Traffic of the Stage in Calderon's *La vida es sueño."* Renaissance Drama, 4 (1971), pp. 155-83.

Piñera Llera, Humberto. "¿Descartes en Calderón?" *La Torre* (Puerto Rico) 6 (1958), pp. 145-65.

Pring-Mill, R.D.F. "Los calderonistas de habla inglesa y *La vida es sueño:* Métodos del análisis temático-estructural." In Hans Flasche, *Litterae hispanae et lusitanae,* Munich: 1968, pp. 369-413.

Salinas, Pedro. "The Acceptance of Reality: Jorge Manrique and Calderón de la Barca." In *Reality and the Poet in Spanish Poetry.* Trans. by Edith Fishtine Helman, Baltimore: Johns Hopkins Univ. Press., 1966, pp. 33-63.

Sloman, Albert E. Introduction to *La vida es sueño.* Manchester: Manchester University Press, 1961.

―――."The Structure of Calderón's *La vida es sueño."* In Wardropper, Bruce. *Critical Essays...*

Strum, Harlan, G. "From Plato's Cave to Segismundo's Prison." *Modern Language Notes,* 89 (1974), pp. 280-89.

Suárez-Galván, Eugenio. "Astolfo: La moral y su ilustración dramática en *La vida es sueño.*" *Hispano,* 38 (1970), pp. 1-12.

Urrutia, Jorge. "Una escena de *La vida es sueño:* Su organización dramática." *Cuadernos hispanoamericanos,* 247 (1970), 173-91.

Wardropper, Bruce. "Apenas llega cuando llega a penas." *Modern Philology,* 57 (1960), pp. 240-44.

Whitby, William M. "Rosaura's Role in the Structure of *La vida es sueño.*" In Wardropper, Bruce. *Critical Essays...*

Wilson, E. M. "On *La vida es sueño.*" In Wardropper, Bruce. *Critical Essays...*

Ziomek, Henry. "Historic Implications and Dramatic Influences in Calderón's *Life is a Dream.*" *Polish Review,* 20, i (1975), pp. 111-28.

Works by Sixteenth-, Seventeenth-, and Eighteenth-
Century Authors Mentioned in this Study

Beaumarchais, Pierre Augustin Caron de. *La folle Journée ou Le Mariage de Figaro,* Paris: 1785.

Boccaccio, Giovanni. *The Decameron.* Tr. by Richard Aldington, New York: Dell, 1930.

Calvin, John. *Institutes of the Christian Religion.* Trans. John Allen. Philadelphia; Presbyterian Board of Christian Education, 1936.

Castañeda, Martyn de. *Tratado muy sotil y bien fundado de las supersticiones y hechizerías y vanos conjuros y abusiones, y otras cosas al caso tocantes y de posibilidad y remedio dellas.* Madrid: Sociedad de Bibliófilos Españoles, 1949.

Cervantes, Miguel de. "El celoso extremeño." In *Novelas ejemplares, Tomo II.* Ed. Fernández Gutiérrez, Barcelona: Juventud, 1962, pp. 25-61.

—————. "La cueva de Salamanca." In *Entremeses.* Ed. Miguel Herrero García, Madrid: Espasa-Calpe, 1962, pp. 185-214. (Clas. Castellanos).

—————. *El ingenioso caballero Don Quijote de la Mancha.* Ed. Martín de Riquer. New York: Las Américas, 1967 (2 vols.).

—————. *La Galatea,* Madrid: Espasa-Calpe, 1961 (2 vols.).

—————. *El rufián dichoso.* In *Obras completas,* 13th ed. Ed. Angel Valbuena Prat. Madrid: Aguilar, 1964, pp. 323-364.

————. "El viejo celoso." In *Entremeses*. Ed. Miguel Herrero García. Madrid: Espasa-Calpe, 1962, pp. 215-243. (Clas. Castellanos)

Ciruelo, Pedro. *Reprobación de las superticiones y hechicerías. Libro muy útil y necesario a todos los buenos cristianos.* Salamanca: 1539, 1541; Alcalá: J. de Brocar, 1547.

Feijóo, Benito Jerónimo. *Discursos y cartas.* Ed. J. M. Alda Tesan, Zaragoza: Ebro, 1958 (Clas. Ebro).

Fuente La Peña, Antonio de. *El ente dilucinado. Discurso único novísimo que muestra ay en la naturaleza Animales irracionales invisibles, y quales sean.* Madrid: 1676-1677.

Gracián, Baltasar. *Oráculo manual y arte de prudencia.* Ed. E. Correa Calderón. Salamanca: Anaya, 1968.

Hobbes, Thomas. *Leviathan,* Chicago: Britannica, 1952 (Great Books).

Kepler, Johannes. *Epitome of Copernican Astronomy.* Chicago: Britannica, 1952 (Great Books).

————. *Harmonies of the World.* Chicago: Britannica, 1952 (Great Books).

Lebrun, Pierre. *Historia crítica de las supersticiones prácticas que han engañado a los pueblos y embarazado a los sabios.* 1702; Amsterdam, 1733-6; 1745; Nouvelle Edition augmentée, Paris: 1750-51.

Leibniz, Gottfried Whilhelm. *Theodicy* (Abridged). In *Leibniz, Selections.* Ed. Philip P. Wiener. New York: Scribners, 1951, pp. 509-21.

—————. *Monadology.* In *Leibniz, Selections.* Ed. Philip P. Wiener; New York: Scribners, 1951, pp. 533-51.

Loyola, Ignacio de. *Los ejercicios espirituales.* Ed. Juan Roothan, Intro. y traducción de las notas con nueve apéndices por Teodoro Toni. 3rd ed. Zaragoza: Hechos, 1959.

Luther, Martin. *De servo arbitrio.* Wittembergae: Apud I. Lufft, 1526.

Machiavelli, Niccolò. *Il Principe.* Roma: A. Blado, 1532.

Mersenne, Marin. *La vérité des Sciences des Sceptiques ou Pyrrhoniens.* Paris: T. Du Bray, 1625.

Molina, Tirso de. *El burlador de Sevilla.* In *Comedias,* I. Ed. Américo Castro. Madrid: Espasa-Calpe, 1963. (Clas. Castellanos).

Montaigne, Michel de. "Apologie de Raimond Sebond." In *Les Essais de Michel de Montaigne.* Ed. by Pierre Villey, Tome II, Paris: F. Alcan, 1922.

Montesquieu, Charles de. *De l'Esprit des Lois.* In *Oeuvres complètes.* Paris: Seuil, 1964, pp. 527-833.

Newton, Issac. *Mathematical Principles.* Chicago: Britannica, 1952 (Great Books).

Pascal, Blaise. *Pensées sur la Religion et sur quelques autres sujets.* Paris: J. Delmas et Cie, 1960.

Pererius, Benidictus (Pererio, Benito). *Adversus fallaces et supersticionas artes, id est, de Magia, de observationes somniorum et de divinatione astrologica.* Lugduni: 1603.

344

Pérez de Moya, Juan. *Philosophia secreta*, II. Madrid: Nueva Biblioteca de Autores Españoles-Los Clásicos Olvidados, 1928.

Río, Martín Antoine del. *Disquisitionum Magicarum, Libri Fex In Tres Tomas Partiti*. Lugduni: I.P. Illechotte, 1604. 1604.

Sánchez, Francisco. *Que nada se sabe*. Buenos Aires: Emecé Editores, 1944.

Shakespeare, William. *Much Ado About Nothing*. In *The Complete Works of William Shakespeare*, ed. by William Aldis Wright. Garden City: Doubleday, 1936, pp. 595-628.

——————. *Othello, the Moor of Venice*. In *The Complete Works...*, pp. 935-980.

Suárez, Francisco. *Disputaciones metafísicas*, Tomos I-VII. Trans. Sergio Rabade Romeo, Salvador Caballero Sánchez, and Antonio Puigcerver Zanón. Madrid: Gredos, 1960.

Torres Villarroel, Francisco. *Vida*. Ed. by Federico de Onís. Madrid: Espasa-Calpe, 1954.

Victoria, Francisco de. *Relectiones Theologicae*. Salamanca: 1565; Lugduni, 1587.

Vives, Juan Luis. *Tratado del alma*. In *Obras completes*, Tomo II. Trans. Lorenzo Riber. Madrid: Aguilar, 1948, pp. 1147-1323.

Philosophical and Historical Background
and Literary Criticism.

Aquinas, Thomas. *Summa Theologica.* Chicago: Britannica, 1952 (Great Books).

Astraín, Antonio. *Historia de la Compañia de Jesús en la Asistencia de España,* VI. Madrid: Administración de Razón y Fé, 1920.

Augustine. *The City of God.* Chicago: Britannica, 1952 (Great Books).

——————. *On Christian Doctrine.* Chicago: Britannica, 1952 (Great Books).

Bentley, Eric. *The Life of the Drama.* New York: Atheneum, 1964.

Caro Baroja, Julio. "Honour and Shame: A Historical Account of Several Conflicts," trans. R. Johnson in J. G. Peristiany (ed.) *Honour and Shame.* Chicago: The University of Chicago Press, 1966, pp. 79-137.

Curtius, Ernst Robert. *European Literature and the Latin Middle Ages.* Trans. Willard R. Trask. New York: Harper Torchbooks, 1953.

Elliott, J.H. *Imperial Spain, 1469-1716.* New York: New American Library, 1966.

Fülop-Miller, René. *The Jesuits: A History of the Society of Jesus.* Trans. F. S. Flint and D. F. Tait. New York: Capricorn, 1956.

Huizinga, J. *The Waning of the Middle Ages.* Garden City: Doubleday, 1954.

Lovejoy, Arthur O. *The Great Chain of Being: A Study of the History of an Idea*. The William James Lectures delivered at Harvard University, 1933. Cambridge, Mass: Harvard University Press, 1936.

McKendrick, Melveena. *Woman and Society in the Spanish Drama of the Golden Age: A Study of the* Mujer Varonil. London: Cambridge University Press, 1974.

Menéndez Pelayo, Marcelino. *Historia de los heterodoxos españoles, Tomo IV.* Madrid: Consejo superior de investigaciones científicas, 1963, pp. 365-70.

Pitt-Rivers Julian. "Honour and Social Status," in J.G. Peristiany (ed.) *Honour and Shame.* Chicago: The University of Chicago Press, 1966, pp. 19-79.

Popkin, Richard H. *The History of Scepticism from Erasmus to Descartes.* N. V. Assen, Netherlands: Koninklijke Van Gorcum & Co., 1960.

Rougemont, Denis de. *L'Amour en l'Occident.* Paris: Plon, 1939.

Russel, Bertrand. *A History of Western Philosophy,* New York: Simon and Schuster, 1945.

——————. *Wisdom of the West.* Ed. Paul Foulkes. New York: Crescent, 1960.

Works Relating to Existentialist Thought Mentioned
in This Study

Barret, William. *Irrational Man.* Garden City: Doubleday, 1962.

Beauvoir, Simone de. *Mémoires d'une jeune fille rangée.* Paris: Gallimard, 1958.

Breisach, Ernst. *Introduction to Modern Existentialism.* New York: Grove Press, 1962.

Brod, Max. *Franz Kafka: A Biography,* New York: Schocken, 1963.

Dostoyevsky, Fyodor. *The Brothers Karamazov.* Trans. Constance Garnett, New York: Random House Modern Library, 1950.

Heidegger, Martin. *Existence and Being.* Tr. by W. B. Barton, Jr. and Vera Deutsch. Chicago: Henry Regnery Co., 1967.

_____ . "Holderlin and the Essence of Poetry," trans. Douglas Scott. In *Existence and Being...*

_____ . "On the Essence of Truth," trans. by R.F.C. Hull and Alan Crick. In *Existence and Being...*

Jaspers, Karl. *Philosophy of Existence.* Trans. Richard F. Grabau. Philadelphia: University of Pennsylvania Press, 1971.

_____ . *Reason and Existenz.* Trans. William Earle. New York: Noonday Press, 1969.

Kafka, Franz. *The Castle.* New York: Alfred A. Knopf, 1965.

_____ . *Diaries: 1914-1923.* New York: Alfred A. Knopf, 1965.

_____ . "The Judgment", *The Penal Colony.* New York: Alfred A. Knopf, 1948, pp. 49-63.

_____. *The Trial,* New York: Alfred A. Knopf, 1965.

Kaufman, Walter. *From Shakespeare to Existentialism.* Garden City: Doubleday, 1960.

Kierkegaard, Søren. *Attack upon Christiandom.* Trans. Walter Lowrie. Princeton: Princeton Univeristy Press, 1944.

_____. *The Concept of Dread.* Trans. Walter Lowrie. Princeton: Princeton University Press, 1944.

_____. *Fear and Trembling.* Trans. Walter Lowrie. Princeton: Princeton University Press, 1941.

Marcel, Gabriel. *Le déclin de la sagesse.* Paris: Plon, 1954.

_____. *Journal Métaphysique.* Paris: Gallimard, 1935.

Mann, Thomas. *The Magic Mountain.* Trans. H.T. Lowe-Porter. New York: Random House-Vintage, 1969.

May, Rollo. *Love and Will.* New York: W.W. Norton & Co., 1969.

_____. *Power and Innocence. A Search for the Sources of Violence.* New York: W. W. Norton & Co., 1972.

Nietzsche, Friedrich. *Ecce Homo.* Trans. by Walter Kaufmann. New York: Random House-Vintage, 1967.

_____. *Joyful Wisdom.* Trans. by Thomas Common. New York: Frederick Ungar Publishing Co., 1964.

_____. *Thus Spoke Zarathustra.* Trans. Marianne Cowan. Chicago: Henry Regnery Co., 1965.

Ortega y Gasset, José. *Ideas y creencias.* Madrid: Espasa-Calpe, 1964 (Austral).

Sartre, Jean Paul. *Le Diable et le bon Dieu.* Paris: Gallimard, 1951.

—————. "L'Enfance d'un Chef," in *Le Mur.* Paris: Gallimard, 1939.

—————. *L'Etre et le néant.* Paris: Gallimard, 1943.

—————. *L'Existentialisme est un humanisme.* Paris: Nagel, 1966.

—————. *Huis-Clos,* Paris: Gallimard, 1945.

—————. *Les Jeux son faits.* Paris: Nagel, 1947.

—————. *Les Mains Sales.* Paris: Gallimard, 1948.

Schopenhauer, Arthur. *The World as Will and Representation,* Vols. I & II. Trans. E. F. J. Payne. New York: Dover, 1958.

Unamuno y Jugo, Miguel de. *Cómo se hace una novela.* Buenos Aires: Edit. Alba, 1927.

—————. *Del sentimiento trágico de la vida.* Madrid: Espasa-Calpe, 1967 (Austral).

—————. "Nicodemo el Fariseo" in *La agonia del cristianismo.* New York: Las Américas, 1967.

—————. *San Manuel Bueno, Mártir.* Madrid: Espasa-Calpe, 1963 (Austral).

—————. *Tres novelas ejemplares y un prólogo.* 11th ed. Madrid: Espasa-Calpe, 1964 (Austral).

—————. *Vida de Don Quijote y de Sancho.* Madrid: Espasa-Calpe, 1966 (Austral).

TABLE OF CONTENTS